DESIGNING AND
SPACE PLANNING
FOR LIBRARIES

DESIGNING AND SPACE PLANNING FOR LIBRARIES

A BEHAVIORAL GUIDE

Aaron Cohen   *Elaine Cohen*

R. R. BOWKER CO.
New York & London, 1979

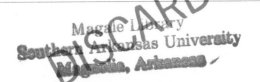
Magale Library
Southern Arkansas University
Magnolia, Arkansas

DISCARD

129858

To our children,
Rachel and Chip,
who helped to research the book and whose
criticism was deeply appreciated.

Cover and text design by Edward A. Butler
Artwork by Aaron Cohen

Published by R. R. Bowker Company
1180 Avenue of the Americas, New York, N.Y. 10036
Copyright © 1979 by Aaron Cohen and Elaine Cohen
All rights reserved.
Printed and bound in the United States of America

Library of Congress Cataloging in Publication Data
Cohen, Aaron, 1935–
   Designing and space planning for libraries.

   Bibliography: p.
   Includes index.
   1. Library planning.   2. Library architecture.
3. Libraries—Space utilization.   I. Cohen, Elaine,
1938–   joint author.   II. Title.
Z679.5.C64   022'.3   79-12478
ISBN 0-8352-1150-9

CONTENTS

PREFACE

Libraries are furniture- and equipment-intensive facilities. The interior design aspects—furniture and equipment layouts, people and material traffic patterns, work flow, lighting, acoustics, and even color—affect how users and staff work in the library. Obviously it is easier to find something in a well-organized facility than in a poorly organized one. It is also easier to concentrate in a quiet space where the lighting is adequate than in one that is perpetually noisy and dimly lit.

This book concentrates on the interior design aspects of library planning. There is a special emphasis on do-it-yourself techniques, important for librarians who do not have the funds or the wherewithal to hire outside help. It should be understood that most planning principles are the same whether the library in question is large or small. The only real difference between the two is the extent of the planning process. The time spent planning a one-room, 5,000-volume facility should be relatively small compared to a great library with a million volumes or more.

This text is a survey of the many different elements that go into setting up a library facility, from the initial report presented to those in charge to the completed renovation or to move-in day. Differing space arrangements, floor loading requirements, book stack spacing, furniture and equipment selection, as well as power and energy requirements, are explained. Discussions touch upon floor plans, in-depth cost analysis, and pictorial documentation. *Designing and Space Planning for Libraries* is intended for librarians, members of the board, college administrators, corporate managers, and even professionals such as interior designers and architects. All too often, libraries are erected that are either functional or aesthetic—not both. Librarians tend to err on the side of functionalism, setting up lines of stacks in uninspired rows. Interior designers and architects err on the side of aesthetics, playing with diamond-, triangular-, or circular-shaped arrangements that destroy the workability of the spaces. This book tries to meld both aspects.

While writing this book we depended upon the aid of two young information scientists—our children, Rachel and Chip. They helped us research the subjects and offered intelligent advice. We would like to thank them for their help, and especially for their patience and fortitude. A thank you to Educational Facilities Laboratories, the source of many of the photographs in this book. We would also like to thank Corinne Naden, our editor at R. R. Bowker, for her editing abilities. Corinne kept syntax clear and our thinking straightforward, so that chapters flow logically and to the point.

Croton-on-Hudson, N.Y.   Aaron Cohen
April 1979   Elaine Cohen

INTRODUCTION

The idea for this book originated in a series of Space Planning and Practical Design Seminars, which the authors conducted at universities across the country as part of a postgraduate program of continuing education. One set of seminars was geared for library administrators, to introduce librarians to the technicalities of planning and design so that they could better understand, and even control, a process with which many had to contend on a continuing basis. Another set of seminars, for office facilities planners, introduced interior designers and architects to the behavioral implications of design, especially the interaction of people with the enclosing space and objects of the work environment.

In other words, both seminars dealt with two distinct groups who looked upon similar problems from opposite vantage points. The librarians tended to be the "clients," while the facilities planners tended to be the "designers." Both were usually one step removed from direct contact with each other by managers who acted as mediators in the planning process. For the librarians, the managers often took the form of trustees, administrators, or corporate officers.

An impressive exterior image such as this can be enhanced by a smoothly functioning interior. All too often, however, the exterior image overshadows the concept of habitability. Particularly in relation to library function, architecture and interior design may translate into a monument (Peabody College, Nashville, Tennessee).

To say that the experience became a learning process for the authors as well is a major understatement. The seminars taught us new insights about the realities of the workaday world, particularly the problems of funding, bureaucratic strictures, and even government legalities. Librarians, especially, often have to work through and around very inflexible hierarchies.

As an architect and a behaviorist (and a husband and wife team as well), we went to the seminars with a holistic view. We believed then, and are even more convinced today, that the planning process for any structure depends upon three elements: the aesthetic, the functional, and the behavioral. To separate any one of these elements from the others in the various stages can cause a breakdown in usability.

Often it is the behavioral elements that are little regarded and even less understood by those involved in the space planning process. As we came to realize, buildings that "work" usually do so because someone—designer or client—understood those behavioral aspects, if only intuitively. For example, if standards require that libraries offer so many seats per users, it matters very much how those seats are placed. They cannot be scattered helter-skelter throughout the facility, nor can they be set too close together. Chairs too near each other often are poorly utilized. Most librarians know that six-seater tables are rarely occupied by more than three or perhaps four people at any given time. There is just not enough "psychological" room.

This viewpoint is part of a relatively new school of thought—behavioral architecture/interior design. Until fairly recently, most architects and interior designers believed that well-designed buildings could do anything, even change ingrained social patterns. But the excesses of the 1960s and the reevaluations of the 1970s changed that. Certain structures that were hailed as forerunners of a new society lasted less than 15 years.

Libraries in particular are vulnerable to the "good design gone wild" syndrome. That is because they are usually viewed as the "intellectual center" of something: the town, the school, the corporate structure. Those in charge want their library, as a focal point, to be the best anywhere. For many, the "best" translates into the "best looking," never mind the rest.

Such words become a harsh statement; unfortunately, all too often the statement is true. The work of Louis Sullivan, Frank Lloyd Wright, Le Corbusier, Mies van der Rohe, and other modern architectural leaders is a three-dimensional art, habitable at the same time. However, over the years architectural and interior design criticism—at least that offered in the most prestigious design publications—seems to have lost the idea of habitability. Beautifully executed pictures taken with special cameras that elongate or foreshorten the area and emphasize textures and patterns cause buildings to win design awards on the basis of how they photograph. Staff, users, and other interested people are rarely interviewed to discover if the facility "works" in the first place and meets the original program requirements.

More than a few participants in our library seminars worked in buildings that had won major awards from the American Library Association (ALA), American Institute of Architects (AIA), American Society of Interior Designers (ASID), and others. But few of the librarians were impressed. Asked to describe their facilities, they used words such as "inhuman," "sterile," or simply "uncomfortable." (At times a few were more vocal.) Besides such common problems as temperature extremes and water leakage, we came

Architectural and library awards may be granted on the basis of beautifully executed photographs that focus on distinct design features. The actual "living" library (this one in Biloxi, Mississippi) may function as well as it looks, but many times function is simply forgotten.

across several not-so-known ones, an example being oxygen deprivation traced to real physical ills because ventilation ducts were not put in work areas.

On a field trip as part of one of the seminars, we examined a building that had not only won an AIA award but was featured on the cover of a famous design publication and highlighted in the pages of at least one book. On the basis of all this publicity, the architect who designed the building won several other library commissions.

But the building was somewhat the worse for wear only five years after construction. Everything seemed to be falling apart—even the teak floor was buckling. Worse still, the design seemed largely to ignore the function of a library. There was no place for the book collection to expand (the book shelves were hung as in a private residence, leading to dead-end corridors). Even the lighting system, once lauded as extremely attractive, became a headache to those involved in library service or energy conservation. Hundreds of unshaded incandescent light bulbs, artfully strung across the ceiling, glared into everyone's eyes and cost more in electricity than the library could afford. And then there were those "little" things, the most laughable being the location of the light switches in a box in the closet of the director's office. Anyone wishing to open the building after dark needed a flashlight to navigate the width of the facility to find the office, locate the closet, open the box, and turn on the lights. The architect did not think switches were aesthetic—therefore, he really hid them!

In the office planning seminar, several of the facilities space planners found themselves dealing with similar problems. It is not unusual for large corporations to hire outside architectural/interior design firms to design the buildings and then employ their own in-house staff to "fine-tune" the result. At the headquarters of a huge international corporation, for example, we discovered a beautiful building with approximately 50 percent of the interior space devoted to such nonassignable things as lobbies, atriums, and corridors. In fact, the corridors were so long that maintenance personnel had to walk a number of miles a day; they wore out their shoes. (Shoes were demanded as part of the new union contract!) Most window walls were saved for the executives' offices or for the corridors. The majority of employees were situated in small, interior offices they likened to dungeons.

A facility planner at one of the seminars explained how he changed his ideas after fine-tuning such a building: "I know it sounds ridiculous, but I used to think, someone needs a light, push the desk under the light; someone needs a phone, move the desk closer to the outlet. I never realized this could hamper an employee's productivity or could make the work station uncomfortable. To tell the truth, the hardest thing about this job is dealing with people."

To be fair, the fact that so many famous structures have real service and behavioral problems is not the fault of architectural or interior design firms alone. A goodly portion of the blame can be placed with the powers in the library field, including the boards of trustees, administrations, and even library directors, who offer little guidance. No group, no matter how talented or experienced, can understand the service and behavioral aspects of every facility. It is foolish to tell a design team to "construct a library" and offer no control whatsoever, either in the form of a specifically worded and carefully adhered to program or constant interaction between the staff and designers. There are more than a few instances where the same architectural team designed a first-rate facility one year and a poor one the next.

The implication, then, is that if the library management or staff does not believe they have the time, inclination, or knowledge to coordinate this work, they should hire a library consultant who does. And that consultant should be on the job from the program stage to the final day of construction.

In addition, we have come to see this interaction as so important that we advise libraries not to depend solely upon a firm's reputation, but more upon the "feel": Is the firm willing to work closely with management, staff, or consultant, or is it high-handed? Our favorite public library in the state of Connecticut was designed by a relatively unknown group working closely with the library director. A beautiful building, a New England gem, it is also a first-rate facility (and to our knowledge has not won any awards).

For a facility to work, the planners, beginning with the program stage, should consider the following points:

1. The program should be followed; the place should ultimately function as expected—within reason. This may sound logical, but it often is not the case in real life. One library in New York turned into an audiovisual center simply because there was no room to house any other materials.

2. The facility should be comfortable—or behaviorally usable—for both users and staff. The users should find the library inviting, of course, but it is not mandatory that the staff be relegated to subterranean spaces and treated as second-class citizens.

3. The facility should be attractive. Although we have complained mightily about aesthetics running rampant, on the other hand, beauty plays a significant role in the functioning of a library. A library housed in a structure that is ugly and ill-kept says something about the management and staff, such as disorganization and poor morale.

These three elements—function, usability, attractiveness—should be viewed in a give-and-take relationship, all roughly equal. Here and there a functional aspect may give way to a point of aesthetics; for example, sloping ceilings are more attractive than flat, uninspired ones. Comfort may sometimes override beauty; in harsh winters, facilities stay warmer if windows stop somewhere before the edge of the floor.

Of course, no one is perfect and even the best of work, taking all these elements into view, will still have some problems. We suggest that somewhere between six months and one year after occupancy, the original designers and the library consultant return to the job to fine-tune the place. This postoccupancy evaluation should point out areas to be redone—and the original funding for the project should have monies set aside just for this purpose. Otherwise new funds will have to be sought, and they may be a long time in coming.

It would also be a good idea if library associations, state libraries, library schools, or some such group keep records of these evaluations so that somewhere a source would exist to delineate what went right and what went wrong in the most up-to-date facilities. Thus, the same mistakes, especially those that photograph well, need not reoccur over and over. (Skylights over microform machines or computer terminals are a particular personal bugaboo.)

In the following pages, to some extent we have done some of that. In a very limited way, we have come up with a list of dos and don'ts. However, we realize that in this fast-changing world, what is definitive one year is old hat the next.

This text is not limited to entire library buildings, per se. We have tried to deal with the gamut, from those in giant facilities, to those housed in small rooms in an attic of the corporate structure. We have tried to deal also with new building, additions, renovations, and rearrangements, for, to some extent, the precepts concerning the layouts, even the physical aspects of lighting, acoustics, ventilation, or for that matter the behavioral reactions of the users and staff, are universal. (What is the difference to a reader who cannot see because of a too-bright light whether the library is housed in a big building or a small room?)

Finally, after leading so many seminars we have found that one of the most important aspects of good design has to do with the interpersonal relationships of staff and administrators. Therefore, although this book is nominally a text about library design, it skims over aspects of reporting to management and justifying expenditures.

THE
PSYCHOLOGY
OF
CHANGE

Anyone reading this book, the library administrator, staff member, trustee, office planner, interior designer, or architect, is likely to be contemplating change — the library needs renovating, rebuilding, a new start. Possibly it needs only minor revisions to the physical plant (furniture rearrangement), or perhaps a major new facility is required. In any case, whatever the plan, it has to do with some aspect of change.

The change factors

There is a so-called psychology of change. It deals with change itself and how people react to it. Anyone who is facing change of any kind should be aware of, and be prepared to deal with, the following points:

Change may be for its own sake. Some changes are beneficial; others are not. Everyone recognizes that. But, by and large, change appears to be neutral. Whether or not an individual or people in general recognize the fact, a great deal of change is made simply for its own sake (the room should be painted a different color—was the original shade so awful, or has it just become boring?). Even the most staid, stick-in-the-mud individuals eventually get bored with some aspect of that which is known, and they desire something different. In other words: It often doesn't matter what you do, as long as you do it!

Such a viewpoint may sound cynical, especially considering the rapid rate at which libraries and library science have grown over the last 50 years or so. Besides, there are certainly many good reasons for wanting to change the library. Some of the reasons may have to do with a definite need for expansion, access for the user, staff productivity, building maintenance, and even building ambiance—or a combination of these. However, one should realize that the final result may be only slightly different than the situation that now exists.

Construction involves dust, dirt, noise, and inconvenience.

Change may bring uncertainty. Underneath it all lurks another possibility. Change causes a taste of uncertainty. "Why am I running around like this?" "Is this right? Is that wrong?" "What have I gotten myself into?"

Even without uncertainty, the construction phase may be an especially unhappy time; all too often the library is thrown into turmoil with dust, dirt, noise, and plain inconvenience. In the process of moving, important documents may become lost or misplaced. At times the whole idea seems quite distasteful.

Change causes stimulation. If change can bring turmoil and if the process can be so distasteful, why proceed? One reason is the desire for a successful conclusion (people grow through change), and, for another, the stimulation can be enjoyable.

Whenever people change something, there is a flow of interest, a stimulation that makes the inner juices flow. And if nothing more, in the case of library administrators, they become more visible to the community at large. Those not in a position of power are more noticeable because funds are flowing their way. For those already in a position of power, they become more visible than before to the legion of realtors, architects, contractors, and salespeople who keep calling. The adverse side of stimulation is that the attention people have created pulls them away from their offices, and work goes undone.

Change may increase staff. Change may also bring about some unlooked-for results. A librarian, for example, may envision greater productivity from the original staff in the updated facility, but may end up dealing with more personnel than anticipated. More space always seems to mean an increase in staff, a problem that does not trouble libraries alone. (One library in Westchester County, N.Y., planned a lunchroom for nine employees. Within a year 30 people were trying to eat in that space.) Increased space allows for a faster growing collection; more staff is needed to work with it. Extra space also provides room for programs long resting on the shelf. More maintenance personnel seem to be required immediately.

So, for those contemplating change without planning to hire new people, it is well to face the realities. In the long run, more than likely more employees will be needed.

Change may increase morale and cooperation. Not all change implies something to worry about. Change (construction or otherwise) has some very positive aspects, too. In a series of experiments at Western Electric's Hawthorne Works in Chicago, conducted in cooperation with the National Research Council of the National Academy of Science from November 1924 to April 1927, an interesting discovery was made about what motivates people. The original experiments dealt with the effects of lighting upon employee efficiency. First, the lighting levels were increased for the experimental group, and the group's output rose, which was not unexpected. But to everyone's surprise, so did the output of the control group, whose lighting had not been touched. In another test, illumination was gradually reduced. Again, the output of both groups rose.

It soon became obvious that lighting changes were not causing the employees to work more efficiently. They did so simply because management was showing an interest in their work habits and reactions. Today, we know that this so-called Hawthorne Effect colors nearly any change—good, bad, or neutral—*at first*. That is why an upgraded or new library usually means better staff morale, increased user attention (circulation generally increases immediately), and a nicer ambiance.

Whether these benefits remain depends more upon the policies of management than the pros and cons of the physical space. That is why a post-evaluation of the facilities should be held a minimum of six months or a year or two after moving in.

In other words, bringing departments together, reducing congestion in the library, or housing a bigger and better collection is all well and good. But in the end, keeping good morale is dependent upon good management policies, not the configuration or even the upkeep on the place.

Change and realism work together. If expectations are unrealistic concerning what the new or changed facilities will mean, the letdown may be difficult to handle once the library is completed. Such was the case at a new public library in California. Designed by an architect with a worldwide reputation, the library is a relatively handsome building with few shortcomings. But almost immediately upon completion, the employees began to complain about how badly the building performed. This was wrong, that was awful. Nothing was right, nothing worked. The truth was that the staff had been led to expect a *great* library, and when they received something even slightly less than great, they viewed the whole place with prejudiced eyes.

The point is that change must be viewed realistically, without investing too much wishful thinking into the actual situation. If things do not turn out as planned, the approach is to search for a solution calmly, instead of blaming the space.

BEHAVIORAL
ASPECTS
OF
SPACE

Any building that works well integrates function, usability, and attractiveness to varying degrees. These are the important elements to consider in planning any change of space. But in order to do so, to make space really work, whether in the library, the office, or the home, it is necessary to understand how, in fact, humans feel about space and how they act within it. With that knowledge, it is possible to rearrange space so that it works better for people and people work better within it.

The personal space concept

Most people might agree that there is such a thing as human territoriality—if they understood what it was. Since the 1950s, an increasing number of researchers has been examining the concept of human territoriality. For example, Stanford Lyman and Marvin Scott[1] distinguished four types of territories commonly found in human society: public, home, interactional, and body. *Public* territories—parks, beaches, streets—allow citizens freedom of access, but not always of action (it may be against the law to litter or to play ball on the beach). *Home* territories are public places taken over by particular groups or individuals, such as makeshift clubhouses, gangland turf, or even a special seat in the library. *Interactional* territories are areas where social gatherings may occur, but they have clearly marked boundaries and rules of access as well as egress—libraries, theaters. *Body* territories are the very personal spaces, the most private and inviolate belonging to an individual. Depending upon interpretation, these territories may be large or may describe only the spaces around an individual's body.

The idea of body territories—personal spaces—is not particularly new. Most people know from history that in long-ago days the bodies of royalty were not to be approached too closely, especially by mere commoners. (In fact, the murder of kings was given a special name: regicide.) For centuries in India, the body spaces of a class of people known as the Untouchables were considered impure. (That is still largely true, although the name and the practice are now outlawed by the Indian constitution.) The idea that we *all* have body spaces, and that each space has a different definition, is, however, decidedly new.

Distance zones

In his 1966 book,[2] Edward Hall described the personal space distance-sensing processes of a group of middle-class, healthy adults, mainly living in the northeastern United States. Most of the men and women were in businesses and the professions. Each of Hall's four distance zones were divided into near and far phases, but for the purposes of this chapter, only whole zones are explained in the following list.

1. Intimate distance: up to 18 inches away. Anyone less than 18 inches from another person is in close proximity indeed. These distances usually are reserved for family members, lovers, and extremely good friends. (Sometimes intimate distance is "forced," as on a crowded subway or bus.) For some people, at these very near distances it is impossible to focus the eyes, which accounts for some of the physical discomfort people often feel when others get too close—"They make me cross-eyed!" In addition, at this

distance, one can feel another's body heat and can detect personal odors. Even up to 18 inches the voice is held to a low level. Less than 6 inches, most speech is in a whisper. Intimate distance is shunned by most Americans in public; it is not considered proper, except, perhaps, in relation to children. In fact, other people entering these distances are viewed as not only bad mannered but possibly hostile.

2. Personal distance: 18 inches to 4 feet away. At the closer limits, one can still touch another person. The farther limits allow one to keep "an arm's length away." For most people, the eyes can easily focus and the normal details of the other person are seen, including small imperfections. Another's body heat is not perceptible, and the voice level is moderate. Breath odor can sometimes be detected. This is the distance at which most Americans conduct friendships.

3. Social distance: 4 to 12 feet away. At the closest distances, only the head, shoulders, and upper trunk can be seen; beginning at 7 feet, the same visual sweep will take in the whole body. Body heat, breath odor, and other intimate features are not noticeable. On the other hand, the fine features of skin and hair and the condition of the teeth and clothes are still visible. At the farthest distances, the voice has to be raised. Most Americans conduct business at this distance, the farthest limits being more formal. There is more personal involvement in the closer phases. (One of Hall's subjects felt that the demarcation between personal distance and social distance was the "limit of domination.") An interesting feature of social distance is that it can be used to screen people from one another. The farthest distances allow people to work in the presence of others without appearing rude. (As the space between receptionist and visitor lengthens, the receptionist is less inclined to chitchat.)

4. Public distance: 12 to 25 feet or more. Here the fine details of the other person are no longer visible. At the closer phases the voice is loud, but still not a shout. Beyond 30 feet, the voice must be exaggerated, and much of the communication shifts to gestures and body stance. Somewhere beyond 30 feet, people become part of the scenery.

Robert Sommer,[3] professor of psychology, took Hall's thesis one step further. During a two-year period at a midwestern university, he measured personal distances systematically in a series of experiments. Enlisting the aid of graduate students, he set up situations that forced unwitting subjects to defend their personal distances, or as Sommer calls them, personal spaces.

The general method involved sending a researcher into the main reading room of the library when it was not crowded. A subject was chosen at random, and the researcher would sit as close to the subject as possible. (To minimize sexual overtones, both the researcher and the subject were female.)

At first, most subjects, more than a little displeased and obviously aware that there were any number of empty tables and chairs about, would attempt to ward off the researcher simply by changing body posture. Elbows pointed outward, legs moved. If that did not work (meaning the researcher did not move away), the subject changed the direction in which she was facing so that now she had turned away from the researcher. Some subjects rearranged books and clothing to form barriers. Eventually, all the subjects packed up and moved books, pencils, and coats elsewhere.

Sommer reports that it usually took 15 minutes to dislodge a subject. But since his work, others have performed this experiment. A speech therapist reported that at the Ossining (New York) Public Library, it takes only 5 minutes to dislodge a subject! That figure has been supported by others who have used public rather than university libraries.

The point is twofold: First, work has been done to explain the nature of personal spaces, and second, because of the nature of the university library—a place with a controlled group in a setting where individuals can be easily observed—an important part of this research is specific for librarians.

Age and status differences

Personal spaces are by-products of cultural heritage. For example, most Europeans stand closer to each other than most Americans would dare. To be in such close proximity has definite sexual overtones for Americans, or else they feel there is something not quite "proper" about smelling the breath or feeling the body heat of people who are only acquaintances. (That is one reason why few relationships begin on public transportation during rush hours!) The closeness of body to body, especially of strangers, is considered potentially hostile. And in the United States, unlike many foreign countries, it is rare to observe two men embracing one another. Americans tend to view such closeness as improper.

Personal spaces and society's view of them may change from group to group. For instance, those waiting on a line may become very hostile if loud, poorly dressed people try to push ahead. Yet they will rarely complain if the people who try to move in have just stepped out of a limousine or are recognized as celebrities. Americans often endow high status with actions considered unacceptable for others. And, in fact, people in the highest society levels generally demand—and get—more personal spaces than the majority.

We accept the fact that those of great wealth often live in mansions, or that high-level corporate executives work in offices two to three times as large as those of their immediate subordinates, whether or not they need the extra space. As a matter of fact, the corporate/bureaucratic structure is extremely cognizant of personal space. The lowest level employee may receive only a simple desk, even without a place to put personal belongings. A middle-level manager may rate an office with a window, but the high-level executive usually works in a suite of rooms, sheltered from others by a secretary. On the individual level, law librarians know that one self-assured attorney working on an important brief can easily dominate an entire eight-seater table, preventing anyone else from being seated by artfully spreading out books and papers.

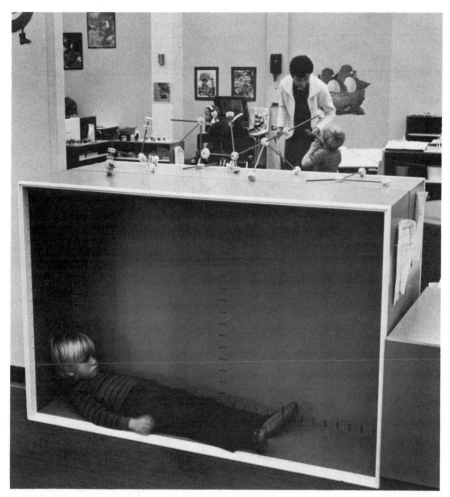

Children treat their bodies differently than adults. It is not unusual to find small children working—or thinking—in unusual situations (Melody Village, Toronto).

Personal spaces and viewpoints regarding them also change with age. Children, for example, have different views of personal space than the adult majority. As children grow, however, their knowledge of how one is expected to act around others increases until their personal spaces are the same as the majority's. Most children's, young adult, or even college librarians are aware that many of their users work only in groups (often very raucous), unlike generally more sedate adults, many of whom are alone when they come into the library. Small children not only want to work at the same tables as their friends but they also want identical books. Conversely, in some elementary school libraries it is not uncommon to open a closet and find a child working happily away!

Somewhere near old age, personal spaces change once again—they decrease and increase simultaneously. This has to do, in part, with a

Undergraduate college librarians are aware that what is applicable in their situations (as here at Williams College, Williamstown, Massachusetts) does not necessarily work in a graduate research library.

change in body abilities and fear of harm. Because elderly people do not hear or see as well as they once did, they may walk up to a stranger and stand too close. They may even steady themselves by holding the other person's arms and hands. Yet, at the same time, their moving spaces grow. In a supermarket, elderly people may use shopping carts as both a crutch and a barrier, extending the forward space, which others may not enter, around their bodies. One elderly woman living in an inner city is so afraid of being mugged that she threatens anyone who steps over an invisible line— about 36 inches—with her cane.

Healthy elderly people are generally less inhibited than younger people. For example, in a library an elderly person might seek out a sturdy chair. If the chair happens to be in another part of the facility, he or she will think nothing of dragging it to wherever it is the most comfortable. Older citizens might like the look of a soft, deep lounge chair, but such chairs are usually difficult to get out of, so they generally prefer chairs that look sturdy and have a straight back.

Library space and personal space

Some researchers claim that personal space around the body is hourglass-shaped, fairly large in front, narrowing at the sides, and flaring out in the back (although the front always remains substantially larger than the back). In other words, people will allow others to come closer if the approach is to the side and the back rather than the front.

Anxiety seems to increase distances between people. In one experiment, students who had been told they had done poorly on a test before going to a private interview with the teacher sat farther away from the instructor than students who had been told they did well. The distance of the teacher's chair to the rest of the class modifies how students pick out their seats on the first day. After the first few days, there is more familiarity and a definite movement toward the instructor's desk.

Nearly everyone can use the implied notion of personal space to mark out public territories, and these territories generally will be recognized. In one experiment, Sommer found that he could mark out a personal territory in the university library even under the most crowded conditions—at the height of exams. All that was necessary was to place a jacket on a chair and leave an open book topped by a pair of glasses on the table in front. The space remained vacant for 2 hours.

This technique may also save a seat in a movie theater or a fast-food restaurant. However, the same experiment does not work as well when high-status groups or the elderly are involved, especially if they have reason to believe that the seat is being saved for convenience (a place to keep coats

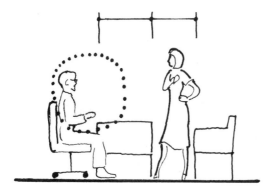

A person's "bubble" of personal space is widest to the front, narrowing at the back and sides.

while the movie is in progress) or that the user may not come back for quite a while ("I'll get up when someone returns").

Everyone seems to have a tendency to find personal territory in public places. Many students return to the same carrel over and over again, often leaving personal objects from day to day to mark the space as theirs. In a hospital emergency waiting room, people may leave the room to be examined or ask a question. They invariably return to the same seat, and if that is occupied, to one as close as possible to the first.

Men seem to be more expansive than women about personal territories in public. David Canter[4] states that women stand closer to mere acquaintances than do men. Law librarians report that freshman male students spread their books farther and take over more library table space than do female students.

Furniture size and placement

In any library, research shows that rarely will more than two people sit on a three-seater library lounge, unless the people know each other. Strangers will sit as far apart from each other as possible. This indicates that, as far as adult libraries are concerned, small tables in the reading rooms and club chairs in the lounge often work best, although all large tables or big couches should not be eliminated. But rather err on the side of small furnishings than large. (This sometimes presents a difficulty: Most architects and interior designers like to use larger objects because they look better in space. They

People space themselves to define personal territories and to minimize eye contact. Two people will sit in close proximity on a three-seater couch only if they know each other (Dunster House Library, Harvard University).

Chairs positioned with backs to an open walkway are perceived as unprotected and, therefore, often remain empty.

often see smaller furnishings as so much "clutter.") It might also be well to consider a few footstools scattered about to be used with the club chairs. Most people like to be fairly horizontal when they relax. Many library club chairs do show matching footstools at furniture showrooms, but most librarians, to save money, do not purchase them. However, users often pull other chairs near and use them for footstools.

Observers at the University of California Library, at Irvine, noted several seating areas, most of which were poorly used because of overcrowding. In fact, the stack master's weekly duties included a roundup of chairs. The carrels were positioned so close together, and in such psychologically vulnerable positions, that students not only refused to sit in them but also moved the chairs to other locations on the same floor where they felt more at ease. The number of chairs and carrels was not the important factor. Much more important was the orientation of chairs and carrels to one another and the square foot allowance of floor and aisle space for each. In one area with nearly 50 chairs and carrels, only 15 students were working. In another area with the exact footage, but containing only 17 chairs and carrels, 15 students were also seated.

A carrel with no protective barrier between the chair back and the walkway through the library spaces will remain empty unless the walkway is rarely used, or the user needs only a small piece of information and will leave quickly. People like to sit with their backs and sides protected, all things being equal. In other words, if the view out the window is pleasant and the sun not too bright, a user may overcome protective instincts and turn the seat toward the window, allowing his or her back to remain vulnerable to the space at large.

Work in office design confirms this. When specifying office landscape furniture where the desks hang from the 5-foot-high cubicle partition, many

Carrels placed perpendicular to walls are heavily used. They provide territorial protection while allowing visual control of access (Skidmore Library, Colorado College).

desks face into the cubicle wall rather than toward the door. Employees have difficulty getting used to such an arrangement. Quite often, if employees also have visitors' tables set in the middle of the cubicles, they will use the tables as the main work spaces, seated so that they face the door.

On this finding, Sommer's work disagrees. He noted a preference to sit with one's back to the door rather than toward it. Sixty percent of his sample faced away from the door. However, in the test Sommer only *asked* the students where they would prefer to sit (via questionnaire). There is no way to know what physical aspects of the reading room may have modified the students' answers—location of the door (in many libraries there is no door; one may enter from several orientations), location of the major walkways within the reading room to the chair backs, and location of the windows.

There seems to be a desire by many people to control access into a space, although they will also sit to the side of the door (so there is control from the corner of the eye). For instance, alone in a classroom at night, a student rarely faces completely away from the door. And in offices, where windows are so desirable, workers nearly always position their desks so they face toward the door (and, ironically, away from the window).

Sommer did find that there was a decided preference for chairs toward the rear of the room (as far away from the door as possible)—79 percent selected chairs in the rear. In addition, 62 percent chose tables against the wall.

Americans nearly always arrange furniture around the periphery of rooms. This inclination is not universal; Japanese, for instance, tend to place furniture toward the center of rooms. In the United States it usually is easy to find the top executives of a corporation—they have the corner offices. In

Americans tend to position furniture around the periphery of a room, which often results in a sea of space at the center (Sonora High School, California).

Paris, where office buildings often form a star pattern, Hall says to look for the person in the middle. Unfortunately, in new buildings with too much new square footage and not enough furniture, American librarians almost unconsciously arrange furnishings and equipment around the periphery, leaving a sea of space to flood the middle. By placing the first furnishings around the periphery (and rarely, if ever, moving them again), the positions of the next furnishings are set. In that case, a functioning plan worked out by a good architect or interior designer can disintegrate into a poorly working interior.

Library tables

Research shows that rectangular tables seem better for work and concentration, while circular tables are best for conversation. On a rectangular table a person can clearly mark his or her territory: "This is my work space. Don't enter it." A circular table makes it more difficult to mark out territory (or status, for that matter: At the Round Table, all the knights were considered equal).

An exception may be the interior design of elementary school libraries. There, a good mixture of circular and rectangular tables in the work spaces may be the best choice because children like to work together and because researchers such as Sommer found that children like to sit side by side when conversing (the barrier of the table is too big even when scaled down to size).

If the library is to be a congenial place where active socialization is expected, space and furnishings should be arranged with that in mind. A nearly even mixture of small and large tables, round and rectangular, should be set here and there so that some people can talk or be physically close, while others study or read. (Many business people depend upon their public libraries to finish overtime work. They do not use library materials, but bring their own office work to a quiet place.)

On the other hand, if the library is a research facility, where serious concentration is the goal, the setup should consist primarily of small tables, with a few larger ones. (Occasionally, some people like to see what is going on, to be in the middle of things, while studying; others need to socialize.)

Library carrels

In a research facility, 90 percent of the small tables may be carrels. Carrel size is very important. Most public libraries use carrels that are only 3 feet wide and 2 feet deep, not large enough for anyone wishing to concentrate for long periods of time. The size does not allow space to spread out. Furthermore, many public library carrels do not have any shelves upon which to store other books. Unfortunately, the public library carrel is all too often used as a standard for other facilities, with poor results.

Some people use a library nearly every day. Many university students, for example, require space to store other books. A minimum carrel for this purpose could be 4 feet wide and 2^1/$_2$ feet deep, with 9 or 10 inches of depth to be taken up by one or two shelves that rise above the desk top. Such a carrel, particularly if the shelving can be removed, is a bit more flexible. Microform readers can be used on them.

For graduate students and researchers in special libraries, carrels should be at least 5 feet wide with right and left pull-out shelves and shelving

A person of high status can dominate even an eight-person table indefinitely. Corporate executives, scientists, lawyers, and doctors tend to spread out their belongings more than others, making it impossible for anyone else to be seated.

If the first person to sit at a six-seater table chooses the center chair, that person will dominate the table longer than if an end chair were selected. An end chair is in close proximity to only three chairs, leaving the other end chairs available for the next person.

above the desk top; such people may need to work with two, three, or more books open at once. Furthermore, they often arrive at the library laden with other texts and paraphernalia. An even better carrel is 5 feet wide and has a secondary work space at right angles, 18 inches deep and 4 feet wide, with lockable drawers, book shelves, and/or cabinets to keep books, paper, pencils, and even confidential material.

Carrels have become popular pieces of library furniture because they are so behaviorally correct. They provide each person with his or her own marked-out territory and, because they are cubicles, they are not too claustrophobic. Besides, if the front wall of the carrel is 5 feet high, the seated individual does not have to look up and stare into the face of someone else. Most people do not mind other people's faces, but they do mind looking into the eyes of people they do not know (or do not wish to speak to). To look into another person's eyes is to invite that other person to speak. People who go to the library for a particular study purpose often want to be left alone. They do not want to socialize. Thus, the carrel defines their territory, especially if they have a great deal of reading and writing to do, and gives them the isolation they require. (Using a carrel as a place to write or take notes is its purpose. Otherwise an isolated club chair would be fine.)

One library consultant feels that a 5-foot-high front and side wall on a carrel is too tall for public libraries. The height of the wall should be 4 to 4½ feet above the floor. At this dimension the carrel wall provides eye protection for the seated user, but visual control for librarians. Even short people can see over the tops of these carrels when standing. (The average line of sight is 5 feet for women and 5 feet 6 inches for men.)

Study/lounge seating

A workable system can be found in the Columbia University Library in New York City. A group of wing chairs is placed facing out around a column. In front of each chair is a footstool and to the side a small table over which swings an ordinary lamp on a pivot. Not only does each chair face away from every other (allowing a reader to look into empty space) but each chair has an individual place to put one's legs, store belongings, and also has a separate light to move at will. Rarely are these chairs empty. They are heavily used even when normal user seats and tables are unoccupied.

Encouraging patrons

Some libraries want to attract patrons, but do not want anyone to hang around. (As one mayor of a town said: "I want them in, and I want them out!") But for those libraries that exist to attract people and have them stay, they should consider light, color, noise, and social interaction as important factors. (Lighting, color, and noise are discussed in later chapters.)

Social interaction

A *sociopetal* space, where interaction is encouraged, obviously should be noisier than a *sociofugal* space, where interaction is discouraged. Most people realize this. Lounge areas, for example, often are sociopetal; all chairs face across a coffee table. (The wing chair group at Columbia is sociofugal; all chairs face away from one another.)

In an experiment in a psychiatric hospital, Sommer found that he could change patient interaction by changing the furniture arrangements. Instead of placing all chairs in a row, he turned them toward one another. People

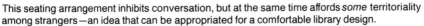

This seating arrangement inhibits conversation, but at the same time affords *some* territoriality among strangers—an idea that can be appropriated for a comfortable library design.

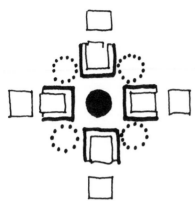

Armchairs complete with footstools and individual lights can be arranged around a column, affording a comfortable, secure reading or listening area. (The column can also provide access for electrical power.)

began to speak, if for no other reason than they were now looking into each other's eyes.

To converse while sitting on couches, people prefer to be opposite one another, as long as the distance between them is no more than about 5½ feet nose to nose. More than that distance apart, they move side by side. On the other hand, if people are only coacting (they do not know each other), they will choose seats on couches that are far apart spatially and visually.

When conversing at a rectangular table, most adults prefer to be opposite one another, as long as the distance between them is no more than 5½ feet. If the distance is greater, they move side by side. (At most round tables, perhaps because of the inability to sit a comfortable distance across from one another, most people prefer to sit side by side.) These figures are important because many of the standard design texts place furnishings as far apart as 8 feet. If lounge seats in the library are not used as expected, this may be the reason.

The idea of sociopetal and sociofugal space arrangements can be used to set up library offices. An office where four people at desks are constantly staring at each other will be full of conversation.

The role of design

Human interaction can be changed simply by rearranging furnishings or the enclosing space. Architects call this "architectural determinism," a theory often applied during the building boom of the 1960s. It indicates that people's actions are modified by the enclosing space or building.

To some extent, this is true. A post-World War II research project at the Massachusetts Institute of Technology indicated that families with doors facing toward the center of the married students' courtyard made more friends in the same building complex than those facing outward toward the street. Because friendship often develops through casual contact, there was greater possibility of friendships forming with people who saw each other every day than with people who did not.

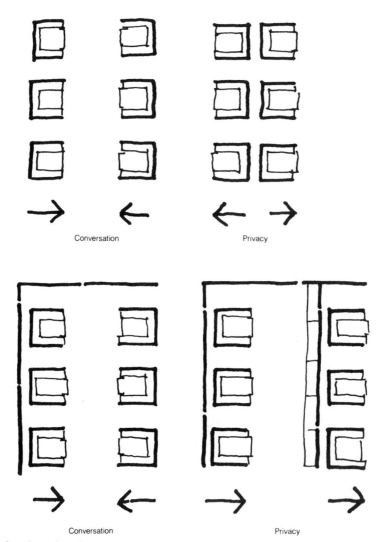

Conversation   Privacy

Conversation   Privacy

A sociopetal seating arrangement encourages conversation; a sociofugal arrangement inhibits it. To discourage conversation, chairs should not face one another, thus minimizing eye contact. If conversation is to be encouraged, chairs should face one another and people should not be seated more than 5 feet 6 inches (nose to nose) apart.

What many designers do not realize is that people take with them a socialization process that often overrides the physical aspects of the enclosing space. For example, some young executives on the way up rarely interact with secretaries in the adjacent space. These executives are too busy trying to impress those with higher status.

Oscar Newman[5] has shown that designers often use the wrong reasoning and thus—not surprisingly—get the wrong answers. Convinced that new housing will somehow turn the poor into the middle class, designers of low-income housing projects have often disregarded the realities of day-to-day living. The most famous example of an architectural determinism disaster was the Pruitt-Igoe housing project in St. Louis. Constructed with an elevator system that stopped at every other floor or so (in an effort to save costs) and with community rooms spotted on isolated floors, the project soon became a vandalized, crime-ridden shell, overrun with gangs. Residents could not protect themselves even in the hallways outside their own apartment doors. The space simply was not defensible. Eventually, St. Louis used dynamite to tear down the project.

One of the most famous comments in favor of architectural determinism was made by Winston Churchill: "We shape our buildings and afterwards our buildings shape us." Actually he was referring to the bomb-blasted House of Commons, requesting that it be rebuilt as it had stood before, complete with all past inefficiencies. The original structure did not have

Architects and interior designers seem unaware that many people carry with them an internalized idea of how space is supposed to be. This library may make eminent sense but may appear sterile and uninviting to others.

enough seats for everyone, and the overcrowding forced members of opposing parties to interact. Churchill felt that this aided the process of democ-
racy because cliques could not easily be formed.

Hall finds that there is such a thing as "internalized fixed feature
space," where, indeed, we may carry around the past inefficiencies of other

*A: The arrangement of architectural elements modifies the perception of space. B and C: Open
environment. A colonnade, for example, appears to have more space for bodily action than an
enclosed room. A psychological feeling of flexibility is created by the indefinite physical confine-
ment. As the fragmented shape appears, it seems to have a potential to grow, but as the
solidity of the mass is increased, the flexibility of use seems to decrease. D: Confined environment. A room is closed in every direction (but the door), so it is limited in ways it can grow. For
some people this limitation affords security, a feeling of territoriality, and a sense of privacy. For
others, it causes claustrophobia.*

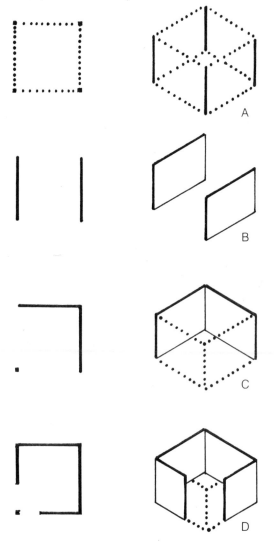

buildings we have known. In other words, most of us have definite ideas of how walls, floors, ceilings, even rooms should be constructed and placed: "I can work anywhere as long as I have a window to see the outside." "I can't stand the smell of new buildings. They're so sterile."

Architects and interior designers often are totally unaware that people carry with them an internalization of how space is supposed to be, ideas probably learned in infancy. It is a problem that causes more than a few arguments and may be, in effect, why many people do not want to have anything to do with "design," per se. They see architects and interior designers working on iconoclastic three-dimensional spaces, where living and working promise to be impossible.

That is one of the reasons why delivering standards should be avoided—standards for the number of square feet, volumes, seating arrangements, and so on. It all *depends*—upon how the library is supposed to be, its philosophies and goals, and for whom it is supposed to function. For example, even in the most beautiful buildings there may be a need to provide some work space without distractions in the depths of the basement. Or in graduate school libraries, even during exam time, not everyone will want to be locked away in a study carrel. A few will always want to sit at large tables near the front door to be in the middle of things. (These may be the same people who learned to study while the television set was on.)

One should also beware of the designer's and one's own physical orientations. In one office complex, an area where panels 5$\frac{1}{2}$ feet high were used, the manager was asked, "Why?" He replied that the panels were high enough for privacy when seated and low enough to allow control and an expansive view when walking around. "When *who* is walking around?" he was asked. The manager was 6 feet 3 inches; he and very few others could see over the panels with ease.

The aesthetic sense

Although a discussion of space often concentrates on function and behavior, aesthetics should never be ignored. And many would agree that a good-looking library—all things being equal—usually functions better than one that is not.

More than a few librarians know that if a chair develops a tiny hole, within a few days, perhaps hours, the entire chair seems to self-destruct. Or to leave a few well-chosen words of graffiti on one rest room wall immediately invites other such scribbles. It is essential that the library look good and be kept up. People respect buildings that are attractive and well cared for. If the librarians and staff do not care, why should the users?

One experiment having to do with the look of space divided a group in two. One group looked at photographs while sitting in a very attractive conference room. The other group looked at the same photographs while sitting in an unattractive janitor's closet. Of the participants in the janitor's closet, very few remarked about the general ambiance. But the different locations made a difference in the results. Those in the conference room found the people in the pictures to be all smiles. Those in the janitor's closet found the same people to be grim and unhappy. The inference here is that perhaps design professionals have a piece of the truth: The look of the space is nearly as important as its functional and behavioral aspects.

Notes

1 Stanford M. Lyman and Marvin B. Scott, "Territoriality: A Neglected Sociological Dimension," Social Problems 15 (1967): 236–249.

2 Edward T. Hall, The Hidden Dimension (New York: Doubleday, 1966).

3 Robert Sommer, Personal Space. The Behavioral Basis of Design (Englewood Cliffs, N.J.: Prentice-Hall, 1969).

4 David Canter, ed., Environmental Interaction (London: Surrey University Press, 1975).

5 Oscar Newman, Defensible Space (New York: Macmillan, 1973).

SPACE
PLANNING
GUIDELINES

Once the decision has been made to ``do something'' about a library — refurbishing, renovation, or new construction — the library administrator should set up guidelines that will help to make the project smooth running and successful. Following are some guidelines intended to lead the administrator and staff through logical, understandable steps in the often bewildering area of space planning for libraries.

Documenting the project

No matter the size or extent of the project, it is going to cost money. And for the library head, that usually means seeking funds from the library board or other administration. So step one is a feasibility study—in other words, documenting the project.

Obviously, the size of the documentation depends upon the scope of the work. One piece of equipment does not require a 40-page report. For most jobs, major or minor, the simplest method is to take photographs of the problem spots in the library (long waiting lines for rest rooms or whatever). Paste the photographs in the report; they are often more eloquent than words.

Make certain that the text of the report is straightforward and clear. Remember that most people are not as print-oriented as are librarians. A too-detailed text often finds its way into the circular file. Provide a summary of all pertinent facts and figures on the first page (some people never read beyond it). See the table on Documenting the Project, which indicates a simple cost breakdown study.

Among the included facts and figures should be a strong indication of the projected scope of the monies involved. For a few pieces of equipment, it is relatively simple to find the prices in catalogs. However, a major rearrangement of space, added space, or new construction requires research. The project may need the services of a library consultant, architect, engineer, interior designer, contractor, or in-house staff (whose functions are discussed in the chapter entitled Who Does What?). Thus the intent of the report may be to acquire funding for such services.

Some service people, particularly contractors and vendors, will provide free "guesstimates" of simple jobs. They will inspect the library and discuss figures to be included in the report. It is not necessary to pay for such services. If the contractor or vendor is told that there will be no advance payment, no problem should arise.

However, architects, engineers, library consultants, and other professionals often receive compensation for their time. Some will be willing to make a "previsit," others will not. This should be discussed by phone or in a letter. If professionals expect compensation for any site visits to the library, their daily or hourly rates and what they will accomplish should be included in the report.

The report should include justification.

What are the objectives of the proposed change? Will it
Increase service to users?

Increase staff productivity?

Reduce operating expenses (by using space more effectively or by being more energy conserving)?

DOCUMENTING THE PROJECT

Architectural and/or Interior Design Elements	Renovations & Additions	Cost Breakdown
Ceilings	Demolition	$ _____
	Rewiring	_____
	Lighting	_____
	Air handling system	_____
	Acoustical tile	_____
Comfort/Aesthetics	Color	$ _____
	Graphics	_____
	Safety	_____
	HVAC (temperature and humidity)	_____
Equipment	Bookstacks	$ _____
	File cabinets	_____
	Microform machines	_____
	Computer terminals	_____
	Electrical/telephone/CRT cables	_____
	Telephones	_____
Floors	Remove old flooring	$ _____
	Reinforce floor	_____
	Carpeting	_____
	Tile	_____
Furnishings	Library armchairs	$ _____
	Library armless chairs	_____
	Office chairs	_____
	Tables	_____
	Desks	_____
Walls	Demolition	$ _____
	Dry wall	_____
	Painting	_____
	Wall covering	_____
	Electrical wiring	_____
	Electrical outlets	_____
Total cost		$ _____

Provide greater access to resources?

Provide better looking facilities?

Bring more status to the library (making it as good or better than possible competition)?

The feasibility study

If a large project is anticipated, a major feasibility study may be next in line.

For a small job, this step is not necessary. No special study is needed to add a small piece of equipment (except perhaps a computer terminal). However, for a large project, it is advisable that someone develop a study in which the library's philosophy is compared with long-range funding. Certain specifics of the proposed renovation or new construction should be outlined at this point (such as how large or extensive, or what is involved), but in a most preliminary way. (Because getting money is generally a political process, it is especially good to have the philosophy, goals, and reality of the situation match.)

Although there are times when any knowledgeable staff member may be able to work up such a report, a library consultant may be a good investment for two reasons: First, the job is time consuming and, second, an outside agent is more objective and probably has overseen this process many times before.

The consultant's role can be detailed or severely circumscribed. In either case, present services and future possibilities should be examined. In addition, the consultant can initiate a more definitive feasibility study in which the possibilities for future expansion are proposed. The consultant should be able to analyze library facilities according to standards set up by various library associations and government bodies. The library consultant can point the way in which the library should turn and can detail how large the eventual project proposes to be. For example, a consultant may be hired initially only to determine whether it is best to renovate the old place or to acquire a new facility. If the consultant recommends renovation, perhaps the library will also have to weed the collection extensively or turn heavily to microforms and computerization. All possibilities should be outlined.

The design process

After a successful feasibility study and additional funds are granted, the design process begins. Obviously, if the job is very small, there will be little involvement with this step. However, for large projects some understanding is necessary concerning how library objects will relate in three-dimensional space.

Now is the time to decide whether the job will be done with in-house staff or outside professionals—architects, engineers, interior designers, design/builders, or vendors. If a library consultant was hired for the feasibility study, he or she should continue to work on the project—continuity is important.

In a major job, librarians rarely hire the professional help. Usually that is the function of the board, administration, or management, although the librarian's suggestions may be taken into consideration. Certainly, the librarian should try to be a part of the hiring process.

Control

Control is the most important word in the entire design process. Essentially it has to do with the chain of command involving librarian, staff, administration, and professional help. Who is reporting to whom? Who knows exactly what

DATA CONCERNING THE COLLECTION (sample form)

Type of Material	Sections	Shelves	Linear Ft. Avail.	Linear Ft. in Use	% Shelving in Use	Size of Collec.	Net Growth Per Yr.	% Net Incr.	Sections 1979	Sections 1990
Abstracts	30	180	540	490	90	2,190	260	11.8	30	60
Bound journals*	267	1,800	5,400	5,400	100	26,000	1,800	6.9	267	504
Current unbound journals	40	200	600	600	100	1,000	—	—	40	75
Microfilm cass.	3 bins	—	—	—	—	—	—	—	—	—
Monographs	80	560	1,680	1,680	100	20,000	1,000	5	80	214
Ref. tools	15	70	188	1,508	80.2	980 vols.	—	—	15	30
Total	432 3 bins	2,810	8,408	9,678		50,170 items	3,060		432	883

*Analysis of bound journals: Of the total collection, 40 percent are 1 to 5 years old and require 2,160 linear feet of storage space; 50 percent are 5 to 25 years old and require 2,700 linear feet; 10 percent are 25 or more years old and require 540 linear feet. Total required space (5,400 linear feet) equals the maximum available space. Since 60 percent of the bound journals are more than 5 years old, the collection should be weeded in this special library.

is going on and when decisions are taking place? Is the role of the librarian passive or is there active involvement?

Because technically professional help, including library consultants, are generally hired by the board, administration, or management, librarians are not always kept informed. The librarian should become intimately involved and aware of all important decisions. Librarians might ask the professionals to mail them carbon copies of every letter and report sent. After the money has been spent, it is too late to become involved. The design process cannot be started over again.

The program

The design stage must be based upon a program that outlines such details as space requirements for people, procedures and equipment, requirements of departments, traffic flow of users, staff, and library materials through the facility, and ambiance of user areas. To write the program the first step is to collect data. (See table on Data Concerning the Collection.)

Present size and projected rate of growth of the collection—5, 10, 20 years.

Library association requirements and/or standards for the collection (per user population).

User population current; projected rate of growth—5, 10, 20 years.

Present size and projected rate of growth of the staff—5, 10, 20 years.

Library association requirements and/or standards for the staff (per user population).

Library association space standards per users, staff, and collection.

Inventory of present furnishings/equipment; future projections.

The next step requires policy decisions.

Collection rate of growth/retention of materials/deacquisition policy.

Space allocation for users (lounge, relaxed study, long-term study, and so on).

Space standards for library staff (managerial, professional, clerical).

Space allocation as a percentage of the facility for special library programs (audiovisual, multi-purpose areas, special departments, and so on).

The third step is to define the work processes that will take place in the library.

How is work done in the library? What tasks are involved in the staff areas and how must they fit together?

Will equipment replace some functions? How will this affect the space allocation or power requirements?

The program can be written by the library staff or by a library consultant. If the job is of any magnitude a library consultant is recommended. In either case, the program should become a major construction document adhered to by the designers. For that reason, if future circumstances require, the program should be updated as design stages proceed. The program is the major source of *written* control modifying the work of the architects and interior designers. (See the table on Typical Program Requirements, a general guide which should be prepared by the librarian and submitted to architects and/or interior designers.)

Preliminary design

Here the design is executed in the most preliminary way. It may be nothing more than a series of sketches, depending upon the scope of the work. On large jobs, a preliminary model, or visuals, may be submitted as well. The librarian, staff, administration, library consultant—anyone involved in the process—interacts with the design if not the designers, making changes where necessary. The program should be updated if it does not cover certain possibilities at this juncture.

Design development

Interaction continues. On a small job this phase may be skipped entirely. For a large architectural project the design development phase is where most of the work takes place. The program should be checked and rechecked to make certain that the design follows specific requirements and/or concepts. The program should be updated if certain decisions supercede those previously determined.

Final design presentation

For a very small job, usually an interior design project, the preliminary design and final design presentation may be one. Here the designers submit finished plans ready to go to contractors and vendors for prices. (The finished plans should match the program. If they do not, either they should be rejected or the program should be changed and updated.) However, for a public library referendum a slightly less finished set of plans and specifications may be submitted; work will be done if the referendum passes. For large jobs where funding has been obtained, more complete renderings and models may be submitted.

TYPICAL PROGRAM REQUIREMENTS

General
  Hours open   Per day
    Library in general   Per week
    Specific depts.   Special

  Security   Unimportant
    Library in general   Important
    Specific depts.   Intensive
                                       Special

  Access   Open
    Library in general   Controlled
    Specific depts.   Restricted

  Disabled patrons   Open
    Library in general   Controlled
    Specific depts.

Collections
  Volume count—growth
    potential   Floor area minimum
  Microforms—growth
    potential   Floor area minimum
  Computer area—growth
    potential   Floor area minimum

User
  Activities   Important
  Interaction—staff   Intensive
  Occupant load   Special

Staff
  Activities   Important
  Interaction—users   Intensive
  Interaction—collections   Special
  Occupant load

Location—depts.
  Adjacencies   Important
  Accessibility   Intensive
                                         Unimportant

Spatial—depts.
  Internal flexibility   Important
                                         Normal
                                         Not required

  Proportions   Square
                                         Rectangular
                                         Special
                                         Optional

  Daylight   Important
                                         Not desirable
                                         Optional

TYPICAL PROGRAM REQUIREMENTS (cont.)

View outside	Important
	Not desirable
	Optional
Ceiling height	Maximum
	Minimum
Access/egress	Ordinary
	Special
Surfaces	Ordinary
	Special

Furnishing/equipment

User seating	Tables
	Carrels
	Lounges
	Stand-up reference
Staff work stations	Clerical
	Professional
	Managerial
	Custodial
	User areas
	Circulation
Equipment	High book stacks
	Low book stacks
	Machines
	Machine tables
	Built-ins
	Special

Performance—mechanicals

Temperature control system	Temperature range
	Special
Humidity	Humidity range
	Special
Ventilation	Air changes per hour
	Percentage outdoor air
	Filtration
Lighting	General
	Task
	Corridor
	Storage
	Incandescent
	Fluorescent
	HID
Acoustics	General ambience
	Special

Specifications

Fire	Building design
	Furnishings/equipment

TYPICAL PROGRAM REQUIREMENTS (cont.)

Electricity	General
	Special
	Emergency
Communications	Telephone
	Intercom
	Security
	P.A. system
	Computer
	AV
Plumbing	Water supply
	Floor drains
	Fixtures
	Sinks
	Other

Cost detailing

Depending upon the scope of the work, whether it be a small addition of furnishings or a huge new building, a detailing of costs should be received from either a contractor or a vendor (of course, depending upon whether construction or just the purchase of equipment and/or furnishings is needed). Some companies may suggest changes in the plans and specifications before the contract is signed. This is often done if costs appear to be much more than the funds allocated. Substitutions of less expensive materials and/or equipment may be made.

Like the program, the specifications must always be kept up to date. Specifications are also construction documents. It can be said that buildings, furniture, and equipment are only as good as the specifications. Furthermore, plans and specifications submitted by designers are the very basis for contractual agreements with contractors and/or vendors. Once they sign the contract no changes should be made in plans or specifications *unless absolutely necessary*. Changes have a tendency to suspend the contractual agreement, and costs can escalate with little or no control.

Once the project is sent out to bid and the prices come back much higher than expected, the library may request the designers to redesign the entire job. If the library was careful to limit the designer's work with an upset price or if the contract signed with the designers specified that the costs should not exceed a certain limit no matter how many times redesigned, the library will not have to pay an additional fee for the redesign. However, if no such agreements were made, the designers will more than likely charge for these extra services.

Purchasing procedures

To some extent, purchasing procedures have been discussed in cost detailing. However, once again the question of control is important. Who knows what decisions have been made? Who is aware of what is to be delivered and when?

Construction

Rarely does the librarian become involved in actual construction except to coordinate the phase and to check that everything is proceeding as agreed. However, the librarian should be aware of the supervisor in charge, existing controls, and the person in the library (company, school, or board) who is approving invoices. Is it important to get a breakdown of trades and the amount of monies spent to make sure that no one is receiving more than what was agreed to in the contract? Must the contractors and/or vendors be bonded?

A "time and action" calendar should be set up, detailing what is being purchased, when it is to be constructed or delivered, coordination details with the building, trades, and/or vendors, and, finally, when the job will be completed. Obviously, if design professionals are handling the job, the library's calendar does not have to be that exact. On the other hand, if the librarian is handling all procedures, the calendar should be accurate.

Delivery of materials

Again, it is important to know: Who is approving invoices, who is in charge, and what controls exist. What about guarantees and warrantees? Has everything been delivered per the agreement? Who is in charge of checking deliveries?

Job completion

Before the job is "signed off," a punch list must be made of the little things that need to be done. Even on the best of projects, things are overlooked. If a design professional is on the job, it is his or her responsibility to make up the punch list. However, usually the professional needs the aid of someone intimately involved—perhaps the librarian and staff—to point out special problems. Often this is done during a formal tour of the facility.

The person in control, who approves all invoices, should not pay anyone a final fee until everything has been completed to satisfaction. Experience shows that if certain workers are paid on time, regardless of contractual agreements, they may leave the job then and not show up for a long period. That is because it is quite common for many of these people to be working on more than one project at a time (they may have to wait for something to be delivered before they can complete the next portion of the job). Therefore, to make sure that people show up when needed, knowledgeable employers hold back on payment until everything is completed to satisfaction.

It is also wise not to render final payment until the proper releases are in hand, stating that any and all subcontractors have been paid. As explained later, some people do not do all the work for which they contract. Instead, they farm out certain portions to others. For example, a general contractor may do only the carpentry portion of the project and hire an electrical contractor to do all rewiring. If subcontractors are not paid, the library can become liable for any unpaid monies due.

Moving and renovating
the library

Moving entails a great deal of planning and work. If the job is large, a moving consultant may be retained to act as agent and to guide personnel as well as moving companies.

Most moving companies work on an hourly basis. They will give cost estimates beforehand, but rarely do they do any job for a flat fee. If the planning is inexact, the hourly rate can build up. Overtime is especially costly.

Moving almost any library is a headache. But probably the worst situation occurs when a library is open, working, and being renovated at the same time. The whole situation is piecemeal—a few stacks, files, tables, and desks are vacated and moved to a cramped area within the facility, re-packed, and expected to continue to function without a hitch. Once the renovation of that space is complete, the stacks, files, tables, and desks are vacated once again, moved, and repacked. This can go on for a long time in area after area in the library, disrupting the place and causing frayed nerves among users and staff alike.

To say that planning is essential in renovation is to underestimate the problem. A specific game plan must be drawn up to coordinate people, places, and things and show exactly who and what will go where—and, possibly, for how long. Obviously, the plan must be flexible to allow for the unknown. The new lighting fixtures may be delayed three months because of a strike, throwing the whole plan out of kilter. Some libraries use a large board similar to the time and action calendar to keep track of all details.

Follow-up

This is the stage most likely to be skipped, especially if the job is minor. Few people check out anything six months or a year after completion to see if it really works as expected (except, of course, if there is a major failure, all the book stacks buckled, for example). Instead, they live with problems and forget about them. They adapt.

That is precisely why so many mistakes, particularly the minor ones that drive people up the wall, are repeated again and again. Americans are a nation of people who desire standards, and if there are none, we make them up.

But it is good sense to keep track of what little things have gone wrong. Specifications can be changed, if not right now, the next time around. And questions should be asked. Are the library facilities performing as expected, or were the expectations unrealistic? Was the work of the library consultant/architect/engineer/interior designer/contractor/vendor/mover satisfactory? What is wrong? What should be changed?

Some of the changes can be made, especially if the original budget specified a sum for just that purpose. Usually, this is not done, but, if possible, it is a fine idea. Too many jobs are considered complete when they are anything but finished. A poorly functioning design may not show up immediately.

Scheduling guidelines

Set up a guideline list to make sure your basic steps in space planning are coordinated. Also see the tables for Typical Time Frames and Time Frames.

1   Establish your target date for move in.

2   Divide the time between the present and the move-in date proportionately among *all* tasks to be accomplished. Establish reasonable time frames.

3   Provide ample time for approvals, reviews, revisions, and final approvals.

4   At the very beginning, develop a preliminary budget. Financial limitations must be established immediately. (It does not make sense to begin a project that cannot be funded.)

TYPICAL TIME FRAMES (approx.)

Documenting the problem	1 week
Approvals	immediate to 1 year (large jobs, 2 to 5 years)
Selecting a consultant	4 weeks
Consultant's visit and feasibility report	4 to 8 weeks
Writing the program	8 weeks to 6 months
Approvals	immediate to 1 year (large jobs, 2 to 5 years)
Selecting an architect/interior designer	7 weeks
Design processes	6 months to 1 year (large jobs, 2 to 5 years)
Construction phase	6 months to 1 year (large jobs, 2 to 5 years)
Purchasing furniture and equipment	8 to 16 weeks
Delivery of furniture and equipment	8 to 16 weeks (popular items, 9 months)
Move in	1 week to 6 months

TIME FRAMES: START TO FINISH

Small interior design job	2 weeks to 6 months
Large interior design job	1 to 2 years
Small library building	2 to 5 years
Major library building	4 to 10 years (up to 15 years)

WHO
DOES
WHAT?

Library X has fallen into a state of disrepair, and it is generally recognized that the entire facility needs to be upgraded. A new building or renovation of the old space are two possibilities. Obviously, outside help will be needed, perhaps a library consultant, an architect, engineer, interior designer, space and facilities planner, manufacturer or vendor, contractor, builder, or special consultant. But who?

For those entering the bewildering area of library building or renovation for the first time, it is well to remember two things. First, it is not uncommon for design professionals, builders as well as tradespeople, to claim that only they understand the problems at hand and for best results all services should be joined under one aegis—theirs. Second, although the majority profess otherwise, most groups in the building industry have negotiable fees. There is always someone who will do the same job for less.

Following is a rundown of the professional people who offer services in the field of library building or renovation. Who are they, what do they do, and what do they charge?

Library consultants

Although library consulting is not new, as an actual profession the major impetus dates from the building boom of the late 1950s and the entire 1960s, when there were money and interest to spend for the "best" libraries possible. Partly to fill the gap between the "ivory tower" study of library philosophy as taught at universities and the down-to-earth nuts and bolts of the building industry, certain groups were attracted to library consulting, first and foremost librarians who already had been in charge of constructing a library.

Armed with a list of what went right and wrong in their own facilities, and with a strong theoretical background as to what a library is supposed to be, librarians with building experience made up, and still make up, the majority of library consultants. These people understand the nature of library service, but usually depend upon others in the building industry to work out individual building elements. (The American Library Association has tried to limit the title of library consultant to librarians with library degrees. However, this is still an unofficial rule.)

Another group functioning as library consultants is made up of certain vendors who sell everything from furnishings to special equipment, for example, microform equipment. Some of these people have been in the field for a very long time and are knowledgeable about specific library problems pertaining to their areas of interest. They may calculate the requirements of the circulation desk, how many book stacks are needed, where the lighting should go, and so on. Their fee is part of the merchandise they sell.

Architects, engineers, and interior designers also practice as library consultants simply because they have designed several libraries. These people have some understanding of library service, but are most interested in the library as a three-dimensional space—they are concerned with the building.

Ideally, the library consultant should act as liaison between the librarian (or board or administration) and the people who will do the constructing, equipping, or even moving into the library. Of course, a consultant's work can entail much more than that, depending upon the particular situation—

from ferreting out the library's central philosophy and matching it with community requirements, core collections, and current services, to fitting those needs into coherent three-dimensional space. Very often library consultants are most concerned with traffic patterns and access within the library—how people, books, and materials get from one place or person to another, whether one department belongs physically next to another, as well as its location in the building vis-à-vis user, staff, and material access.

Obviously if the library is most interested in service aspects, a consultant should be hired who is well steeped in library philosophy. However, for those most interested in the three-dimensional, a consultant primarily concerned with the visual world can be a better choice, especially one who can read plans.

If major construction is contemplated, a library consultant may be retained to write a feasibility report on whether it makes sense to renovate an old facility, add on, or move to an entirely different site, including where the necessary funds will come from. If the construction is okayed, the consultant, through interviews, research, and/or observation, may author a program for the library building so that the services can be accommodated. In this case, the library consultant may delineate square foot standards and type and number of furnishings to house the current as well as the projected collection. Again, it depends upon how one retains the services of the consultant.

Library consultants are often hired to ascertain that which is already known, but because of internal politics must be said by someone outside the library. Sometimes the administration must be prompted by outside people to start large projects. Under such conditions, if possible, the consultant should define the problems carefully, create priorities, and develop control mechanisms to see that the priorities are carried out.

Furthermore, for any kind of major change in the library, there must be continuity from beginning to end. Librarians are often too busy to oversee that chore. This may be the real function of the library consultant—providing a continuity to ensure that the job will be completed, and completed correctly.

For any major construction, it is essential that a good, concise building program be written, and more importantly, that the design professionals be made to follow that program. This can be done if the administration indicates faith in the consultant and explains to the design team that the program is to be part of their resources. After each phase of the design, the plans should be checked against the program to determine whether they match.

Fees

Because most library consultants hold other jobs (they may be directors of libraries or professors in schools of library science), generally their fees are low when compared to those of other managerial consultants. They can be retained in a number of ways: flat fee basis, hourly or daily rate, or percentage of construction costs (usually 1 to 2 percent). In many instances, especially when dealing with libraries that are part of government agencies, consultants will enter a bid competition for a job by offering a proposal, including a fee for services.

It is well to remember that library consultants do not work on a per room or on a per square foot basis, a common practice in the interior design field. The work of a library consultant is conceptual; a written report usually is involved. Whether a library has large areas or small, the fee will depend upon the complexity of the job.

Architects

Most architects are trained at technical colleges or schools of architecture, although in some states a few professionals still gain experience solely by working in architectural firms (as lawyers often used to "read law" rather than attend law school). In any case, all architects must be licensed, usually by examination, in order to call themselves architects, and, in addition, the title is recognized only by the states that issue the licenses. There is a national licensing board, the National Council of Architectural Registration Boards (NCARB), but the state licenses are all-important. In many states reciprocal licenses are granted to architects certified by NCARB. In others, the licensing requirements are more stringent, leading to the practice of associating with local state architects, a procedure that is common in even the largest firms.

Allowing architects to practice only in states in which they are licensed ensures a level of professional competence for that locality. For example, the architect licensed in New York State does not have to have extensive knowledge about earthquakes; the architect licensed in California does.

What is most important to know is that the architect sealing the construction documents has the legal right to do so. For an architect, the seal is the instrument of the profession. Many local municipalities require even more stringent construction documents than do the states. Blueprints of plans affixed with an architect's (or an engineer's) seal may be necessary for construction of any magnitude. Depending upon the stringency of the regulations, "construction of any magnitude" may be as little as from $100 to $500. The seal then implies the accuracy of the drawings—that everything is in compliance with good architectural practices, state laws, and local rules and regulations (including zoning requirements). It should be noted that in some states it is possible for anyone to erect a building of any size without sealed construction documents, as long as they do not pass themselves off as professionals.

The architect is the owner's agent on the job and must adhere to certain ethics. For example, until recently it was considered unethical by the AIA, the most famous of the architectural societies, for an architect to be both designer and builder on a project; in certain states an architect could be disbarred for that practice. The regulation was lifted in 1978, and opened the way for creation of architectural building companies.

Normally, an architect will provide schematic drawings based on the program supplied by the library. If there is no program, the architect can aid the library in developing one (although it is wise to have program goals set

Models are generally expensive to produce and are rarely constructed for small projects. However, fairly complete models often accompany large projects. (This model is for the Hill High School, Connecticut.)

long before an architect arrives). In addition, the architect can draw detailed plans, elevations, and even models and renderings of what the project will look like (the last two elements are not always part of a standard contract). Architects can write detailed specifications and will "let" the contract based on these specifications—ideally on the basis of a bid competition among contractors—if retained to do so. If necessary, an architect will consult with mechanical, electrical, and/or structural engineers and pay them out of the architectural fee (unless specified otherwise in the contract). Finally, the architect can oversee the work of the contractor and report progress to the library (only if the architect is retained for on-site inspection).

The architect's involvement in the job can be limited. For example, if the client feels that the contractor is trustworthy or if the client is capable of doing the work (perhaps the library employs a first-rate carpenter), architects need not be retained for on-site inspection. An architect may be hired to provide concept drawings only, and the material may be turned over to an in-house engineer for translation into construction documents.

However, unless the situation is such that an architect's further involvement would be truly unnecssary, the library should consider otherwise. Limiting involvement may also be limiting the architect's liability. What if the contractor is not performing the job as per the contract? Who is to know and what can the client do? Perhaps the carpenter changes some specifications; an architect cannot be held responsible for something he or she knows nothing about and was not hired to pursue.

And, of course, as in the case of the library consultant, on all jobs it is best to have continuity from beginning to end. If the continuity is broken and different people are hired for different phases, never communicating with each other, difficulties are sure to arise. A lack of communication can prevent the project from ever reaching a successful end. Whenever possible, the architect, as well as all other professionals, should see their jobs through from start to completion.

Fees

An architect can be hired on a percentage of the construction cost, from as high as 20 percent to as low as can be negotiated. The larger the project, the smaller the percentage, so that a job of $100,000 may cost the library 15 percent, or $15,000, for the architect, but a job of $1,000,000, by the same library with the same architectural firm, may cost $7\frac{1}{2}$ percent, or $75,000.

Architects can be retained on a percentage basis limited by a set price. Here the client knows in advance that no matter what happens, the library will not pay more than, say, $15,000. Otherwise, if actual construction costs run to $200,000 rather than the planned $100,000, the architect will be due another $15,000 based on a 15 percent fee.

Architects can be retained on a fixed fee basis (the library will pay a certain amount—no less, no more) or on an hourly or daily rate. If the job is large, an hourly or daily rate is not advised. First, the number of hours will be great, and second, the hourly or daily rate is usually higher than a fixed fee or even a percentage.

There are no standard fees for architects. A Supreme Court ruling found published fees by any professional society to be in restraint of trade; the case in question was against a local bar association. So all fees by any professional in any field are now negotiable.

Engineers

Engineers are capable of handling most aspects of architectural design work; their professional training, licensing requirements, and societies are similar. Although one usually thinks of engineers as designing only the structural loads or the mechanical and electrical specifics, there is a great deal of overlapping between engineer and architect. Some of the larger architectural firms are engineering firms, too; some of the larger engineering firms provide architectural work.

In the engineering field there are several separate specialties and courses of study. For instance, an electrical engineer usually will not do the work of a structural engineer, and vice versa. In some states this may be the law.

Engineers are also bound by a list of ethics regulated by state law, as well as by the professional societies to which they belong. The best-known engineering society is the National Society of Professional Engineers (NSPE). A licensed engineer displays the initials P.E. after his or her name, connoting professional engineer. As with architects, engineers must be licensed in the state where the job is to be done. Otherwise the engineer will have to associate with a local firm to seal the construction documents properly.

Like the architect, the engineer may be hired by a library to do a feasibility study—whether it is best to renovate or move—and which site (or space in the building) would suffice. However, in the case of a new facility, unless a library has particular structural or other difficulties (perhaps a parking garage on the roof), usually the professional engineer works in a consulting capacity only—designing the heating/ventilating/air-conditioning system, checking loads, and so on. In other words, for a new facility the library usually hires an architect and the engineer works as a consultant, paid out of the architect's fee.

In an older building, the library may need the services of an engineer much more than the architect—the mechanical system must be upgraded, the facility needs an energy audit, structural cracks have developed. In this situation, the engineer is the primary professional on the job. If an architect is called in at all, such services may be on a consulting basis to the engineer.

Fees

If engineers are retained on a consulting basis, they usually charge on a daily rate or a fixed fee basis for the entire job. However, if they are designing the building from start to finish, they may go to a percentage of construction costs. If they are working as consultants to the architect, they may be paid a percentage of the architectural fee, which may amount to more than one-third.

Interior designers

Although both architects and engineers can provide interior design services—some do regularly, including layout of individual spaces, designing custom-built furnishings and equipment, purchasing furnishings and equipment, and generally overseeing the decorating—most people think of interior design as a separate specialty.

Again, there is a great deal of overlapping of the various services, but architecture usually connotes construction and/or large object definition (look, texture, height, breadth of walls, floors, and ceilings, as well as the exterior facade), and interior design usually touches on smaller things (look, color, and texture of furnishings and equipment).

Few states require interior designers to be licensed, except, perhaps, for the right to collect sales tax (known in the various trades as the resale number), a right nearly anyone running a business can request. However, the profession has several associations, the most famous being the American Society of Interior Designers (ASID), which has standards and ethical considerations to which an interior designer must comply.

Usually, interior designers are more knowledgeable about layouts and the cost of furnishings than are library consultants, architects, or engineers. (Depending upon past experience, the other professionals may be equally knowledgeable about the cost of equipment.) Interior designers claim a better sense of color and a better understanding of the behavioral requirements of their clients (how people will use the furnishings). However, practically all design professionals—interior designers, architects—share the same fault; they are often more interested in the "look," the aesthetics of the library, than in its function and service, which are the librarian's main concern.

There is a good deal of jealousy among architects, engineers, interior designers, contractors, even library consultants; in fact, between all people in the design and construction fields. But all can work together profitably, and often do. Some of the larger architectural firms have interior designers on staff and many large interior design firms employ architects.

On a job, interior designers often work with a series of prepared forms to list the processes that should take place in specific areas. For example, the forms may indicate the number of workers assigned to a particular area, the various functions that are required, and the furniture and equipment necessary to do the job. Ambiance may be another factor. In the children's area, for example, the tone may be gay and light; in the adult section a more reserved atmosphere may be desired.

Next, interior designers usually produce layouts that show every piece of library furniture and equipment in place. These drawings are in addition to any architectural or engineering construction documents, and although lighting design is rarely shown (except in the case of special lighting design), a tracing paper overlay should be made in addition to the layout drawings. In libraries the lighting is always a particular concern, and if the furnishings and equipment are put in place without consideration of lighting, problems will eventually follow.

Besides the layout drawings, a sample board often displays all fabrics, colors, and textures. Swatches of fabric, pieces of carpet, samples of paint, and so on are graphically displayed so that everyone involved with the library design will understand what that design will eventually entail.

Interior designers can prepare models also, although for a small library this is usually not part of their normal services and would have to be paid over and above the fee. (This depends upon the contract. If the interior design contract specifies a model will be built, the model is part of the agreement and should be provided at no extra charge.)

Fees

There are various ways in which an interior designer can bill the library for services:

1. The interior designer can buy all the furniture and equipment wholesale and sell it to the library retail. In effect, the designer is acting as a vendor and not charging the library for design. This is a very lucrative practice, as the markup can be as high as 40 to 50 percent. The library as part of a municipality, school, or even a corporation may be able to buy the same equipment and furnishings at a much lower rate. For that reason, the most prestigious interior designers rarely work in this way. Besides, it puts the designer in the position of a vendor and not a professional being paid a fee.

2. The designer can charge a fee as a percentage of the furnishings and equipment costs. The figure may be as high as 30 percent to as low as

the library can negotiate. In this case, the designer may buy on discount and pass the discount on to the library.

   3. The designer can charge a fee on the basis of interior square footage. Thus the price is more in the nature of a flat fee. (For example, if the fee is $1.50 per square foot and the library has 10,000 square feet, the fee would be $15,000.) Again, the designer may buy on discount. Depending on the nature of the work, the fee may actually be on the basis of a sliding scale—$1.50 per square foot for, say, an intensively designed audiovisual area, 80¢ per square foot for the rest of the facility, and perhaps 25¢ per square foot for the exterior of the building adjacent to the entranceway.

   4. The interior designer can work on a daily and/or hourly rate.

   5. The fee can be based on a combination of several of the above.

   There is often good profit in the work of the interior designer and more leeway for extra charges than for the architect or engineer. An architect, for example, may work on a job for as long as three years (from the time first approached to final construction), and the interior designer may work for one year, but the designer may receive a larger fee (based on days employed).

Space and facilities planners

Dating from about the 1950s, a specialized group has begun to influence the way in which corporate or government libraries are designed. This group is made up of people trained as architects or engineers, interior designers, or some with no design training at all. By and large they are employees of the greater corporation or government agency of which the library is a part, members of planning departments, which may oversee the design of, say, up to one and a half million square feet of interior space. The library is only a very small part of their overall responsibilities.

   In most cases, the corporate or government librarians have little control of these individuals. The planners may have rigid corporate or government space, design, and funding standards to which they must adhere.

   Space planners and facilities planners (two names for the same occupation) rarely design the entire facility, particularly the exterior shell and core spaces. An outside architect/engineer is usually retained to design and oversee construction of the building, leaving most floors as empty loft spaces. After the building is erected, the planners lay out the furnishings and equipment of the different departments.

   Interestingly, many of the individual planners do not control the aesthetic design of the interior. Often they cannot choose the type of carpeting, fabrics, materials, or even colors to be used. At times they are severely limited as to the number of square feet they can allocate. Instead, the corporation or government agency has set up fairly rigid standards, which depend upon an employee's grade level and the importance of the particular department in which the employee works. Thus, if the employee is, say, a grade 14 working in a department level 3, the only furnishings that the planner can specify may be light green steel in a total work station covering 48 square feet.

In certain organizations, the planners do only run-of-the-mill work, so it is not uncommon for outside architects, engineers, interior designers, and even consultants to be hired in what is perceived as special situations. The outside expert may only block out the work to be done, allowing the planning department to implement the job. Libraries are often perceived as special situations.

Fees

Because planners work for the same corporations or agency, there are no fees involved. However, for bookkeeping practices, in some organizations the in-house planning department charges the library according to the work hours required and the furnishings allocated. Although no actual monies change hands, on paper the library posts charges against the yearly library budget.

Manufacturers and vendors

Manufacturers may sell the materials they produce directly to the library or they may sell the product only to distributors. The distributor may act as a vendor and sell directly to the library or may work in the middle and sell only to a third party, who acts as a vendor selling directly to the library. There may be as many as four, five, or even more hands touching the equipment before the library purchases it. The more people in the middle, the more the price rises. In the field of merchandising, every time a product passes from one person to another, its price is increased perhaps two to three times.

Obviously, then, it is better for the library to deal directly with the manufacturer. Unfortunately, because of antitrust laws, the manufacturer may be prevented from selling directly to customers. But many furniture and equipment manufacturers or their distributors in the normal course of work will supply interior design services, especially if the library is large. Rarely do they ever supply architectural or engineering services that require sealed construction documents (although they may work hand in hand with an architect or engineer retained by the library).

Some of the services provided by manufacturers or vendors are very good. Who else knows best how the equipment or furnishings should be set up? Also, by going directly to a manufacturer or vendor, costs can be nailed down to the penny, and there may be very few contingencies to deal with later on. Manufacturers and vendors can help the library write up the specifications for all pieces to be delivered, and they know enough to specify all parts. (For example, they will remember that all stack ranges need two starters.) Thus the library can receive an accurate breakdown of monies to be spent long before the job actually begins. In addition, some professionals will install their own merchandise, which cuts down on problems.

However, the library should be aware that manufacturers and vendors want to use merchandise that *they* are selling, not someone else's. Thus, if a particular chair, lighting fixture, or whatever has caught a librarian's eye, and vendors do not have it in stock, they will try to change the buyer's mind, even if the wanted piece of furniture is better than their own. Then, too, it is to their advantage to overestimate the needs of the library, and some vendors do.

Discounts are usually available, and an unwary librarian may pay retail prices for products, even going directly to a manufacturer, that may be discounted as much as 50 percent to the trade. In other words, for their "free design services," the manufacturers or vendors may be receiving their normal wholesale markup and an additional retail markup as well. The practice can be exceedingly lucrative.

Some vendors, acting more or less in the middle, will deal with any furnishings and equipment manufacturer on the library's behalf. Interior designers buying wholesale and selling retail also work in this fashion. Some of these vendors are extremely specialized and deal with only one aspect of the library. There are software firms that will arrange for sophisticated communication systems and recording firms that will set up first-rate studios. In the corporate field, at least one firm sets up only certain types of special libraries. Because they are so specialized, some of these vendors do an excellent job and are well worth the money they are paid—but they do tend to be very expensive.

Fees

It is difficult to nail down the fees in this area. First, the library has no way of knowing how much profit a manufacturer or vendor is making (unless the particular company is on the stock exchange and publishes a profit statement). If the amount of merchandise to be purchased is large, which gives the library some power, prices probably can be negotiated. Another widely used method is the competitive bid, where several vendors submit specifications and costs for the equipment and furnishings to be installed. But here the problem is that the lowest bidder may not be the best. First, the specifications leading to the bid and written by the library may have left out some important points. Second, it is the maintenance and follow-up after installation that can cost the library more money than anticipated. What if furnishings are delivered in a damaged condition? If the lowest bidder does not repair them in good order, who gets the blame? Besides, some equipment needs regular maintenance by someone who is knowledgeable. If the lowest bidder does not provide the maintenance or the parts, who will? Therefore libraries should try to use vendors with a good follow-up record in their area.

Contractors

If the library needs construction, a contracting firm may be hired. Depending upon the scope of the work, the contractor may be a one-person operation or may employ 500 people.

A general contractor is just that, a contracting firm that claims to do everything, all the work. Usually, however, it must hire special subcontractors for the electrical system, plumbing, or perhaps the roofing. The general contractor may be solely an administrative organization, which in turn hires subcontractors, or the principals of the firm may do some of the work themselves. Very often the general contractor is a carpentry group, which subcontracts the other work.

Unless the scope of the work is large, it is wise to use a company where one of the principals works—or can work—on the job. In that way, the library may be assured that someone who understands the nature of the job is supervising the workers. The general contractor will receive a percentage off the top (usually 10 percent for overhead and 10 percent for profit) and, if working on the job, daily wages as well.

The worst thing that can happen to a library is to have the contractor underestimate the job and, as a result, receive no compensation. If the general contractor is hurt, everyone else will be, especially the library. That is why on small jobs it is advisable to use a contractor who works on the job. At least that person is receiving daily wages, and thus there is reason to continue. Otherwise the contractor may simply walk off the job if there is no compensation coming.

The construction phase is certainly the most difficult for all involved. This is when plans become realities. During construction and installation, all misunderstandings are brought out; designs may not be as attractive as they looked on paper or exactly what the staff visualized. Furniture, when in place, looks too large for the rest of the decor. There are times, through no fault of their own, when contractors take the blame.

For most jobs, general contractors sign contracts or agree to do a specified amount of work for a certain amount of money. The work specifications may be supplied by an architect, engineer, interior designer, manufacturer, vendor, or even the library. Unless a particular contractor is desired, most contractors receive work by bid competition (although not all libraries choose on the basis of the lowest bid, if not required to do so by law—a contractor's past work may be evaluated as well). Materials, labor, and profit are calculated and form the bid. Obviously, the contractor must be fairly accurate, but it is not uncommon for one of the estimates to be off by a percentage. If that happens and the library hires that contractor, the library is facing trouble.

In addition, problems develop that are beyond anyone's control, for example, a strike called in a national union or certain materials hit with sudden price increases. Of course, the library can bond the contracting company, and this is often done on large jobs. But unless the project is extensive, insurance adds extra costs and the library may not be prepared to pay.

Someone who is knowledgeable (usually the architect, engineer, or interior designer) should perform on-site inspection and act as a liaison between the contractor and the library. On very small jobs the librarian may be able to oversee everything. On the biggest jobs, the architect or engineer might be asked to provide a clerk of the works, someone who is on the job every day to answer any questions. Design professionals will not show up every day on most jobs. Instead they will perform on-site inspection at regular intervals over the course of the work. However the liaison work is performed, the person in charge should see that all jobs are proceeding and the correct materials are being used. The liaison should keep a time and action calendar and check that suppliers and subcontractors are paid.

A general contractor on occasion defaults and does not pay the suppliers or subcontractors, although the library has appropriated the funds. This can be particularly nasty. A mechanic's lien can be put on the project, and all sorts of legal trouble may follow. Therefore, at the end of the construction phase, it is necessary that a release be received from subcontractors and suppliers to the effect that they have been paid. Then the work can be "signed off," acknowledging that the general contractor has done the work as required. Librarians should avoid contracts stating that once the library takes possession of the facility (moves in), the job in effect has been "signed off."

Fees

Here again, it is difficult to state precise fees. Contractors using union workers tend to be much more expensive than those who do not. (It is not uncommon for a nonunion worker to be paid half as much as a union member.) However, few libraries can use nonunion labor. Some contractors will work for "time and material," a situation in which the library is charged only for the time and material to do the job. For a small project, this may be a good idea, particularly if an upset price can be agreed upon (the cost of the job will not exceed a specified amount) and if the library can offer adequate supervision. But this is not suggested for larger jobs. It is too easy for extra work to be fabricated and nonexistent materials to be billed.

A fixed contract price for work to be done is ascertained by estimating materials required and then calculating the costs. Next, the work hours are estimated and the labor charge is added, topped by 10 percent profit and 10 percent contingency figures. Because all calculations are based on estimates, it is obvious why cost overruns seem to be endemic in the field.

A word of caution—avoid extras. Once the job begins, the contract for proposed work should be followed. Changing one's mind is usually costly; work which is not a part of the original bid may be charged at a much higher rate. The contractor has little incentive to keep the price low.

Design/builders and modular/prefabricated builders

Design/builders are design and contracting firms in one. Similar to vendors who offer design services and installation of furnishings and equipment, design/builders emphasize construction. Some architects and engineers function as design/builders. Interior designers can also be design/builders, although in certain states they need either an architect or engineer to seal the building plans. Some vendors function as design/builders, particularly those who sell modular or prefabricated constructions, but they, too, must have their plans sealed in most states. However, most design/

builders are contractors who feel they can perform all design services as well as the contracting aspects.

By using a design/builder, the client has two decided advantages. First, the library has only one firm with which to deal, and thus the lines of communication are usually better and the headaches fewer. Second, there is better control of costs. Being both designer and contractor, the design/builder can quickly translate plans into cost estimates for labor and materials.

But, as with all good things, there are disadvantages. Certain design/builders have not studied design and may create spaces that function poorly. No one is acting as the client's agent on the job, looking over the shoulder of the design/builder and determining whether the company is performing as it should.

Even so, for the small library in particular, use of design/builders may be the best route. The job is just so small that it does not pay to get involved with other professionals. Book shelves and new lighting can be specified and put up in little time, with very little hassle.

Modular/prefabricated builders fall somewhere between manufacturers/vendors and design/builders. Here the library buys a building, or a part of a building, in kit form already designed. This type of construction has not made large inroads in the library building industry, but it is known in the residential, commercial, and industrial building fields. Entire buildings can be purchased from a catalog and put up in a few days to perhaps a month. This is, of course, one of the reasons they are becoming popular. Also, one can see before construction what has been purchased.

Prefab manufacturers are now turning their attention to the library field. Small buildings specifically for public library use are available from several organizations, as well as modifications of commercial and industrial kits. The manufacturer/vendor may put up the building (or an addition) after proper documents are filed. If the manufacturer/vendor is nearby and will oversee everything instead of hiring a local contractor to do the work, the prefab may be an inexpensive project. By fabricating everything at the plant and minimizing on-site construction, much labor and time are saved.

However, if the manufacturer first sells to a distributor and the distributor sells to a vendor, who in turn hires a local contractor, no savings may be realized. The prefab is a manufactured product, and like all such products, there is a markup for each change of hands. The cost of transporting the building from plant to site must also be considered. For example, if the manufacturer is located in Oregon and the building is to be erected in Florida, shipping costs may eat up all savings. In addition, the building kit may arrive and the site not be appropriate. In other words, although it may appear that these buildings are always cheaper, sometimes they are not.

Fees

Fees are negotiable, but design/builders have a better profitability record than general contractors, architects, or interior designers because they can absorb the design or builder fee. They calculate costs in a manner similar to general contractors. For the prefab builders, it is difficult to talk about fees because these buildings are manufactured items, but the rule of two to three times markup for every change in distribution is about what to expect.

When purchasing a kit, it is important to ascertain if the price refers to the factory site or the library site. In other words, is shipping part of the purchase price or must the library figure that as an extra? If shipping is extra, charges must be figured. Is special equipment necessary? An extra-wide load needs special routing on highways and may add shipping time as well as money to the bill.

Who is going to erect the building? Has that cost been included in the purchase price? What about the costs of bringing utilities to the site? If modifications are to be made to the kit, those costs must also be figured.

Consultants

Except for library consultants (already discussed), the consultation field is difficult to define. There are consultants for just about everything. Depending upon the library's circumstances and needs, available consultants include:

1 Management consultants to deal with administrative problems

2 Lighting consultants to design special effects or the entire lighting system

3 Acoustical consultants to tone down library noise or improve the sound in a proposed auditorium

4 Energy consultants to study heating/ventilating/air-conditioning/lighting systems

5 Moving consultants to relocate the library

6 Weeding or editing consultants to throw away unwanted books, papers, files, or microforms

7 Computer consultants to computerize the library

8 Display consultants to deal with special displays

Some of these people are licensed in their fields and some are not. For example, a lighting consultant may or may not be a licensed engineer. Either way, they may be extremely knowledgeable in their chosen fields. For example, although Buckminster Fuller is considered by many to be a great architect, he is an engineer. Keyes Metcalf, the father of the library building program and probably more knowledgeable about library construction than many who hold licenses in the construction field, is a librarian.

The main concern for the library administration is to comprehend fully how the consultant works. For example, if the library must have sealed construction documents, who is to provide them? Can the consultant find the proper professional, or does the library have to do so?

Special hiring problems

After reading the qualifications and services of the professionals, it still may be difficult to decide which are better for the individual library. Who will fulfill the requirements to the greatest degree?

Much about the hiring process is often illogical, depending upon a special mannerism or personality trait. Some people, for example, do not make a good first impression, even though they are honest, hardworking, and would be careful with the library's funds. People who are personable, whether or not they can do the job, have an easier time selling their services.

Among the important points to keep in mind when hiring are whether management and staff will be able to work with the professional group, and if the group checks out as stable. Do these professionals have a reputation, not uncommon in the architectural and interior design fields, for walking off the job if they are opposed? Some manufacturers, vendors, and contractors who have enough other work may not give a job, particularly a small one, the attention it needs. The monies that seem substantial to a particular library may be very little in the large company's view. Above all, when hiring any professional, the client must retain control throughout the process.

It is unnecessary to spend a long time on the hiring process. Interviews with up to six qualified people should be satisfactory. For a small job, only one interview may be necessary, and even for the largest jobs, where prescreening is a necessity, sound initial selections will help to whittle the possibilities down to six. A small school library should not contract an 80-man engineering firm to upgrade the lighting; should the firm accept the job, which is unlikely, it will either charge too much or pass the work on to someone very low in command. In the same way, a large university library should not choose a one-person architectural firm to redesign the entire building. One person will not have the resources upon which to draw to satisfy the large library's requirements.

For libraries that must hire on the basis of bid competition, it is best to make specifications as detailed as possible for the largest projects. For small jobs, overly detailed specifications are often ignored or overcharged by the bidder. A responsible company reading an extremely detailed specification will take the document at its word and enter a high bid. A fly-by-night concern, little worried about legal implications, may enter a low bid and get the job. Either way, the library loses.

PLANNING
AND
ARRANGING
LIBRARY
SPACE

As work environments, libraries are "difficult." On the one hand, they embody the mystique of the written word. People tend to think of libraries as great soaring buildings and monuments to knowledge. On the other hand, today's libraries are complex

Some libraries feature book stacks radiating from a central point like spokes on a wheel, a configuration that often limits the amount of usable area (Plantation Middle School, Ft. Lauderdale, Florida).

organizations, equipment intensive and becoming more electronic each day. Because of this reliance on equipment, a valid argument can be made that planning library interiors is something akin to planning factory interiors. Where factory layouts must depend upon the proper position of machinery to help produce goods, libraries rely upon row after row of stacks, cabinets, files, tables, and machinery to store and access collections—to produce knowledge. What good is a factory design so complex that the manufacturing processes are impeded? What good is a library design so difficult that there is little room for the current collection, much less future growth?

Unfortunately, some of the most renowned American library buildings have been poorly designed vis-à-vis function. Many architects and interior designers find book stacks, file cabinets, storage bins, map cases, and index tables boring in shape. They want to create interesting, attractive interiors to delight the eye. And so, many of them "play" with space—book stacks radiate from central cores as spokes on a wheel, others form pyramids, still others are diamondlike, placed in a square with opposing angles to the walls. Too many libraries designed in these ways have problems with shelving, accessing, and especially growth. The square footage is there, but not in any usable manner. Wasted space may account for up to 25 percent of the total.

No one advocates only factorylike libraries. However, the bottom line for any library facility is space for its collection. Sometimes designers, builders, and planners lose sight of the fact that books, materials, and films are the reasons that the library exists in the first place. The collection makes the library—and needs space. The second priority is space for users to *use* the

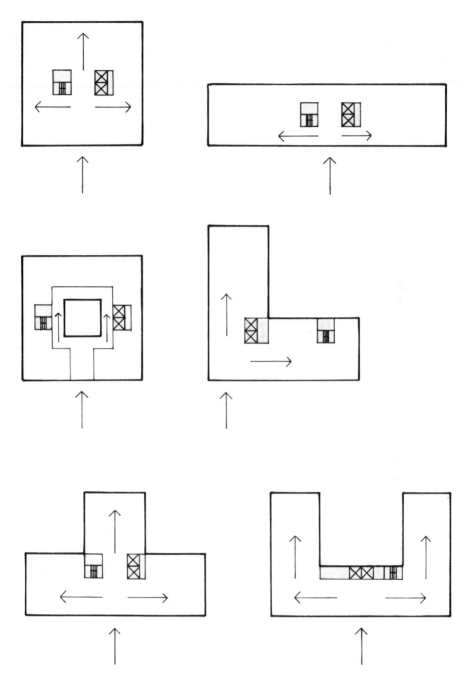

The shape of the floor determines waste space. A long rectangle, doughnut shape, "L" shape, "T" shape, and "U" shape require more corridor space than a simple square. The location of entrance and vertical access (stairwells, ramps, elevators) is another determinant. Traffic patterns control the amount of usable space.

A reader area can be a pleasant oasis (AT&T Corporate Library, Basking Ridge, New Jersey).

library. Libraries with little room for users lose their patrons, the very people who pay to keep the library open, or, at least, the people for whom the library was created. The third priority is space for staff, the people who keep the facility functioning.

Book stack spaces should be simple, utilitarian. The lobbies, corridors, reader areas, lounges, or meeting rooms may be visual delights, but the areas designated for book stacks should be straightforward. Being both utilitarian and handsome need not be a design problem. Bookstores often incorporate both. Retail store design is different from library design, but a good store is set up to attract customers, utilizing every inch of space. As stock changes, so must the design. Store design must be flexible. A good library interior should be flexible as well.

The square as flexible space

Library areas of heavy traffic and book stack spaces should be square or large rectangles, everything else being equal. Other library areas can take more pleasing shapes. The square is the most flexible interior space, espe-cially in a library. Book stacks and files tend to be long rectilinear objects. If the space in which they are housed is square, they can be run in either direction, north-south or east-west, without difficulty. A good lighting system works best in a square arrangement (see the chapter on lighting, power, and energy). The square is also good acoustically (see the chapter on acoustics). A square minimizes walking, all points being equally distant from the center. This centralization makes a square easier to control—all spaces can be viewed equally from the center. (A circle has some of these advan-tages, too, but a circle is an extremely costly form to build. Most construction

A square allows greater flexibility for spatial arrangements, with greater visual control as well, as shown in the top two diagrams. A square is acoustically better than other shapes. Because the center is equally distant from all walls, sound does not reflect at odd angles. In a long rectangle, sound bounces back and forth, creating noisier space. A square is also easier to control than an irregularly shaped space, and it minimizes distances.

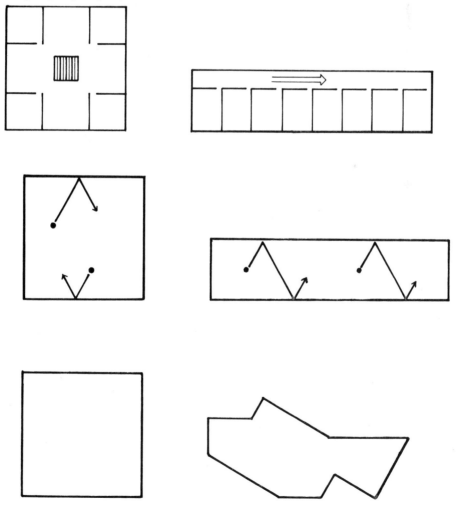

materials are fabricated in square or rectilinear shapes, making the square or rectangular form the least expensive to construct. There is less labor cutting things down to size. Circles and irregular shapes require custom work and increased labor costs.)

Unfortunately, both squares and large rectangles are, in general, uninteresting forms and not especially aesthetic. Most libraries have L, T, or U shapes, or are narrow rectangles or doughnutlike structures (for aesthetic purposes). Or some have "just grown," without planned design. If a square was planned in the first place, there may have been circumstances why the library had to take another shape: a triangular site, fire requirements, zoning setbacks, other facilities too close by. The point is that anything that changes the basic square or large rectangle creates wasted space for the library, particularly in the stack areas and areas of heavy traffic. This increases the nonassignable space.

Nonassignable space

Nonassignable space is space that cannot be used for library purposes—corridors, stairwells, elevators, rest rooms, mechanical rooms, and such. Nonassignable space also implies unusable nooks and crannies. In a few instances, nonassignable space has been planned for aesthetic relief. A huge atrium six stories tall can be exceptionally attractive, but it is space that must be maintained—heated, ventilated, air conditioned, and lighted.

Most space planners agree that it is best to keep nonassignable space to a minimum. A good tight facility, and also one that is attractive, should not

An atrium causes nonassignable space—space that must be heated, ventilated, air conditioned, and lighted (Skidmore Library, Colorado College).

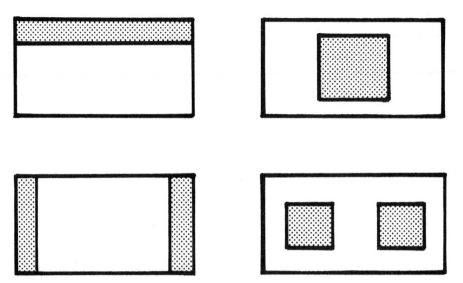

If an atrium is planned, the most important consideration is its placement. The resulting space should be simple and not be cut into fragments. In this diagram, the atriums (shaded spaces) on bottom right create the worst space arrangement of all.

consist of more than 25 percent nonassignable space. A full 15 percent of the total area of the building must be relegated to corridor and simple traffic circulation; the other 10 percent is divided into areas such as rest rooms, mechanical rooms, and aesthetic details. As the total percentage of nonassignable space begins to rise over 25 percent, the planning begins to be wasteful and the work flow ineffective. Too much nonassignable space implies walking—lots of walking—lack of control and major increases in staff.

The great academic facilities of yesteryear may have huge reading rooms, perhaps six stories tall, but in relation to the amount of space available to house the collection and provide areas for library functions, many of them are, nonetheless, space conserving. Out of more than 300,000 square feet of interior space, only a few thousand may be used for aesthetics. A case in point is the two buildings that make up the National Gallery of Art, Washington, D.C. Both the gallery's old and new structures have impressive lobbies, but the older facility has more exhibit space to hang paintings than does the newer, much-acclaimed wing. The Massachusetts Institute of Technology began a program to track space, and to the staff's great surprise they discovered that within the entire campus only 2 percent of the interior spaces were classrooms, 17 percent for laboratories, 17 percent offices for staff and faculty, and 18 percent for corridors.

Any shape that spreads out wall space increases the nonassignable areas. More wall space implies more corridors. But with a square, there is more floor area in relation to the confining envelope than other easy-to-build configurations. A square is also simple to divide and rearrange. Cut in two and the result is two small rectangles. Cut in four and the result is four small squares. No matter if the library is large or small, to be built from the ground up or simply rearranged, the square always works.

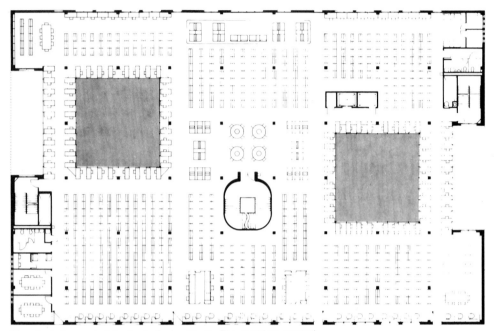

The shaded areas in this plan indicate atriums. The corridors created along the exterior walls near the atriums limit the flexibility of space. It is unlikely that such areas can be used for anything but carrel seating.

The central square

Workable or not, space saving or not, most people do not want plain, square library facilities. They are too "workmanlike." A solution is the concept of the "central square" for the areas of heaviest user activity and the places most likely to change. These are the spaces requiring the most control. Large staff areas, operations functions, meeting rooms, departments that require acoustical and/or visual privacy, do not belong in the central square. Those places need quiet and some confining walls. The central square should be the focal point of the library from which all user activities radiate, an open place where people and activities converge. The central square concept can be applied everywhere in the library; each individual department should have its own central square to aid work flow. In a multilevel facility, each floor should have a central square. Technical process needs a central square also.

Furnishings and equipment in the central square should be loosely fitted because this is an area of change. Future requirements may cause the card catalog in the lobby to be replaced by computer terminals. The circulation desk may divide into circulation and information areas.

To find the central square on any plan, draw an outline around the periphery of the library on a piece of tracing paper and locate the main entrance, stairwells, elevators, and other major points of traffic flow. The central square is superimposed upon that area. The main entrance is the most important access point. Because it controls traffic, it is essential that the main entrance be located at the heart of the central square. It is the point of orien-

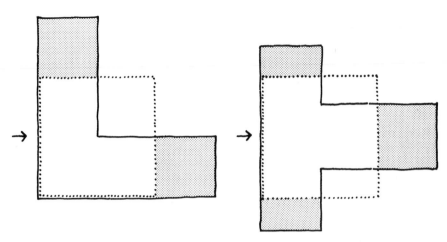

The central square should be the focal point of the library from which all user activities radiate. Departments that require less user interaction should be located away from the central square. Such departments belong in the shaded spaces.

tation for nearly everyone. If it is the only entrance/exit (except for fire doors), everyone must pass through it at least twice a day. The main entrance is the point at which the majority of users enter the library. It may not, however, be the largest door. In a public library, the majority may drive to the building and enter through the parking lot door. The door by which the majority enter and leave, no matter where it is located, is the main entrance.

If the main entrance is in a difficult area, particularly one where a central square would not be possible because it would be divided by many walls, the main entrance might be moved to reroute traffic or the walls may be able to be moved. Here the services of an architect or engineer are often required.

Movement patterns

After locating the main entrance and central square together, the next step is to review the movement patterns based upon departmental locations. In a multistory facility, the stairs, elevators, and ramps determine access and, literally, where people and materials go. Usually it is best to locate the elevator and stairs adjacent to one another as one point of vertical access. In a very large facility, there may be more than one elevator/stair combination in

The main entrance, which controls traffic, is the most important access point. Wherever possible, it should be located at the most central point. The main entrance and major corridor (shaded area) on the left are well located; the entrance and corridor on the right are poorly located.

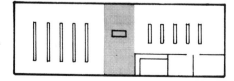

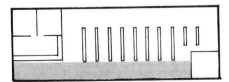

different parts of the building. These combinations form vertical cores, minimizing nonassignable space on each floor. A good example of this kind of planning can be found in multilevel office buildings. Not only do stairs and elevators relate to one another but so do all entrance/exits, rest rooms, and mechanical facilities. By grouping all structural elements that rise vertically through the building, including plumbing pipes, electrical wiring, and ductwork, each floor can be "opened up" and made more usable in terms of available square footage. Nonassignable space, particularly in corridors, is reduced. Here, the major difficulty is the location of this large "bulk." If the core is placed in an inconvenient site for later renovation or even rearrangement, flexibility may be limited. The proper location must be planned carefully.

Common sense says that the corridors or walkways running through the library, or through each floor of a multilevel facility, can be reduced in size if related directly to the departments strongest in demand. Departments that generate the most traffic should be closest to these corridors, starting with the main entrance and radiating toward the rest of the building. As one walks farther and farther away from these points, the activity levels should reduce. In other words, it does not make any sense—as one library was set up—to store bound periodicals right next to the front door, the most valuable user space, and to keep new periodicals upstairs in the back (unless, of course, bound periodicals form a special collection that is in constant and heavy demand—not the case in this instance). This also implies that in larger libraries, those staff functions that do not relate directly to the users can be removed from behind the circulation desk and placed elsewhere in the facility.

The location of the technical process area is a key to the difference between layouts of public, academic, special, or school libraries. Public and academic libraries tend to hide staff areas, usually behind closed doors. Special libraries and some school libraries are organized differently. Staff functions are displayed in full view. Users may walk through these areas to get to the collection. The essential reasons for this difference are that special and school libraries are located in office environments and it is important for users to understand that the library is also a place of work; and one person may serve as a reference librarian, cataloger, and acquisitioner, a rare setup for public and academic libraries, except for the very smallest. One courthouse library actually has 100,000 volumes, 16,000 square feet of space, and one staff member! Of course, that is an extreme example.

If the library has more than one entrance/exit, and means to keep it that way, common sense also says that those entrances/exits should relate to the user populations they serve, for instance, a public library with a parking lot door. Most adults ride to the public library, entering through the parking lot door; many children walk, entering through the street side door. Often adult services are located to the "front" of the building, on the street side, while the children's services are located to the "rear," close to the parking lot. Adults cross the entire length of the facility to get to their areas of interest, while children cross in the opposite direction. Loss of control, as well as books, results.

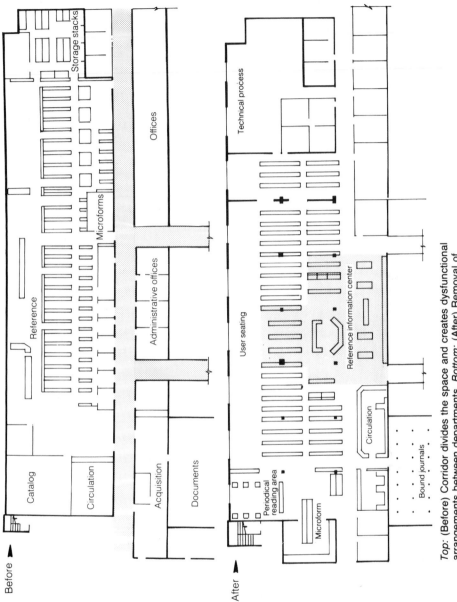

Top: (Before) Corridor divides the space and creates dysfunctional arrangements between departments. *Bottom:* (After) Removal of walls simplifies the arrangement and work flow between departments.

In some libraries, similar but more serious situations may occur where services are available for the handicapped. In one facility, handicapped patrons can enter the building in a wheelchair only by means of a ramp in the basement. The special areas set aside for the handicapped are located on the third floor, at the opposite end of the building. If for some reason the ramp entrance cannot be changed, why must the services be on the third floor, so far from the elevator? Usually this type of situation is the result of someone's not thinking.

Being able to visualize how something will work in real life is essential to a designer. First-rate architects and interior designers "see" spaces as they draw them, mentally picturing which areas go where, how people, materials, and "things" will move through the library. Although most librarians tend to be print oriented, the technique of visualization need not be limited to the artistic. Anyone can mentally walk through the facility in question. Exactly what do you "see"? Which areas are the most popular? Who goes where? Which areas are decidedly nonfunctional and unattractive? It is a good idea first to walk through the facility as a user and then as a staff member; the two groups often use different spaces and do not interact with the same objects.

When visualizing, the first general view is usually the most important. That is why areas around entranceways and lobbies often are well decorated; they are the first areas to make user contact. In a multilevel facility, the first floor or the floor where the main entrance is located is the most important user space for the same reason. When feasible in a multilevel facility, the most important user services should be located on that floor. Other ser-

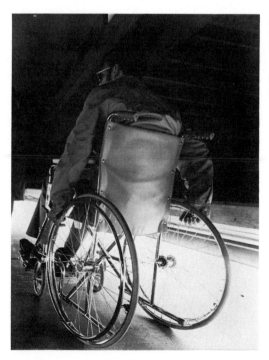

A barrier-free environment implies ease of access. Requirements for the physically disabled can be viewed as a positive factor in the arrangement of space; a staff member pushing a book truck has many of the same accessibility problems.

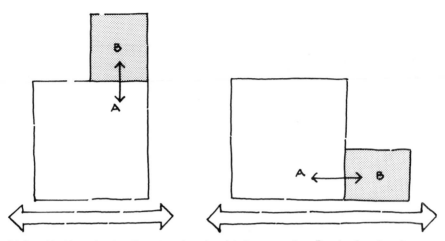

It is important to understand how departments relate to one another. Popular departments should be located next to a corridor (as A is here). Users should not have to walk through one department to get to a heavily used but rather small room (shaded area B). A better arrangement is to have A and B side by side, both on the corridor.

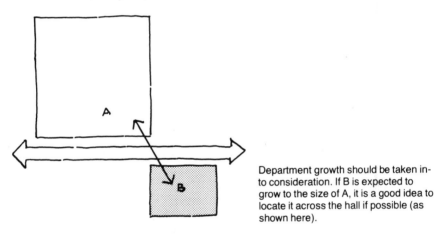

Department growth should be taken into consideration. If B is expected to grow to the size of A, it is a good idea to locate it across the hall if possible (as shown here).

vices not in such heavy demand can be placed elsewhere. (The same holds true for areas around heavily trafficked stairwells and elevators on other floors in a multilevel facility. Those areas serve as the most important for the floors in question and require the most popular services to be close by.)

Relating space in the library

What library services are the most popular, how should they relate to one another in space, and how do they relate to their satellite departments? Are any of these services or departments expected to expand at a quicker rate than others? Are any expected to be phased out over the next few years or substantially reduced in size? All this information must be gathered and the relationships charted. In this way, the librarian can relate spaces in the library for the most efficient operation.

CHARTING LIBRARY X

	Main Entrance Complex				Periodicals			
	Entrance	Circ. Desk	Info. Desk	Fiction	New	Bound	Study	Comments
Main Entrance Complex								
Entrance	/ /	A 6,1	E 6,1	I 6	I 6	X 4	X 4,1	Circ. & Info. desk close by; bound periodicals & study far away
Circ. desk	A 6,1	/ /	E 6,5,4,3,1	I 1	I 1	X 4	X 4,1	Main entrance & info. desk close by; bound periodicals & study far away
Info. desk	E 6,1	E 6,5,4,3,1	/ /	I 1	I 1	I 6,1	I 6,1	Main entrance & info. desk close by
Fiction	I 6	I 1	I 1	/ /	E 6,1	X 4	U /	New periodicals close by; bound periodicals far away
Periodicals								
New	I 6	I 1	I 1	E 6,1	/ /	E 6,5,3	O 6	Fiction & bound periodicals close by
Bound	X 4	X 4,1	X 6,1	X 4	E 6,5,3,1	/ /	E 6,5,3,2,1	New periodicals & study close by
Study	X 4,1	X 4,1	I 6,1	U /	O 6	E 6,5,3,2,1	/ /	Bound periodicals close by; main entrance & circ. desk far away

Value   *Closeness*
A   Absolutely necessary
E   Especially important
I   Important
O   Ordinary closeness
U   Unimportant
X   Undesirable
/   Repeat or not applicable

Code   *Reason*
1   Security and control
2   Relation of staff to equipment
3   Require electrical/telephone/plumbing
4   Noise
5   Relation of staff to one another
6   Accessibility of user

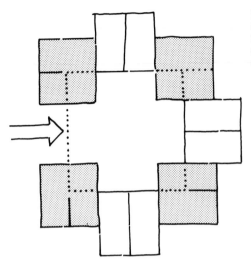

In this arrangement, all departments work off a central square, and each interacts freely. This concept is not applicable in all situations, only where clustering of activities is effective.

The Muther method

There are a number of ways to chart data for relating library space. One system, developed by Richard Muther, an industrial engineer, and his associate, John D. Wheeler, is widely used by facilities planners, architects, engineers, and interior designers.[1] The system is applicable for libraries of any size, but because the charting method was basically set up for plant engineers, the layout has been modified here for simplicity (see Charting Library X).

With the Muther method, every large department or function is rated with every other large department or function according to "physical closeness in space." Muther and Wheeler suggest using vowel letters as ratings. Next, a numerical code should be set up indicating why the relationships are valid. The reasons are left to the individual librarians and/or designers. See, for example, the six reasons shown in Charting Library X. Other reasons can be added, but the total should reach no more than about 10 (5 for a small library); otherwise the chart will get too complex. Whenever possible in planning, keep it simple.

At this point the librarian and the designer should be charting only generalized activities. They want to get a "feel" for the essential services. They need to understand which departments and functions should be physically close to one another and which should be farther apart.

In the sample (Charting Library X), the study area is to be located next to bound periodicals, but far away from the front door. It seems obvious that the study area is a place for long-term, quiet work. That means that it should be in the depths of the facility. On the other hand, bound periodicals should be located next to new periodicals and the study area. The chart should indicate how one department relates to another in space.

At this stage, a diagram can be drawn to show relationships in space. The diagram is not concerned with the size of the various departments, but is a series of circles connected to one another by lines. Muther suggests

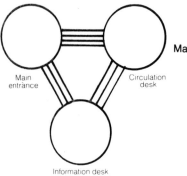

Main entrance complex.

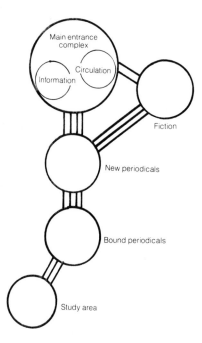

Main entrance complex and relationship to other areas in a nonsquare space.

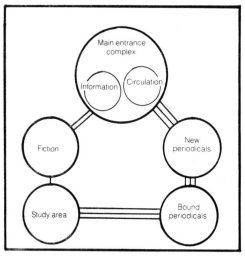

Optimum floor plan as a bubble diagram.

using four lines to show absolutely necessary, three lines for essential, and so on. A wavy line would indicate X or undesirable. Because most libraries are not as complex as manufacturing plants, all that is necessary at this point is to chart the A and E relationships along with the Xs (see diagram of main entrance complex). Four lines show that the circulation desk must be placed as close as possible to the main entrance. Three lines indicate that the information desk should be close to the main entrance, but not as close as the circulation desk. Three lines between information and circulation indicate closeness, but again, less close than the main entrance and circulation. Next, the other relationships can be charted (see diagram of main entrance relationships).

Muther and Wheeler suggest that square footage should be determined at this point. But the authors believe that a circle chart can be set up first without regard to square footage in the outline of the floor plan, realizing that some of the departments may not fit, to plot the optimum floor plan.

Even if the library is anything but square, this diagram will work, as indicated in the diagram of nonsquare space.

Determining area sizes

The next step is to ascertain square foot relationships to find the minimum areas needed. It is essential at this point to know the collection size, staff size, user requirements, and the estimated growth potential for each over the next 5 to 20 years.

Growth potential is the most difficult data to determine. At the rate the information industry is changing, it is difficult to make a good estimation of needs even five years in the future. Many periodicals, for example, now available only in hardback, will be published in micrographic form; many now in micrographic form will be placed directly on-line. There is a strong indication that certain back-dated shelving requirements will become minimal. On the other hand, changing populations and changing requirements sometimes increase the use of library facilities. How does one estimate— reasonably?

Book collection space

To make any estimates, one must know the number of volumes and other materials to be housed, the number of staff, and the number of patrons at any given time. The figures vary from library type to library type. In a public library, for example, adult book stack areas are expected to house between 15 and 18.5 volumes per square foot; law libraries house only 5 to 7 volumes per square foot. (Books are thicker in law libraries.) The same is true of staff and user requirements. In an academic library a few staff members may need two desks, one out on the floor and one in the office area to get work done. In a school library, the librarian may have only one desk. Counter space for quick reading is essential for many corporate libraries; in a graduate research facility, nearly every student is assigned a permanent carrel.

A bubble diagram should be blown up
and traffic patterns drawn in relation to
the main entrance and vertical access
points. The next step allows inclusion
of furniture arrangements. Again, traffic
patterns are shown.

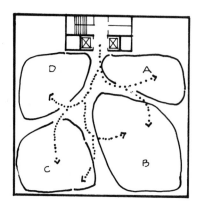

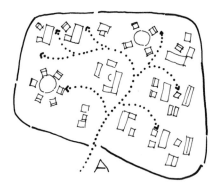

The number of volumes per square foot depends not only on the size of
the books but also on the size of the book stacks—the number and depth of
the shelves—and the length of the ranges and width of the aisles in between. According to Metcalf,[2] a range 66 feet long, divided by one 6-foot
cross aisle so that the lengths of the subranges are only 30 feet, made up of
book stacks double-faced, 7 shelves high, each stack 3 feet long, 9 inches
deep, placed 4 feet 6 inches from book stack center pole to book stack
center pole, contains 15 volumes per square foot. Here, the aisle between
stack faces is 3 feet wide. But if the stack shelves were 12 inches deep, the
center pole spacing would increase to 5 feet, reducing the volume per
square foot ratio substantially.

To convert lineal feet to square feet using a module of space, follow
these steps (see also book stack layout diagram on page 80).

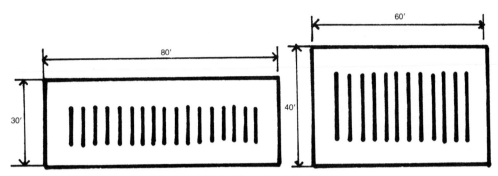

Two plans with the same square footage. The facility on the right, 40 feet by 60 feet, can allow 1,056 square feet for book stacks; the facility on the left, 30 feet by 80 feet, can allow only 768 square feet. Planning a more square shape and noting the configuration of extremely large pieces of equipment (such as long runs of book stacks) results in greater usability of square footage.

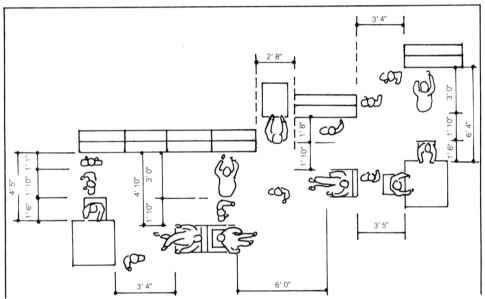

Typical dimensions for seating arrangements and standing requirements.

1. Measure the distance between columns. Multiply length by width to determine square feet enclosed. If the distances between all columns are the same, the square foot area between each column will make up one bay or module of space. In the book stack layout diagram, the space is 20 feet by 20 feet; one module contains 400 square feet.

2. Lay out book stacks by marking out the center pole of one double-faced range to the center pole of the next. In all cases, the minimum aisle should be 3 feet. Thus, if the shelves are 12 inches deep, from one center pole to the next the space to be spanned will be 5 feet.

3. Count the number of book stacks one can lay out in the space. In the diagram, there are 24 double-faced stacks.

4. Count the number of single-faced stacks. In the diagram, there are 48 single-faced stacks.

5. Determine the lineal feet of shelving in each section. In the diagram, all stacks are 3 feet wide and 7 shelves high. Each single face contains 21 lineal feet.

6. Multiply the number of lineal feet in one single-faced section by the number of sections. In the diagram, there are 21 lineal feet × 48 single-faced sections, which equals 1,008 lineal feet.

7. Determine the number of volumes per lineal foot (using standards or random sampling of shelves). In the diagram, there are 7 volumes per lineal foot; 1,008 × 7 = 7,056 volumes in the collection in that module or bay.

8. Divide the number of volumes by the square feet in the module:

$$\frac{7{,}056 \text{ volumes}}{400 \text{ square feet}} = 17.64 \text{ volumes per square foot}$$

Many libraries prefer to run very short ranges, which is wasteful. But by simply filling in a few of the cross aisles, the volume count can be increased. Many libraries also prefer to run single-faced stacks around the walls, which also reduces the volume count. Besides being quite costly (most cost almost as much as a double-faced stack), single-faced stacks are not an efficient way to house books. The wall space should be saved for "people" activities, and double-faced stacks should be used whenever possible.

If, for example, a 5 percent per year collection growth rate is figured, a library with 2,000 square feet of collection space would require an additional

Book stack layout (see steps 1 through 8 in text).

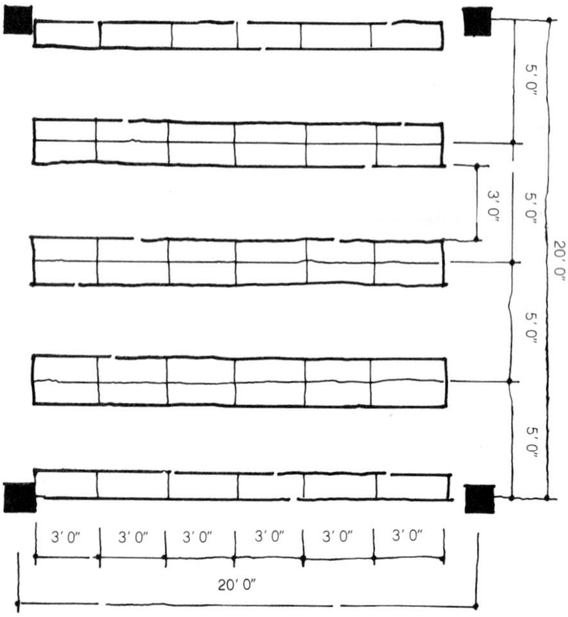

COLLECTION SQUARE FOOTAGE ESTIMATE
(20-year projection)

```
    2,000 square feet to house the already existing collection
  +2,000 square feet to allow a 5% growth rate per year for 20 years
  ─────
    4,000 square feet
  ×    6% configuration loss
  ─────
      240 square feet configuration loss

    4,000 square feet subtotal
  +   240 square feet configuration loss
  ─────
    4,240 square feet to house the collection in book form
```

2,000 square feet in 20 years (a 5 percent growth rate compounded annual-
ly means the collection will double in 14 years), bringing the total to 4,000
square feet (assuming the library continues to grow at the present rate and
does not turn to new areas that require additional collection increases).
Adding a 6 percent configuration loss (assuming the interior space will not
be square because of aesthetic or other reasons), 4,240 square feet would
be needed to house the collection in 20 years (see Collection Square Footage Estimate). In all calculations, a minimum 6 percent configuration loss is
used. Sometimes the figure is a good deal higher, more than 25 percent if
the building is circular.

   Note the use of the term "book form." An ordinary microfiche cabinet
with 9 drawers, 4 sections per drawer jam packed, holds 36,000 fiche. A
more reasonable figure would be about 30,000 fiche (including some space
to move around the width of envelopes to hold the various titles). Using 400
pages per title (obviously, this varies from library to library), an ordinary
cabinet standing in about 4 square feet of space can hold 7,500 titles, or
reduce the space required to house the book collection by about 500
square feet. (This is an optimum figure, not taking into consideration the
access required around the microfiche cabinet.)

Wherever possible, save the walls for people. (In a small room, one has no choice but to ring the
walls with books.) Walls are prime study and work areas.

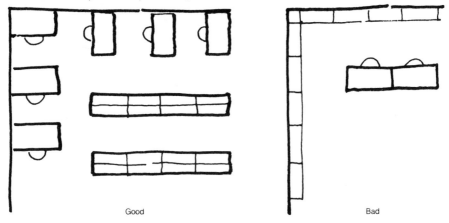

Good   Bad

Staff space

After determining the collection square footage, the next step is to estimate the areas required by staff. There are three ways to calculate staff requirements—on net basis, net/gross basis, or gross basis. On a net basis the minimum estimate is 50 square feet per person. A 5 foot by 2½ foot desk and a 3 foot by 1½ foot runoff uses 27½ square feet. But that does not include any file or storage space for the employee or any walkway space around the desk. Each library employee uses about 6 feet or more of personal file and storage space, without considering that which is shared by others. Walkway space around the desk requires at least a 3-foot aisle on one side. There is a need for about 1½ to 2 feet of sitting space behind the desk (although in the case of a runoff this has already been provided) and 2 more feet to pull the chair out. That is why 50 square feet per person is a viable net square footage requirement.

But 50 square feet per person does not include any generalized corridor (as opposed to localized walkway) space. This adds an additional 15 percent to the total. There is also equipment that must be shared with others: bookstacks, copying machines, reader printers, card catalogs, shelf lists, and book trucks. What about space for office paper supplies and specialized work functions such as binding? Adding up all the extras totals a 10 foot by 10 foot space, or 100 square feet per employee on a net gross basis. And there are rest rooms, lounges, and kitchen areas. Has the circulation desk been figured into the staff requirements? (It is a staff/user area.) Are those extra desks out on the library floor? What about a loading dock or space for a bookmobile? A gross estimate may double the 100 square feet per employee figure.

Facilities planners in large corporations often use gross figures when calculating space requirements. As the size of a facility increases, the gross figure per person drops. A library employing 12 people does not need a much bigger loading dock than the library employing 6. In a largely clerical

When planning furniture and equipment space requirements, local access must be considered. For example, a 3 foot aisle is sufficient for one person to use a book stack, but a 3 foot 9 inch minimum is required for one person plus another pushing a book truck. A 4 foot 4 inch aisle is required for carrel seating, allowing a person to pass behind.

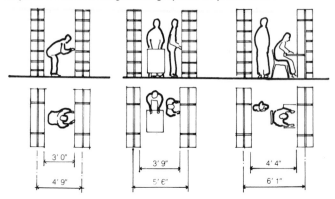

STAFF REQUIREMENTS ESTIMATE
(20-year projection of square footage on net/gross basis)

600 square feet (6 staff × 100 square feet each) current
+600 square feet additional (6 staff × 100 square feet) future

1,200 square feet of space
× 6% configuration factor

72 square feet additional (configuration factor)

1,200 square feet of space
+ 72 square feet (configuration factor)

1,272 square feet—total required on a net/gross basis

office building employing 1,000 people, the gross figure may be 150 square feet per person, supplying space for everything required in the work areas, mechanical rooms, elevator corridors, and even cafeterias and gyms, while a facility employing 3,000 people may need only 125 square feet per person.

The ALA and other professional organizations have space standards usually calculated on a net/gross basis rather than a gross basis, figuring the other requirements as extras. So do some state agencies. Unions sometimes are explicit in their contracts about square footage allowances, also on a net/gross basis. It is important for the librarian to be aware of any such "standards" and to realize that more space may be needed for special facilities.

For an example, library X now employs six staff members. The present projection is for the staff to double over the next 20 years (although with automated systems it is just as likely that staff size will remain the same or reduce). Using the net/gross figures favored by most agencies, staff space can be projected (see Staff Requirements Estimate). But an additional 400 square feet is required for unspecified extras—a lounge, conference room, or space for a small special collection.

User space

Some libraries, particularly those housing large archival collections, need to seat very few users, but those users do heavy research and need long-term study space, perhaps with locked storage. Other libraries, particularly some corporate facilities, may serve many users who drop into the library for a few minutes and request extensive searches. Still others, such as law school libraries, are required to make room for many users—in a law school library, 65 percent of the student body must be able to be seated. The librarian must survey how many user seats are required, what type and other considerations, by making a daily count at intervals throughout the year (or at least over a period of weeks) and by researching pertinent texts as well as organizational and state standards.

Space requirements for different seating arrangements vary considerably. For example, a common 2 foot by 3 foot table top takes up only 6 square feet of space on a net basis; a larger table top (3 foot by 5 foot), meant for long-term research, takes up 15 square feet of space. In certain instances, one person doing research may use a 4 foot by 6 foot table, or 24 square feet of table top. These figures do not include any seating space or real traffic circulation space, etc.

The size of the chairs is also important, and changes space requirements. Armchairs usually take up more room than chairs without arms. It is also essential to know whether seats are to be bolted down. In an auditorium where the seats are bolted to the floor, $7^1/2$ square feet is allotted per chair, allowing circulation space and some crossover aisles. But in an auditorium when a person is seated in a chair, there is virtually no room to pass down the row. Multipurpose rooms are calculated generally at 10 square feet per person, allowing room to move around. But even this figure is not accurate for all chairs. A lounge chair to be used with a footstool can take up an area as large as about $2^1/2$ feet by $6^1/2$ feet, or 14 square feet, without considering local access.

Using the 2 foot by 3 foot table top space allotment, and figuring large tables that run down the length of the room with seating space and local access, the reasonable seating space totals about 15 square feet per person—a very tight situation often found in large academic and public libraries (such as the main reading room in the New York Public Library). If the spacing is adjusted, using more small tables and widening the aisles, the total is a more comfortable figure of 25 square feet per person, a popular estimate. Loosening the spacing even more, to form carrels that are as wide as an average work station, a practice found in some special libraries, the total may be as high as 50 square feet per person. (In all cases, these are net/gross estimates.)

For library X, using 25 square feet per person, after daily checks and research on standards, it is ascertained that the library needs to seat about 50 people at present and, in 20 years, at least 100. Therefore a minimum of 2,500 square feet must be available to seat users, with an additional 6 percent added for configuration loss. The total for user seating space on a net/gross basis is 2,650 square feet (see User Seating Estimate).

USER SEATING ESTIMATE
(20-year projection, net/gross)

  1,250 square feet seating space (50 seats × 25 square feet) current
+1,250 square feet seating space (50 seats × 25 square feet) future

---

  2,500 square feet seating space required
×   6% configuration loss

---

    150 square feet configuration loss

  2,500 square feet
+   150 square feet

  2,650 square feet required for user space

Calculating total space needs

At this point, library X can estimate square footage requirements (see Square Footage Estimate).

The library now has some idea of its needs. After adding all the "specials," it has even more of an idea. But to make the figures completely accurate, it is necessary to break down each area, using the same methods, emphasizing work flow, functional arrangements, and specialized areas that do not appear under staff, user, or stack headings (multipurpose rooms, for example). In other words, the entire interior design must be examined. But this is rarely effected at this stage. Such calculations are usually not arrived at until the project is well underway, long after the program is completed and the schematic designs are done. It is simply too complicated. That is why some departments end up with less space than they need. The departmental breakdown often does not jibe with the original estimate.

This also explains why cost overruns occur. Estimated budget figures for the whole project can be determined by multiplying the total estimated square feet by the current estimated square foot cost of construction and/or furnishings in the local area. If the cost for construction alone is, for example, $100 per square foot, the building estimate is $1,020,300. Furnishing and equipment costs are additional. But the square foot calculations may be inaccurate. They are estimates, and estimates are guesses. Although administration and management want hard cost figures, until everything is completed, no such figures exist. (See the seven illustrated steps for analyzing a library plan.)

The planning process

As we have said, the procedure that determines departmental requirements often occurs long after initial estimates are made, and after the size of the space can no longer be changed. That is where trouble occurs. Suppose

SQUARE FOOTAGE ESTIMATE
(20-year projection, minimum estimate)

    4,240 square feet to house the collection in book form
    1,672 square feet to provide staff space
+ 2,650 square feet to provide user space

    8,562 square feet
× 25% nonassignable space (mechanical rooms, toilets, lobbies, circulation, etc.)

    2,141 square feet, nonassignable

    8,162 square feet
+ 2,141 nonassignable square feet

    10,303 total (without considering extras such as meeting rooms, audiovisual screening rooms, special areas, etc.)

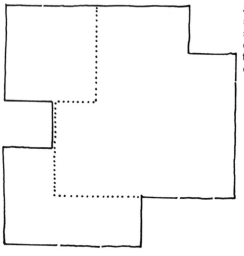

Step 1: Draw the outline of the library space. Divide the library into user and staff areas (user areas are shaded in diagram). Remember that simple rectangles are easier to plan than more complicated shapes.

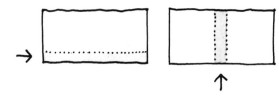

Step 2: Locate the entrance, placed so that interior spaces are accessible from one major central point.

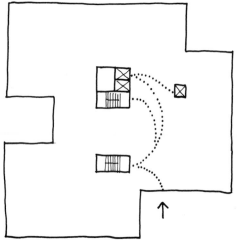

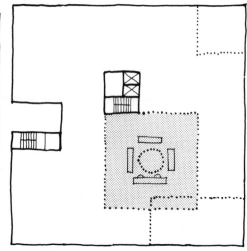

Step 3: Locate elevators, stairs, ramps, and other entrances and exits. Map traffic patterns. Wherever necessary, locate stairs and elevators together (it is cheaper to move a stair than an elevator).

Step 4: Where possible, add space to simplify the library shape. Block out the central square. If necessary, relocate the stair out of the central square.

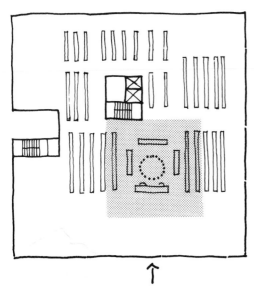

Step 5: Locate the collection. The most heavily used resources should be closest to the central square.

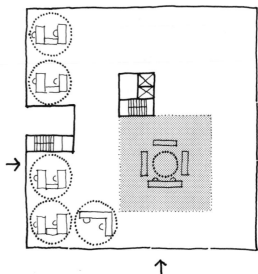

Step 6: Locate staff and delivery areas in relation to the central square. Consider work flow arrangements. (In some libraries, steps 6 and 7 should be reversed.)

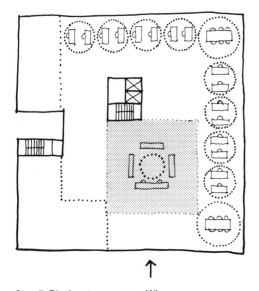

Step 7: Block out user areas. Wherever possible, save corners (especially) and walls for users; save windows for users and staff.

the initial estimates were too broad? To avoid such problems, the planning process should be as follows:

1 Determine broad figures

2 Determine departmental figures

3 Check broad figures, departmental figures, possible budget, and possible space against one another

4 Write the program

5 Schematic design stage

6 Check schematic drawings against the program

7 Revise drawings or revise initial priorities. Redraft program if necessary

8 Preliminary drawings stage

9 Recheck preliminary drawings against more specific departmental furnishings and equipment requirements

10 Detailed drawings stage

11 Final design stage

Schematic drawings are only quick concepts. They can be redrawn if they do not follow the program. Some concepts in the program may have been incorrect, and the architect or interior designer may have a better insight in this area than the person who wrote the program in the first place. In that case, the program should be redone. But in the end, program and drawings should match. The program is the only document that controls the architect, engineer, or interior designer. If the program is not updated and specific, it becomes useless.

The next stage depends upon the size of the project. If a large building is planned, the structural framework of the building must now be constructed, after which the interior design is implemented. If the library is going into interior space where construction is minimal, most of the work involves placing the furniture and equipment. Often in a small job, several steps are condensed (the contractor or furniture supplier may do the design work).

What if the project is well underway and only now is it discovered that something won't fit? Obviously the original priorities have to be reexamined, and those departments most essential to the adequate functioning of the library should be given the best space; those less important may have to be cut. Will there be enough space for the collection? Will there be good access for users and staff? What about reading and study areas? Is there enough room for their proper utilization?

As an example, library X determines that it needs an additional 445 square feet of space. Because this building may be constructed from the ground up, perhaps it is possible to add another story, even as an afterthought. A vertical building, one with more than one story, is cheaper to build as far as the interior space is concerned than a horizontal building on only one floor, all things being equal. The breakoff for a functional library building is somewhere around 15,000 to 20,000 square feet per floor. Besides, foundations are more costly than walls. By spreading out the building on one floor, there is more foundation and roof than there would be if the building rose vertically; this also adds more walking for user and staff. Library space arrangements become less effective.

Is it possible to build a smaller building now and add on in the future? If the building is to have an addition, when at all possible it is better to plan the addition for only one side. It is less expensive because the mechanical system will need to expand along only one side, and it will cut down the size of the original equipment, ducts, pipes, and wires. Heating, ventilating, air conditioning, wiring, and plumbing costs can make up to 60 percent of new building construction. In any building, the four walls, roof, and foundation enclose empty space; the larger the space enclosed, the less it costs per square foot in relation to the confining envelope. By expanding two sides, more wall area will have to be built. That is why it is better to proceed along only one side; the cost of wall construction is decreased.

If library X is being located in already existing space and the area allocated is too small, perhaps new priority relationships can be drawn to limit the size of the facility but not interfere with absolutely necessary, essential, and undesirable relationships. If that is not possible, can more space be gained in the future? To gain space in an existing structure, after space has already been allotted, is very difficult without encroaching on another's territory. Indeed, more space may not exist because of lack of funds. Even so, all is not necessarily lost. Perhaps an outside corridor can be narrowed, a terrace enclosed, or a storage closet appropriated.

When planning any facility, the librarian must realize that politics are a fact of life. Getting the funds, receiving more space, or adding extra staff often encroaches on others and is viewed as a threat. Architects, interior designers, and facility planners claim that the most difficult aspects of their jobs are dealing with people!

Floor loading

The single most important factor modifying the proper allocation of space in a library is the ability of the floor to bear the weight of equipment loaded with books, film, and paper.

In the last several years, there has been some serious trouble in respect to floor overloading due to increases in the number of libraries housed in buildings not designed for library service. Cost-cutting methods in the construction industry, along with more accurate structural calculations, have resulted in more buildings' being designed to bear only the minimum loads required by local, state, and national codes. On the other hand, the installation of compact shelving and the demand for more efficient use of smaller areas have been on the increase. The cost per square foot to rent or to buy space has forced libraries to make do with what they have, and the possibility of extending into larger areas has been limited.

The ability of any structure to bear weight can be divided into dead load and live load. The dead load of a building is the weight of the structure itself—all elements such as steel, concrete, and wood that make up the building fabric. Roofing materials, siding, mechanical systems, windows, are all part of the dead load. The live load consists of elements that can be moved around the building—furnishings, equipment, even people. On occasion, the "people load" may be separated from the live load, especially in circumstances where the added weight of too many people could cause the building to collapse. In an auditorium or a dance hall, the number of people occupying the structure at any one time may be limited. The partition load also may be separated from the live load. With easily movable walls that do not bear the building weight, the partition load calculations can be an important factor in office building construction, especially in cases where offices are ever changing in size, and partitions are constantly erected and pulled down.

Calculating floor loads should be the responsibility of the engineer or architect. The possibility of collapse is too serious. In any case, it is the live load that concerns the librarian, as it is unlikely that any librarian will make structural changes without calling in proper professionals. Housing air-conditioning machinery on the roof, adding an elevator core, or cutting in a new stairwell usually requires building department or local agency approval. But simply buying a few more stacks or adding a large file room does not need outside okay, and that is where the live-load problems occur. The previous design may have strained the limit of the live load, and no one thinks to check if new pieces of equipment will strain it beyond capacity.

In normal library construction, floor live loads should be 150 pounds per square foot; for compact shelving, about 300 pounds per square foot. In other words, other than compact shelving, the weight of objects such as stacks, files, and furnishings on the floor should not exceed 150 pounds per square foot, averaged across the floor. This does not mean that in a specific square foot the weight could not rise to 450 pounds. But if there is nothing on the floor on the two adjacent square feet, the average of the three spaces does not exceed the 150-pound limit. (Here we are speaking about the entire floor supported by girders and beams working together, not about the puncture of 1 square foot. Although floors can puncture, a much more serious situation occurs when the entire floor collapses.)

Paper weighs 58 pounds per cubic foot, and a normal double-faced book stack, 3 feet long, 20 inches deep (counting the width of the center poles and shelves), and 7 shelves high, weighs about 2,320 pounds fully loaded. The dimensions of the book stack are very important, concerning its fully weighted capacity. As the dimensions vary, so does the cubic volume. A double-faced stack with 8 shelves is much heavier than one with 7 shelves. One with 3 shelves is, obviously, much lighter.

If most stacks are estimated at about 85 percent full, the weight in the average book stack drops to 1,972 pounds. If the book stacks are spaced 4 feet 6 inches on center, with a 3-foot aisle between, the average per square foot becomes 146 pounds. Should the aisle size be increased to 4 feet, the weight is redistributed at 120 pounds per square foot, the live-load rating for some library facilities. By placing the stacks 8^1/$_2$ feet apart—10 feet center to center—the weight per square foot drops to 65.7 pounds. If the area is decreased and goes to compact shelving, where stacks stand about 2 feet apart center to center (counting one open aisle), the floor load is 329 pounds per square foot. Here it matters very much as to the number of closed stacks in relation to the size of the one open aisle.

Most buildings designed specifically for library use can handle 120- to 150-pound live loads without difficulty. Many of these buildings can also

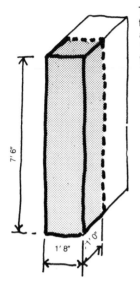

The dimensions of the book stack are very important in figuring weight. An average book stack, 7 shelves high and 85 percent full, weighs about 1,972 pounds. A 1-foot section of that stack weighs 657 pounds (paper weighs 58 pounds per cubic foot).

handle compact shelving in the basement or on a first floor that rests directly on the ground. The major problem may be the load-bearing capacity of the soil beneath the building. In areas such as Houston, Texas, where the ground tends to be swampy, the building may settle after all the equipment has been fully loaded on the floors. A structural engineer must calculate the load-bearing capacity of the ground if there is any question at all, especially in cases where compact shelving is to be added after the building has been occupied.

In the case where a building has not been designed as a library facility, it is rare that the floors can handle 120- to 150-pound live loads, unless the structure was a factory, garage, or, for some reason, had the floors reinforced. Most office buildings in the United States can handle only 50 to 80 pounds per square foot, depending on local building codes. File rooms, record storage areas, and micrographic storage facilities far exceed these live-load limits. It is surprising that librarians, aware of book stack weights, often do not comprehend that file cabinets can be heavier. Equipment salespeople also seem unaware of this fact. An informal survey conducted at an SLA convention showed that most salespeople regarded cabinets as

As book stacks are spaced farther and farther apart, the weight per square foot diminishes. Here the major consideration is the whole floor working together as one unit. Puncturing the floor in one spot is not considered.

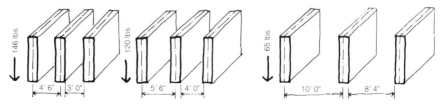

the same weight loaded or empty. Some seemed to realize that paper files were heavy, but the majority thought microfiche files to be very light. The opposite is true. All film is extremely heavy when compacted. Mylar maps at Harvard brought the weight of certain map cabinets to over 1,200 pounds when loaded. Obviously, libraries in office complexes must be designed carefully to stay within floor loading parameters.

There are many types of construction, but the most popular uses girders and beams to tie floors and walls together. Filler material between the girders and beams is, in the case of general building construction, most often a metal pan over which concrete has been poured. Carpeting is glued on top to form a finished floor. Because the girders and beams tie into the building's superstructure, they are inherently stronger than the filler. Most areas around the superstructure—the outside walls, the elevators, and stairwell cores—are also strong. Vertical columns carry their weight to the ground below.

Depending on the type of construction, it may not be necessary to reinforce the floor or to spread out all book stacks 10 feet on center if the live load is only 65 pounds. Areas over beams and girders can take more weight, as can outside walls and elevator and stairwell cores. It is possible that book stacks can be arranged around these stronger areas. But such determinations should always be made by a structural engineer and/or architect.

If the floors must be reinforced, especially for concentrated film or paper storage, usually the ceiling is removed from the floor below and more beams are added to reduce the filler area. Then a second floor made of some structurally strong material is placed so that it rides several inches above the original floor. The reinforcements are tied into the building superstructure.

There are times, when the building is a large multistory facility with many tenants, that it matters a great deal whether others have also reinforced their floors. The building superstructure has its own dead-load capacity. Vertical columns running down the length of the building may not be strong enough for all the added weight. A survey of other tenants may be required.

It is relatively simple to discover if a facility is overloaded. If the aisle spacing between 7-shelf stacks is only 3 feet, the area fully loaded will need at least a 150-pound live-load capacity. Look at the structural plans. The live-load capacity should be noted on them. The plans should be on file with the building engineers, with the renting agent, or at the local building department. If they cannot be found, a call to the original architectural or engineering firm should give the answer.

Many times an overloaded floor does not sway or cause cracks in the ceiling below, but any bending or deflection in the floor should make one suspicious. Stacks standing slightly askew are one indication. Furthermore, most ceilings in the working environment are acoustical false ceilings, hiding the true problems in the space above. If a floor is suspected of being overloaded and the structural plans cannot be found, it may be necessary to remove the false ceiling and have a structural engineer check the condition of the girders and beams.

Fire safety

Another limit on space allocation is national, state, local, and insurance company fire safety codes. Some areas of the country impose strict earthquake codes, too. Sometimes certain areas must be walled off, extra doors built, and sprinklers or other fire extinguishing apparatus added.

In the case of fire safety, a common provision is an area of refuge in another building on approximately the same level, or a way of passage through or around a fire wall to an area that affords safety from fire and smoke. The National Fire Protection Association Life Safety Code[3] requires that travel distance from any point to an exit must not exceed 200 feet if not sprinklered or 300 feet if sprinklered. The maximum length of dead-end corridors cannot exceed 50 feet. This means, in effect, that any large library must have more than one major door, although the other door may be an alarmed, one-way exit. This also means that libraries placed in large office buildings may have to provide open access to fire doors and cannot close off certain corridors. When another exit is required, the code specifies that it must be located as far as possible from the first one.

There are special provisions applying to the length and width of fire corridors and doors and outside egress. The undivided floor area is also determined for educational and business facilities. Special provisions are required for windowless and high-rise buildings.

Because of the variety of fire and earthquake codes in local jurisdictions, as well as specific insurance companies, not all requirements can be listed here. When planning any interior, the librarian should become familiar with those that apply in his or her area.

Notes

1 Richard Muther and John D. Wheeler, *Simplified Systematic Layout Planning* (Kansas City, Mo.: Management and Industrial Research Publications, 1977).

2 Keyes D. Metcalf, *Planning Academic and Research Library Buildings* (New York: McGraw-Hill, 1965), p. 335.

3 John A. Sharry, ed., *Life Safety Code Handbook* (Boston: National Fire Protection Assn., 1978).

FURNITURE
AND
EQUIPMENT

Traditionally, library furniture has been large and solid and made of wood. Although many librarians still prefer that solid look, many more want the flexibility to move furnishings around as activities change or different demands are made upon

Traditional library furniture is large, solid, and made of wood.

departments. Rearranging is difficult with wood, as wooden furniture tends to be heavy. The bulk and weight limit the possible arrangement in a given space. Then, too, wood costs have risen to such an extent that it is doubtful if any but the most well-to-do libraries can afford solid wood. That is why most furnishings on the market today are not exactly what they appear to be. They are imitations of the real thing. Solid wood generally means hardwood veneer hiding a less expensive lumber core. Wood-appearing furniture may be only a thin veneer affixed to metal or to some type of composition material, or may contain no wood at all. Laminates often replace veneer as a surface material.

Furniture suppliers and systems

Changes are occurring in the library industry because of all the changes that have occurred in the manufacture of furnishings. For that reason, some of the larger contract houses, especially those companies selling to the office market, have made inroads in the library market.

A contract house is what the name implies. It is a furnishings company that supplies specified pieces of furniture/equipment on signing a contract. Usually the work is commercial or institutional, as opposed to residential. Buying on contract implies buying in large numbers. Although most houses do have catalog or add-on sales where customers can buy one piece at a time, their major concentration is on larger orders and big clients.

Contract furnishings tend to be more sturdily built than furnishings for residences. The reason is obvious—contract furnishings are expected to take the heavy wear of many different people. Finishes often do not require polishing, and materials rarely have to be dry-cleaned. These furnishings are bought by offices, hotels, schools, libraries, and others.

Some contract houses concentrate on the library field. Often the lines of the other companies overlap, so that a library furnishings company may be called in to supply the shelving and equipment for a records management division of a corporation, while an office furnishings company may supply all the tables, desks, and chairs for a library. Surprisingly, certain library furniture and equipment have wide use in other fields. Compact shelving may hold chemicals, equipment parts, office supplies, and computer printouts. Microfiche readers are the everyday working tools of insurance adjusters and meter readers.

On the whole, the library companies do tend to be more aware of library needs. Usually smaller in size than other furnishings companies, many library furnishings houses can be quite helpful. Small libraries may find the service divisions more dependable, and they are often encouraged to buy on an as-needed basis. But to cut down on overhead, as small sales do not make large profits, a few of these companies have gone into other fields in the library sector. At least one library furnishings company is a major book jobber. Another is a cooperative venture for the residents of a small town. Because there are so many different companies selling materials that can be used in a library, it is important for libraries interested in purchasing furniture and/or equipment to check sources beyond the traditional library companies. Systems developed for other fields may be particularly suited to specialized requirements. The librarian should have an understanding of what is available.

The work station concept

In an office, records management and paper flow have top priority. Several office contract companies have developed modular furnishings systems that offer great improvements over the more traditional types of furniture and equipment. Desks can be purchased with more than one work space, shelving above and below, slotted areas for paper storage, rollaway files, lazy Susans for shared terminals, built-in lockable cabinets, prewired electric/CRT/telephone facilities, and even walls. These modular systems have components that can be slipped in and out as needed. They offer variations for a new type of desk/office arrangement known as the work station concept, meaning that the furnishings supply all surfaces and spaces required for an employee to do his or her job.

The work station concept is different from the office/desk arrangement. Traditionally, employees are supplied with a desk, either in a confined space (cubicle or office) or in a large open area with many other desks (bull pen arrangement). Little use is made of the space beyond 30 inches above the floor, or desk top height. This "air space" is wasted. Furthermore, as an employee's responsibilities increase, so do the pieces of furniture. It was not

A typical technical process area—book trucks ring work stations.

Modern offices often do not have floor-to-ceiling walls. The "walls" are formed by movable partitions, which can be demounted in minutes.

(and still is not) unusual to see staff working at several different pieces of furniture and equipment spread all over the place. For instance, because book shelves are often in short supply, staff members tend to ring their desks with book trucks and machine tables of differing heights to hold incoming, outgoing, and in-process materials.

In the work station concept, the furnishings make good use of the square footage available, including the space above and below the desk top and "walls." L- and U-shaped arrangements are common, so that a staff member has only to swing around to find materials at hand. There are no real walls, but the furniture and equipment form partitions for offices of different sizes. The partitions can be rearranged easily, many in a matter of minutes with one simple tool.

Office landscape systems

Partitions divide office space into what is known as office landscape design. In office landscape, the confining space is only a loft; furniture and equipment divide the space. Most spaces formed by such systems have partitions that are not ceiling high. The "walls" have openings but no doors. The idea is to form offices that do not divide, but allow complete interactions. (Because of consumer demand, a few companies do offer doors with higher partition heights. Some even offer whole rooms with integral ceilings, lighting, and ventilation systems that can be quickly installed in any loft.)

There are two basic types of modular or office landscape furniture/ equipment systems. One type consists of furniture and equipment made in the traditional manner, where parts are glued or clamped in such a way that few pieces are interchangeable. A desk is ordered with a certain number of drawers and cannot be changed. The work station is formed by ordering matching furniture, equipment, and partitions. This system tends to be less expensive than the more unitized designs; individual pieces are usually stock items. Also, the system more readily can reuse furnishings and equipment already in the library. A bank of files, for example, can wrap around a desk to form an office. In certain cases, the library can reuse all furnishings and equipment, and can buy stock partitions to achieve the landscape look. There are numerous partitions and entire walls that can be put up and taken down quickly. Some walls are plasterboard and demountable. Without a practiced eye, one cannot tell them from the real thing.

In the second type of office landscape furnishings, basic units are panels; everything else either attaches to or rests on them. The panels come in different heights: about 30 inches high, desk top height, to 42 inches high, counter height, to well over 64 inches high, or privacy height. (Different manufacturers offer different sizes.) The desk tops, drawers, cabinets, legs— everything that goes into one work station—come in components. The panels form everything, including the confining space. Often only one tool is required to put up or take down the whole thing.

The panel system is exceptionally good for a large library, as everything can be made from a few parts. Even user carrels and tables and the circulation desk can be made out of the same parts. The system offers the utmost in

The items that make up an individual work station must be specified when ordering from the contract house. A terminal usually requires an L-shaped arrangement with primary and secondary work space. The work station should be able to supply electrical, telephone, and CRT wiring.

flexibility and maximum use of space. At the very least, four small work stations can be created from one central panel. With such good space utilization, employees can have more individual area in less total square footage. And there is less waste.

There are, however, drawbacks to the panel furniture system. Rarely can panels stand alone. They must have some L or T form to give them stability, or they must attach to something else. On occasion, a panel that

In this system, panels make up the basic unit. Everything either attaches to or rests on the panels. Panels form desks and even the walls of the offices. Such systems offer the ultimate in flexibility and are suggested wherever constant rearrangement of space is a necessity.

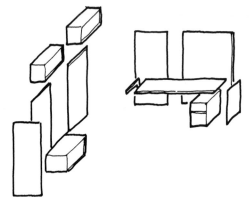

has a heavy weight such as a file hanging from it on one side must have another on the other side for balance. Then, too, different manufacturers supply different height panels. Clamps are positioned in such a way that even different lines produced by the same manufacturer may not fit together. Generally, if you begin with one system, because of this inability to match, the same system has to be continued throughout. Also, because of the many parts that must be ordered, the purchase of panel work stations can be expensive, difficult, and certainly complicated. For these reasons, the panel system is not recommended for small libraries. Simply ordering and keeping track of all the separate parts take too much time and may become a handicap. But for a large library, where constant rearrangement of staff and user areas is common, panel systems pay for any additional expense in a very short time.

Following is a list of priorities when purchasing furniture and equipment (order is not important).

Functional design

Quality of manufacture

Quality of materials

Depth of manufacturer's line (matching pieces)

Ease of installation

Ease of demounting or rearrangement

Space-saving arrangements possible

Availability (time required to receive order)

Manufacturer's commitment (service) and warrantee

Price

Tax advantages

Many librarians like the work station concept essentially because it simplifies construction. Duct work and lighting arrangements can be simpler. Many modular systems are equipped with snap-on electrical raceways; others have prewired telephone and CRT installations, minimizing the cost of such additions. Floors do not have to be torn up to hide wires; the furnishings can contain them. In fact, many common construction elements such as acoustical treatment can be purchased as part of the furnishings. This decreases some of the up-front capital construction costs for nonprofit agencies and adds a substantial tax benefit for libraries that are part of profit-making organizations. In the government area, construction budgets can be decidedly different and come from other sectors than furnishings and equipment funds. The furniture and equipment may be easier to get. For businesses, the Internal Revenue Service allows a 20-year depreciation for building construction and an 8- to 10-year depreciation for furnishings and equipment. The implication is clear. Any building element that can be con-

sidered as part of the furniture/equipment system can be written off in quicker time, saving tax dollars.

Furniture construction

When buying furniture or equipment, whether the more traditional type or the
modular type, it is important for the librarian to understand basic furniture
construction. For libraries in the nonprofit sector and for a few private libraries, a bid competition must be conducted, giving the furniture and equipment contract to the lowest bidder. Therefore the specifications from which
the bidder makes estimates are of the utmost importance. Because furniture
making features a variety of production methods, and because there can be
any number of interchangeable parts or designs, if one forgets to itemize
something, an order may be delivered incomplete or furniture of lesser quality may be substituted.

For example, in a panel system a carrel space of 28 square feet may
have five major items that must be specified: color, size, built-in lights, finish,
and composition of the desk top, supports, shelf, and panels. In addition, each carrel may require acoustical surfaces, built-in wiring, or some
provisions for growth. At this point, unless the library has someone knowl-

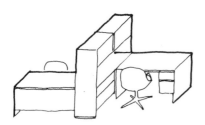

One type of office landscape furniture
system consists of furniture and equipment made in stock sizes. Individual
units are bought to match. Work stations or entire offices can be created
with these matching units.

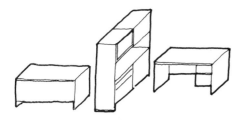

edgeable on the staff, outside help in the form of an architect, interior designer, or furniture specifier usually is required.

Of course, one can deal with contract houses directly. Library companies in particular have sales forces that will help clients prepare layouts and specifications. There is nothing wrong in the method. But in the case of the lowest bid contract, it is often against the law to write specifications so that only one company's products will fit the bill. When the company's salesperson does the writing, the company gets preferential treatment. Then, too, it is to the advantage of a salesperson to sell a customer as many products as possible. Because furniture companies offer substantial discounts to the trade—especially to architects and interior designers—a professional's services may not cost the library as much as expected. Products can be purchased using this discount.

In any event, whether the librarian hires an outsider or relies on a salesperson, it is always beneficial to have some working knowledge of furniture construction. Plastic, for example, is used in many ways in the furniture/equipment industry. Most people tend to think of plastic as a cheap material, but it is not. High-quality plastic is used to form molded chairs, which have become increasingly popular. At the very least, plastic is used to form the insides of drawers, glides on which the drawers slide, and casters on which the entire cabinet rests.

Laminates are often plastics. Some laminates are made of paper impregnated with resins under heat and pressure to form wood-grain patterns that imitate the real thing. Others have wood grain stamped directly into the plastic; still others are injected with dyes or paints to offer a variety of designer colors. There are plastic laminates such as Formica covering desks, table tops, and cabinets. Very often the top-of-the-line steel desk will have a laminated desk top and enameled or painted sides. Enamel or paint tends to be less expensive than laminates, and as the side panels do not have to take the same wear as the tops, they may be so treated.

On wood veneer, instead of laminate, a catalytic finish is used. Here the veneer is stained and then sealed. The catalytic finish, often some form of plastic—a urethane—is applied over the sealer for a fairly transparent but durable surface. Furniture polish is unnecessary to keep the wood looking good, although pieces have to be cleaned occasionally.

As already discussed, a wood veneer is a piece of thin wood, sometimes less than $1/16$ inch thick, applied to the surface of a desk or chair or other furnishing by heat and glue. The illusion is that the wood is one solid piece. As hardwood is the best wood for furniture and has become too expensive for most pieces, it is sliced thin at the factories to provide veneers. For example, few libraries can afford a solid oak door. More than likely what appears to be one piece of oak is a thin veneer covering two thin pieces of plywood with an air space between.

Plywood is made out of layers of wood glued together, with the grains of the plies at right angles or at wide angles to one another. If it is made correctly, plywood is very strong. It is commonly used as subflooring in new house construction. Unfortunately, if water somehow gets behind the glue,

The fronts of all drawers in a card catalog may be made of fabricated
hardwood known as density wood. A soft wood such as pine is compressed and dried so that it takes on the characteristics of hardwood. It will last a long, long time.

the plywood will delaminate. In furniture, special plywood is often made and can be steamed and bent to make exceptionally sturdy pieces.

Particle board or flake board is also used as the subflooring in new house construction. Variations on the same thing, they are nothing more than wood chips—large or small—bonded by glue. The ratio of glue to wood may be more than 4:1, so one can say that it is really the wood that is bonding the glue. But because glue is extremely susceptible to water, depending upon the composition, particle or flake board can absorb water like a sponge. In addition, over a period of time it may sag.

Also a glue composition, but this time in combination with paper, is fiberboard. Not particularly strong, at least in contrast to flake board, it is commonly used in furnishings. One might find it as the dividers inside desk drawers or even the inside of the side and back panels.

The lesson here for the buyer is that the "real thing" may be fake. Most people recognize plastic (and some are extremely good looking and durable), but how many recognize real wood? Because few large pieces of wood are available, most wood furnishings of only one type of wood all the way through are made from separate strips only 2 to 4 inches wide. They are glued together in a butcher-block-type process and given a fine finish. The key is that the grain of real wood is discontinuous, as the pieces that make up furniture are rather small. If the grain appears to be large and sweeping, more than likely the furniture has a thin veneer above a cheaper lumber core. It is all wood, but it is not all hardwood. It may only be a thin veneer of oak protecting a softer core of poplar. For this reason the edges, particularly on desk and table tops, can be very important. These edges protect the veneer from delaminating.

Edges

Edges are separate, and sometimes special pieces are used to cover the ends of tables or desks so that one cannot tell the different layers that make up the piece of furniture. One of the most common edges is known as the "self-edge." It is also the least durable. Here the manufacturer simply glues a piece of the same veneer or laminate that covers the top of the desk or table onto the edge. Because a table or desk edge gets tremendous abuse—people, machinery, things, tend to bump into it, tear at it, or even burn it—the self-edge is easily destroyed. Liquids such as coffee may be spilled and leak into cracks and behind the edge. It loosens and peels.

Two of the more durable methods of edging are known as bull-nose and metal edging. In both cases, the edging materials are pounded into the desk and table tops and held there by a system of internal teeth. For bull-nose edging, the process is fairly expensive because hardwoods are used. Metal edging, where metal makes up the entire edge, is less expensive and relatively durable. Although fairly common at one time, today metal edging is not so often used. Designers do not like the look.

Another edging process uses a thick piece of harder wood, perhaps as much as 1/2 inch thick, glued under pressure to the softer lumber core. This is particularly common in the library industry. A manufactured wood called density wood may be used. In the manufacturing process, soft wood such as pine is compressed and dried so that it has all the characteristics of hardwood. On a card catalog, for example, all the frontispieces on the drawers may be made of density wood. It is extremely durable and will last a long, long time. When used as an edge for a table top upon which a hardwood veneer is used, the impression is that the entire piece is made out of one thick plank of wood.

One edging system is no edging at all. A piece of strong metal, perhaps steel, makes up the table top and is turned to make a rounded edge. A laminate is then applied to protect the surface from rust and scratches or to give it a pleasing color. Wherever two joints appear, a piece of plastic may be slid into a slot or glued on. The furniture may be durable, but also may look old before its time because the plastic has a tendency to fall off.

Steel and other metal furniture may have special edging problems caused by their manufacture. Inexpensive metal cabinets, files, shelves, and desks can have very sharp sides and edges. Some cabinet doors, shelving systems, and table tops are extremely sharp; such furnishings and equipment are to be avoided. Most better metal lines are manufactured with rolled sides and edges to eliminate the problem.

Joinery

Joinery is what most edging hides—the joints, which hold the pieces together. There are two common ways to bind a joint, either by glue or by screws, bolts, clamps, or pegs. Because it is best to buy what can be dismantled easily for shipment or simply to obtain replacement parts that can be quickly installed, glued joints are not always recommended for libraries. Some of the best furniture is made with glued joints, but because the joints cannot be taken apart, another type of joinery may be preferred.

Left: Table and desk tops made of particle board tend to be weak and more cheaply made than other types. The legs should be tied to a frame or stretcher upon which the particle board rests, rather than connected directly to the particle board. *Right:* Legs can be affixed directly to solid core wood table or desk tops. Metal bushings are often used.

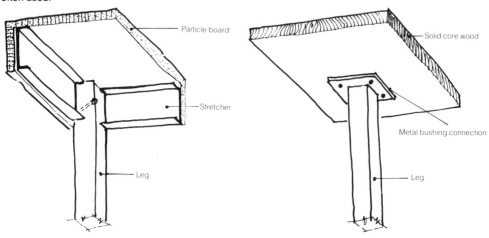

The top-of-the-line office chairs tend to be well upholstered and completely adjustable. Seat, back, and arm supports can be raised or lowered, tilted forward or back. Parts can be replaced easily.

What type of frame holds the joint? The simplest and most rigid is a triangle. If pinned properly, a joint in a triangular frame is particularly sturdy. This type of joint forms the structure for most folding chairs. The next most rigid construction is a rectangle. Whereas a desk, table, or chair seat only has to support downward weight, the frame must support sideways as well. A series of stretchers connected somewhere near midpoint of each leg on an ordinary chair will help to resist sway. In other words, the rectangle is formed out of the top rails, leg post, and at midpoint of the legs with stretchers. To enhance the rigidity even further, at least two of the stretchers should be connected along their midpoints. This is the main reason that most desks are more rigid than tables. The drawers, files, and panels forming the desks act as stretchers.

The least rigid construction has the legs tied only into the table top or chair seat. There is nothing to prevent sideways sway when the top or seat is nothing more than particle board. The screws work themselves loose, and the whole construction falls down. Then, too, metal should be tied to metal and wood to wood. If one is to use a particle board table or chair, the board should rest on an all-wood or metal frame. Thus the particle board does not have to withstand sideways sway, only downward pressure.

Chairs

Stretchers are extremely important for lounge or library chair construction, as opposed to the office chairs that swivel and roll. Because most chairs are moved around quite a bit, a common four-legged chair gets a great deal of sideways pressure. Of course, many chairs that are made of metal do not have stretchers, and they last a long time. Heavy gauge metal is more rigid than wood, and such chairs may be extremely durable. But even here, if a

Stretchers that form a brace between chair legs make the construction more rigid. The legs are not as vulnerable to sideways sway.

chair is expected to take a great deal of abuse, stretchers are often recommended unless they destroy the chair's design.

For metal chairs or chairs with metal legs, one can choose either hollow steel or aluminum. The heavier the gauge, the better the metal. Aluminum is found in cheaper chair construction because the light weight will not pull away from the cheaper flake or particle board as easily as steel will. Unfortunately, to save money, manufacturers generally use light gauge aluminum. The lighter the gauge, the softer the legs. They snap off quickly if given any kind of abuse.

Less expensive chairs may have legs that are not equipped with glides, pieces that adhere to the tip of the legs and make it easier for the legs to slide over the floor. Heavy chairs, in particular, need good glides that will not pit and scar over a long period of time. Older chairs tend to have glides that cause tears and rips in carpeting. For this reason, some prefer to use chairs with sled-type bases on carpeting. Others pay for the best glides available, usually made out of Bakelite, Teflon, or other such material. Good glides often are relatively wide in relation to the dimension of the legs, distributing the weight. The better casters also are relatively wide; 5-inch casters are recommended for book trucks that roll over carpeting. There are some fine double-wheeled casters on the market. Some office chair manufacturers equip the bottoms of their chairs with double wheels. Although these casters tend to be expensive, they do less damage to the carpeting and pay for themselves in this respect in a very short time. Rubber wheels are recommended for tile floors.

Most office chairs are constructed quite differently from library chairs. Office chairs swivel and roll. Their ball bearings and casters must always be of good quality. Otherwise the chairs will break down. The frame usually is made of steel (some chairs use hardwoods). The molded seat rests on only one post. A large screw may hold the seat in place, allowing it to be raised, lowered, or removed. The back support may depend on another screw to provide the same type of adjustment, and may have a lever that allows forward or backward positioning. The top-of-the-line chairs usually are designed to alleviate as many sitting difficulties as possible. For that reason, whenever possible, the top-of-the-line office chairs are recommended. Most are simply the better buy.

Because the connections in an office chair are so important, at least once a year the connections, which may have loosened, should be checked. In fact, all over the library this should be a policy. Most furnishings suffer from "people use." All too often furnishings break down simply because the connections have worked loose.

When buying office or library armchairs, it is essential to make certain that the arms will fit under the desks or tables they are to match. Buying desks and tables from one manufacturer and chairs from another can cause a problem. Arms that will not fit can become a major headache. They damage easily, and they also damage the edges of tables and desks.

For general library chairs, it is always best to buy a variety if the library is large enough. Not only are people made differently but a library uses different chairs for different purposes. Straight-backed chairs may be favored by those who study and write. Lounge chairs are for those who wish to do recreational reading. Office chairs that swivel and roll are best for using microform readers and computer terminals—all machines that are fixed in one position. For the elderly it is essential to have sturdy, fairly high-off-the-ground chairs. Many elderly people have difficulty getting out of seats that are too low.

Buying and maintaining furniture

Many chairs are upholstered. Furniture panels and wall partitions may be upholstered as well. If the library chooses upholstery, it is a good idea to select material that can be removed for cleaning. Many of the better companies feature chair upholstery that simply pops off (the same is true for their panels and partitions). A hidden piece of elastic or one or two screws hold the material in place. Clean upholstery is one way to keep the library looking

People use library furnishings in a host of unanticipated ways. It is advisable, therefore, to offer a variety of seating types and arrangements.

good. Even an expensive chair can look worn out rather rapidly if it gets dirty.

All library furniture and equipment should be bought with an eye toward service and maintenance. Often there are not enough personnel available to keep the library in first-rate order. Therefore, if pieces can be taken down or put together with ease or if components can be ordered without difficulty, the library is ahead in the maintenance game. For that reason, built-in, custom-made furniture is not suggested. If furnishings, equipment, and even building parts are stock items, they can be reordered and replaced without trouble. Many of the better furniture and equipment companies give service contracts. Custom finishers do not. Repairing custom furniture requires special materials and extra labor. Even if a custom furniture job appears inexpensive at first, in the long run it may be more costly.

When buying equipment, check all movable parts. Office chairs that swivel with difficulty, drawers that seem out of whack in the showroom, cabinets that do not close properly, should all be avoided. Check all glides, slides, and rollers. Look for sharp edges.

Upholstery

What is the best buy in upholstery? Of course, different libraries have different needs. One of the most durable and easily maintained fabrics is nylon. Nylon can look very good; it can be produced to look like the finest wool. Only a professional can tell that it is not. Nylon is often blended with other synthetics such as polyesters, acetates, Dacron, or rayon to cut the cost of manufacture. These blends do not wear as well, but they are cheaper to buy.

What is important to know when choosing upholstery is the use a particular fabric is expected to take. For example, a major museum once ordered extremely fine wool carpeting. Within the first eight months after installation, three million people walked over it. The wool was not durable enough to take that much stress. The purchase was a costly mistake.

Nylon is a synthetic fabric. Unfortunately, synthetics give off toxic fumes when they smolder. Others are quite flammable. Nearly all library fabrics must be as fireproof as possible. In most instances, the fireproofing requirements are set by law. Federal, state, and local governments have codes with which the library must comply. Insurance companies may have even stricter codes. The librarian must be aware of the laws that define fabric use within the institution.

Wool tends to be fairly fireproof and quite durable under most circumstances. More expensive than nylon, wool upholstery is one of the two most favored luxury upholstery fabrics for library use. (The other is leather.) However, wool has drawbacks, not the least of which is the expensive price. Also, many people are allergic to wool, so it is not recommended for warm climates where patrons are usually apt to be dressed in thin clothes.

Leather is even more costly than most wools, but is extremely durable. Some leather upholstery requires almost no care. Furthermore, unlike its synthetic counterpart, vinyl, leather "breathes." People are less apt to stick to leather seats in warm weather.

Some vinyls approach and even surpass the durability of leather and are much less expensive. This depends upon the manufacture and the thickness of the upholstery. Vinyls are widely used as acoustical wall coverings, for example, where durability is essential. Furthermore, vinyls are made in a variety of colors and prints. The specifications for vinyl are all-important. Cheap vinyl seems to self-destruct the moment it hits the library floor.

Several of the synthetic fabrics can be washed rather than dry-cleaned. For some libraries, this may save money. Cotton, a natural fabric, also can be washed. Canvas and denim are two of the tougher forms. Unfortunately, nearly all cotton fabrics lose their bright colors and good looks quickly. If they are specified, make sure replacement is a simple matter.

Carpeting

Surprisingly, carpeting tends to be easier to maintain than most other floor finishes. Most tile floors, for example, have to be washed and waxed often. Carpeting has to be vacuumed often but cleaned only periodically.

For carpeting, as for upholstery, nylon tends to be the most durable fiber. It has a very high resistance to wear, but because nylon is a synthetic, it builds up static as one walks across it, especially in dry, cold weather. Therefore an antistatic agent must be built into the structure. It is advisable

CARPET SPECIFICATION SAMPLE

Color: Blue

Weave: Tufted through primary backing

Surface texture: Multilevel looped pile, 7/32 inches high to 5/32 inches low

Face yarn: Antron III

Face yarn weight: 35 ounces per square yard

Total weight: 76 ounces per square yard

Backing: Primary, cap-coated polypropylene; secondary, 36-ounce polyurethane. This carpet
is a direct glue down.

Flammability: ASTM*, E-84-61, DOC*FF-170

Acoustic rating: ASTM *D 424-68, NRC .20, direct on concrete

Tuft bind: 20-pound pull

Static protection: 3.0 kilovolts, as 20 percent RH at 70° F

Fastness: AATC*80 hours, zenon arc, fadeometer test

Description: Nondirectional pattern

*Government and professional codes

for all carpeting to have antistatic protection, even wool. (In the case of wool, wires are woven into the carpeting to avoid static electricity.) Nylon's other drawback is that it has poor colorfastness, and although it can hide dirt rather well, daylight tends to make it appear old before its time.

Wool, on the other hand, has good colorfastness. A luxury carpeting material, wool can be made in a variety of colors and designs. Antique rugs prove that colors can look good even after a long, long time. But wool is very expensive. It may cost more than three times as much as nylon, and will offer only half the wear.

Polypropylene is an indoor-outdoor carpeting material. It is durable and hard-wearing, but has poor resilience and texture retention. It is best for utility areas, ramps, and corridors where looking good is not as important as its antislip function.

Two other synthetic materials often used in the manufacture of carpeting are acrylics and polyesters. Both can look good initially, but they wear quickly. These fibers are often blended with nylon, or even wool, to form less expensive carpeting. In any case, they should be used in moderate to light traffic areas.

Often a library may choose two different types of carpeting, for high-use and for low-use areas. Extra durable carpeting or carpeting that can be easily replaced is often specified for places of traffic wear, such as the entranceways to buildings, in and around the main lobby, or near the circulation desk. Often it is a good idea in some places to use a complementary carpet color, so that when the main carpeting is replaced, one does not have to search for an exact match for the rest of the facility.

Specifications for carpeting should indicate pile height. The deeper the pile, the more one sinks in. Luxury carpeting is not particularly good in a library. Book carts cannot roll over it. It is also important to know how closely the carpet is woven. Tight weaves are the best (the same is true for fabrics).

They are denser and therefore last longer. Note pile construction. Cut or loop pile performs well under commercial conditions as opposed to residential, which does not have need for extreme durability. For instance, a shag rug is not advised for a library (see the Carpet Specification Sample).

There are many different ways to manufacture carpeting. If the carpeting is woven, it should be woven directly through the backing so that the face yarn cannot be pulled away. However, some very durable synthetics are manufactured in which the face materials are glued to the back. If such carpets are to be used, the amount of pull that the glue can withstand matters very much. If the glue is weak, the materials will delaminate. Again, specifications are all-important.

Many carpeting types do not need underpadding. They can be directly glued to the library floor. Although "glue downs" tend to be less acoustically absorbent and have harder surfaces than those that cover padding, they are more suitable for libraries. They tend to last longer, and book trucks roll on them more easily. A quick-release adhesive is available so that the entire carpet can be removed without trouble.

There are some carpeting tiles that are not glued down. They simply rest on the floor. The tiles around the outside must touch something steady, such as a wall, to keep the whole thing from moving out of line. Unfortunately, carpet tiles do not work well where heavy book trucks are used. The trucks push them out of line. Therefore tiles are not recommended for areas where book trucks roll. However, because of the ease of installation and ease of replacement, they are recommended elsewhere.

If a new space is being designed, it is much simpler to purchase carpeting that is the size of the space and let it run under the stacks. There is less labor involved than cutting and shaping the carpeting around the stacks. However, if the library is only going to be refurbished, it is easier to cut the carpeting around the stacks. It is too difficult to remove all the books, take down the stacks, lay the carpet, and reinstall everything. (However, more cutting does mean more seams and more places for the carpeting to tear.)

If book stacks are to go over carpeting, the stacks must be leveled. Therefore carpeting pins should be ordered as part of the stacks. As a matter of fact, all pieces of equipment should have some type of leveling device whether or not carpeting is involved. An out-of-level piece can topple over.

When purchasing carpeting, it is essential to get a seaming diagram from the supplier. All too often the supplier tends to cut the carpet so that the least amount of material is used. This is not often to the library's advantage. Seams should be avoided in areas of heavy traffic and in front of such important objects as circulation tables. If the seams cannot be avoided, it is best to place them so that they get the least amount of wear. In a corridor, seams should run perpendicular to the line of march or should parallel the length of the corridor no more than 1 foot from the wall. But seams should be placed over a power access. Too often, carpeting has to be cut to reach such ac-

Direct glue-down carpeting is suggested for areas of heavy use. Quick-release cement that pulls away with 25 pounds of pressure is widely available.

cesses. (This is where carpet tiles are perfect.) Some libraries have experimented with small carpeting runs of another color over the grids so that the carpeting marks where the grids exist, and the carpeting can be replaced with ease.

Carpeting often hides flaws in the floor. One of the first indications that a floor is overloaded is out-of-whack stacks or lines of file cabinets. In large installations, except earthquake areas, book stacks should be tied together with cross pieces across the top. File cabinets rarely are tied together as they are more stable than book stacks. But some manufacturers, particularly those that produce modular panel systems, provide cabinets with drawers that lock when one drawer in a cabinet is opened. This is annoying for anyone who has to file all day long, but less annoying than when a cabinet falls down.

Stacks

When one is buying stacks, just as in other purchases, specifications are all-important. The number of shelves and the height of the stacks are only two important things to consider. Do stacks made of wood have shelves of lesser quality, only veneer hiding composition materials? Some metal stacks are poorly manufactured so that sideways stress causes them to collapse. Metal frames can be either welded together or cross braced between two faces to prevent this. The supports for the shelves are important. They should be at good intervals to prevent sag. If fiberboard or particle board stacks are ordered for basement areas, water can be a definite hazard. Although both wood and metal stacks are also damaged by water, the effect on the glue in fiberboard or particle board can be horrendous.

There are several cost details to remember when buying stacks. Starters, or stacks that affix to the ends of ranges, cost more than the adders, or central stacks. To be the most cost-effective, ranges should be allowed to run in longer lengths. A single-faced stack costs nearly as much as

Types of stacks. A: Bracket shelving with closed base, the easiest to rearrange. Closed base acts as a shelf, spreading the weight more evenly along the floor, but can cause floor damage. Fairly stable if corners are welded; units can be taken apart and stand alone. If sway braced, stacks cannot stand alone, but can be demounted and stored in small sections. B: Bracket shelving with open base. Stacks rest on pedestals, allowing better air circulation and easier cleaning. Recommended for very large runs of stacks, but pedestals may puncture floor. C: Bracket shelving with open base, resting on elongated pedestals for greater stability. Weight distributed more evenly with less possibility of front and back sway, but pedestals may be a hazard for people walking in aisles. D: Slotted or standard shelving with welded corners or sway bracing. Braces are unnecessary with finished bases, end panels, and canopy tops, or if section corners are welded. Units may stand alone; look more durable than bracket shelving. Can be made of wood or metal. Shelves more difficult to adjust than bracket type. All stacks may have various end panels— metal, wood, or fabric. If fabric is used, acoustical material may be applied underneath for greater noise control. Long runs of book stacks should be tied together except in earthquake areas, where codes may require that each stack be tied independently to floor, walls, or ceiling.

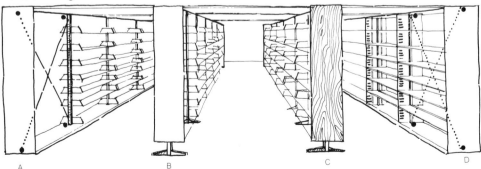

A   B   C   D

a double-faced stack, so that wherever possible, it is better, in terms of money and space ulitization, to order double-faced stacks. Stack end panels can be ordered in a variety of finishes or fabrics. Expensive end panels for long runs of less costly stacks create a look of richness. Steel stacks are relatively easy to refinish. A process called electrostatic painting sprays on new color quickly. Librarians have had metal stacks repainted over night. The same process also refinishes steel desks, cabinets, tables, and chairs.

Some stacks can be purchased with built-in lighting. They are more expensive than the ordinary stacks. However, built-in lighting does allow the possibility of providing individual switches for every stack face and may save substantial energy for a large library. The other possibility is to provide individual lighting for separate aisles, running the lights on the ceiling or along the cross ties, providing every other range with a switch. This is less expensive. In either case the stacks are electrified. As microforms and computers become ever more common, the fact that the stacks are electrified may prove to be beneficial. Eventually, it may be logical to integrate microform/computer installations with the stacks. Stacks with their own power hook-up ability will make the process simpler.

Furniture and equipment layouts

Furniture and equipment layouts are difficult. Not only must building structures, floor loading limitations, available area, and other requirements be

The location of all furniture and equipment should be drawn on the floor plan to scale (Lafayette College Library, Pennsylvania).

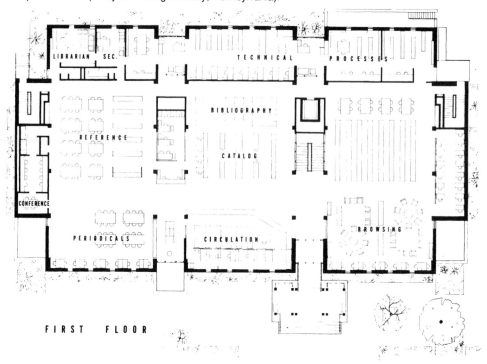

FIRST FLOOR

taken into consideration but so must individual needs. Linear shelving requirements must be translated into square footages, which, once drawn into the plan, become exact dimensions. A staff member's work station for incoming, outgoing, and in-process materials must be changed into exact measurements for desks, cabinets, files, chairs, and book carts. And details describing the exact makeup of furniture and equipment are essential for proper ordering.

An inventory must be taken. If the library is already in existence, the inventory for new furniture and equipment can be based on the old. A more difficult situation occurs when the library is being started new. How people will work and interact in space can only be guessed at. There is a great possibility for error.

The inventory describes in detail the height, length, and width of each staff member's and department's current holdings; what is to be kept, discarded, stored; and what is to be ordered new. When more than one person shares furniture and equipment, a separate sheet should detail that information (see Shared Equipment Inventory). The requirements for electronic equipment should also be detailed, because power must be supplied to provide energy for these items to work (see Electronic Equipment Inventory).

After the inventory process is completed, the librarian should know how many and exactly what types of user and staff furniture and equipment exist, what processes should be changed or rearranged, and, using projections, what additional furniture and equipment must be ordered. Exact dimensions of chairs, tables, carrels, and work stations should now exist for each user

SHARED EQUIPMENT INVENTORY   Department_____
                                  Date _____

Individuals	Shared Equipment and Furniture	Comments

ELECTRONIC EQUIPMENT INVENTORY

Department_____

Date_____

Tally Group	Individual	Equipment List	Shared with (Individual or Group)	Remarks

and staff member (see Furniture and Equipment List). Cabinetry, storage, and out-of-the-way file space should be delineated for machinery and for temporary and archival storage. For example, a clerical function may require a 30-inch by 60-inch standard double-pedestal desk, and two 3-foot shelves on a shared double-faced book stack in the technical process area. In the library proper, the inventory may indicate that two people at any one time require a stand-up counter for quick reference. A 6-foot minimum counter space would be needed.

The next step is to create space and work-flow standards. For example, on the corporate level an executive often is accorded 200 square feet, a professional is given 100 square feet, and a clerk is apportioned 50 square feet. It may be corporate policy to allow no more than two 5-drawer file cabinets adjacent to a work station. The rest of the files must be relegated to a more central departmental records management area.

After all information is merged, the next step is to transfer it to a layout. In the chapter on planning and arranging library space, an outline of the building floor plan (which includes all windows, columns, entrances, exits, and other immovable objects) was discussed. This outline should be drawn on graph paper, and scale templates (predrawn replicas of furniture and equipment) can be moved around on the paper to view various possible arrangements. These templates are easy to create. Most furniture manufacturers supply scales of their own product lines with which to draw them. Art supply stores sell scales that feature the most common outlines for furniture and equipment.

Department _____
Date _____

FURNITURE AND EQUIPMENT LIST

	Exist	Discard	Store	Add	Exist	Discard	Store	Add	Exist	Discard	Store	Add
Book truck space												
Typewriter												
Typing table (size)												
Machine table (size)												
Chairs (type & no.)												
Credenza												
File cabinet (size)												
Shelving: above/below desk top (size)												
Bookcase (size)												
Desk run-off (size)												
Table (size)												
Desk top (size)												
Mail (type)												
Telephone												
Terminal												
Individual (name)												
Tally Group												

Templates can be fashioned out of paper, Mylar, or other two-dimensional materials, or they can help to form three-dimensional cardboard models. Three-dimensional models allow for quick understanding of a layout and are helpful in explaining the layout to others. They are recommended, although the two-dimensional templates are easier to create.

Graph paper is used because it makes calculations easier. Every $1/4$ inch on a graph paper equals 1 foot. Here one must make certain that the graph paper comes in $1/4$-inch blocks and that the scales of the templates match. When the layout is considered to be as good as possible, it can be copied to form a permanent record from which all the necessary specifications will be made.

If the final layout differs from the interior design program, either one or the other should be updated. Remember that the program is one of the forms of written control and it should match the layout. Then specifications can be written and the work sent out for bid. It is not uncommon to solicit several different grades of furniture and equipment. Items that are intended to be situated in user areas are often more luxurious looking than those considered for the staff. Even staff furniture and equipment may be divided into grades. Archival storage can be housed in cheaper equipment that is not subject to the wear and tear of everyday use.

Often, before bids are even solicited, the furniture and equipment industry is researched for cost estimates. It may be that one's idea of interior design is too expensive for the library and a new layout must be drawn. This is a practice especially recommended for large libraries, as the cost differences may not be as enormous for a small library.

Once the contract is awarded, the next steps occur in the installation process. The librarian must keep a time-and-action calendar—who is delivering what, and when it is being delivered. For example, book stacks should not be in place before the space is painted. Often such work is done by the interior designer, but there are areas where the librarian must get involved. Which areas can be set up first with minimum disruption to the library? The following list shows five of the main elements of concern involving interior space.

Collection space: stacks, files, etc.

User space: reader seats (carrels, seats, lounges, etc.)

Staff space: work stations (technical process, administration, user areas)

Support space: copy room, mail room, etc.

Internal circulation: access to all areas and individual pieces of furniture and equipment

After the move in is completed, the librarian, with the architect, interior designer, contractor, or furniture salesperson, must inspect the premises to see if any last things must be done. A "punch list" is written, and those in charge of specific work areas are assigned the tasks.

Following are start-to-finish steps for an interior design installation:

Program development: defining needs (visual survey, staff and user input); furniture and equipment inventory (current and projected); space and work flow standards.

Layout: fine-tuning the program; space layouts, plans and specifications; costs.

Implementation: Contract bidding; procurements (installation, time-and-action calendar); moving in; postoccupancy fine-tuning.

LIGHTING,
POWER,
AND
ENERGY

Three of the most important elements to consider when planning any library space are lighting, power, and energy. Without adequate lighting, the library cannot perform its services. Power refers to the electrical or telephone cables bringing electricity and communication to the building. Energy, meaning the fuels necessary to produce lighting and power, is an ever-increasing concern in the fuel-hungry, power-driven world of the late twentieth century. The time to evaluate the need for these three elements is *now*, before the library is renovated or rearranged or constructed.

Lighting

Obviously, any librarian has to be concerned with lighting. When planning a new library facility or renovating an old one, the librarian should find out as much as possible about such lighting details as kinds of light bulbs, ballasts, rated average life of bulbs, how lighting affects the eyes, glare, how light is measured, and any other factors that may improve the quality of light in the library. These details and others are discussed in the following section.

Light bulbs

Light bulb is the common name, but in the lighting industry light bulbs are known as lamps. That is because all light bulbs are not bulb-shaped; fluorescents, for example, are tubular. (Fixtures are known in the industry as luminaires.)

Light bulbs come in all sorts of shapes, sizes, and colors, but their methods of producing light can be broken down into four main categories:

Bulbs most familiar to library users. *A:* Incandescent (advantages—easily available, inexpensive, easy to install, varied applications, good color, steady light, dimming and flashing; disadvantages—short life, expensive to operate, substantial heat buildup). *B:* Fluorescent (advantages—easily available, diffused light source, better energy efficiency than *A,* long life; disadvantages—flickering, needs ballast, ballast may buzz, color is less attractive than *A,* dimming and flashing may decrease life span, life span may depend on hours per start. *C:* High-intensity discharge (advantages—mercurys can substitute for *A,* better energy efficiency than *A* and *B,* long life, excellent for high ceilings; disadvantages—needs time to warm up, most cannot be dimmed or flashed, color not as attractive as *A,* ballasts required, ballasts may buzz, metal halide actinic ray is hazardous, sodiums may have biological hazard [have poisoned certain trees when used outdoors], metal halide may explode, life span may depend on hours per start).

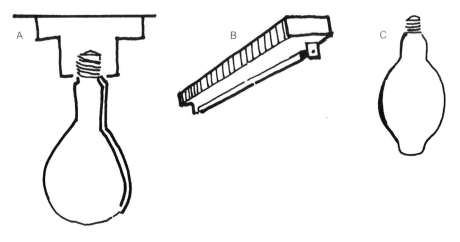

incandescent, fluorescent, high-intensity discharge, and low-pressure discharge.

Incandescent. These bulbs produce light by electrically heating high-resistance filaments to a white heat until they glow. Although favored for household use (they are cheap to buy and easy to install), they are less popular for commercial use because they are too expensive to operate. The ordinary incandescent consumes 90 percent of its electrical energy in the form of heat. More energy-efficient incandescents have been produced, but on the whole, they are not energy-efficient enough. By and large, they raise the electric bill and wreck the air-conditioning system.

Many older libraries, and a few new ones, use incandescents. (One small public library estimated a monthly electric bill of $250. At the end of the first month of operation with incandescents, the bill was over $1,000!) Many people like the illumination that incandescents produce. However, many other bulbs on the market today broadcast similar light. In addition,

This lighting system in the Dag Hammarskjold Library, United Nations in New York City, is made up of incandescents hidden inside recessed fixtures—attractive but wasteful in terms of energy, since 90 percent of the energy consumed is given off as heat.

some people like incandescents because the bulbs do not flicker as they start to burn out.

For library use, incandescent light is relatively easy to control, and incandescents can be put on dimmer switches, which is not the case with all other bulbs. Incandescents are good also for illuminating art in a dramatic fashion. In fact, they are particularly first-rate for galleries, and are recommended in some corridors and closets—but that's all!

Fluorescent. The fluorescents produce light by establishing an electrical arc through gas vapor at low pressure from one cathode to another across opposite ends of a tube. The discharge excites crystals of phosphor coated on the tube interior, which in turn fluoresce and produce light.

Fluorescents are the most common light bulbs used in libraries. They provide at least three times the light per unit of energy, and anywhere from two to sixteen times the life of an incandescent. In addition, because the light emanates along a tube, rather than from a point source such as a filament, fluorescents are less bright in any one spot and more diffuse than the incandescents. However, fluorescents require special ballasting in which an electrical mechanism, separate from the bulb, regulates the electricity flowing into the bulb. (Ballasts are discussed in more detail later in this chapter.) Because of the ballast, fluorescents need special fixtures. One fluorescent does not always fit into another's housing.

Fluorescents also have an annoying habit of flickering as they burn out, which is caused by interruptions in the alternating current provided by the electrical energy. (This is especially annoying in a library without a good light bulb replacement program.) As the current cycles on and off, an incandescent does not have time to cool down and stop glowing. But the fluorescent does, and one that is nearly burned out is strongly affected. That is why two fluorescents are usually tied to one ballast; when one goes off, the other goes on, making the light seem stable. If only one fluorescent is connected to a ballast, such as in a desk lamp, a flicker is apparent even in a new bulb to some people.

Many librarians feel that fluorescent light is detrimental to library materials. But humidity and temperature of the book storage area are even more damaging. Paper disintegration as a result of acidity can be slowed by lowering room temperatures. In addition, many fluorescents on the market have color corrected the damaging ultraviolet light. Of course, any light—incandescent, fluorescent, and especially daylight—will cause paper deterioration, and will attack fabrics as well. Depending on the ability of the specific material to absorb and be affected by light, colors will fade considerably over a period of years.

There are three main types of fluorescents:

1. The preheat or trigger type, which depends on a "trigger" to warm up the cathode before the light goes on. This is the least expensive bulb and in widespread use in homes, but not commercial establishments or libraries. One must hold the button down a second or two before the bulbs light up. A warm-up flicker is noticeable. Preheat fluorescents cannot be dimmed. Turning them on and off constantly shortens their life spans.

Unadorned fluorescent bulbs can be used to advantage in a library if they are set out of the line of sight. For good illumination, only one-third the number of fluorescents shown in this photo need be used.

2. The rapid-start fluorescent, which depends upon a constant flow of electricity—about 7½ watts—to keep the cathodes warm (like instant-on television sets). Once the switch is turned on, the bulbs light up immediately. Even if the bulbs are disconnected, should the ballasts remain in the circuit, the watts of energy will still be consumed. Many rapid-start fluorescents can be used in preheat circuits. However, if they are installed in a rapid-start system, they can be turned on and off without much affecting their average life. In fact, many can even be dimmed. (However, check with the light bulb manufacturer; each one has different specifications.) That is because they are always on. Rapid-start fluorescents are the ones most commonly found in libraries.

3. The instant-start fluorescent depends upon a big surge of initial electricity to warm up the cathodes. When the switch is pressed, they turn on immediately. Such bulbs have been coming into use because they are not "on" at all times. Thus they tend to be more energy-conserving than the rapid-start lights, but because they are not always "on," they have some of the difficulties of the trigger type. They also need larger wires to handle the initial surge.

Fluorescents are affected by temperature. A cool metal object touching a fluorescent bulb may cause dark spots. (One often sees this where metal louvers touch the bulbs.) A too-warm installation may cause the bulbs to blow long before they are supposed to (a problem of fixtures that are not vented to allow the heat to escape). If the bulbs do not appear to be functioning correctly and everything else has been checked, look at the installation. Take note of the temperature in the fixture cavity and ask the manufacturer. The difficulty may be simple to correct.

High-intensity discharge (HID). The high-intensity discharge, or HID, bulbs produce light in a manner not dissimilar to fluorescents. Here the electric arc is under high pressure while passing through a gas vapor. Light caused by an electric discharge results. In an HID bulb, all the "works" are contained in a small tube protected by an outer glass envelope that is heat-resistant and minimizes drafts. The outer glass also helps to absorb harmful electromagnetic rays produced by the tube. Unfortunately, some HIDs will continue to work with the bulb broken and some people have been burned by the so-called actinic rays (somewhat like X rays). Other bulbs have a fail-safe device built in, and cease to operate if the outer bulb is broken.

HIDs are suggested for high ceilings (as shown here in a technical center in Nevada). They have low wattage requirements and long life spans.

Until lately, HIDs were used only in industry; they tended to have a very strange color of light. (The sodium lights with the yellow color seen on highways are HIDs.) But because HIDs are energy-conserving and because many have extra-long lives, the industry has gone out of its way to change the strange color. Some of the best color-corrected bulbs are finding use in the field of merchandising.

Most HIDs require special ballasting, like fluorescents, and therefore special installations (there are self-ballasted mercuries). Another drawback is that they tend not to be interchangeable, and some must burn as long as 10 hours per start or their lives will be shortened considerably. But probably their worst problem is that they are sensitive to current variations.

If the electrical current variations are too great, HIDs will turn off. Once off, the bulb might not light again until cooled, which may be a problem if illumination must be provided for safety. It is not uncommon to find incandescents backing up HID systems.

HID sources also require warm-up before they reach full output, a problem when turning on the bulbs after they have been shut off for even a moment. Some bulbs have a warm-up time of close to 9 minutes. (The bulb may begin as a dark pink and slowly warm up to an almost white glow.)

There are three basic types of HIDs:

1. Mercuries have a remarkably long life, particularly when contrasted with incandescents. Some mercury vapor lights work beyond 24,000 hours of operation. Mercuries often are used as substitutes for incandescents; their light per unit of energy consumed is somewhere between that of the incandescent and fluorescent and their low maintenance makes them very popular. Until recently, mercuries cast a strong blue light, the color of glowing mercury. But this ultraviolet light has been color corrected so that white and warm white (pink) mercuries are available.

2. Metal halides do not last as long as some long-life fluorescents (see details on rated average life later in this chapter), but their light output per unit of energy is far above that of the fluorescent and their color is fairly good. Metal halides are fast finding their way into offices and libraries, particularly in facilities with high ceilings or those that can effectively use an indirect lighting system. Unfortunately, as with all HIDs, the metal halide ballasts tend to be noisier than fluorescents, and if not properly installed, the bulbs have a tendency to explode. Therefore metal halides usually are installed in enclosed ceiling-mounted fixtures or in specially made upward-directed kiosks. In the kiosk, the metal halide light shines up onto the ceiling and then disseminates into the rest of the room. Because these bulbs are so energy-efficient, even though indirect light technically is less efficient than direct light, these systems are very competitive where energy is concerned. Many kinds of light bulbs have special installation requirements. Special care must be taken to install metal halides correctly because of their tendency to explode.

3. High-pressure sodiums are probably familiar to most people because they have been used on highways and can be recognized as the yellow glowing bulb. The sodiums are the most energy-conserving, and

sodiums meant for indoor use have been color corrected so that they broad-cast nearly white light. The amount of light broadcast per unit of energy is far above the others. They are especially applicable for high ceilings. But most high-pressure sodiums have to burn in a particular position, usually horizontal.

Low-pressure discharge. The low-pressure bulbs work similarly to HIDs, except that the electrical arc is under low pressure. These bulbs are the most energy-conserving on the market. Although the sodiums cast an amber light, not especially attractive for indoor use, they have been installed in some libraries. In the future it is likely that their color will be corrected so that the light they broadcast will be more nearly white.

Ballasts

All fluorescents and HIDs need ballasts to regulate electrical current. In-candescents do not. As the current in an electrical arc through a fluorescent or HID increases, the resistance of the arc decreases, allowing more current to flow. If the electrical current were not limited, an arc passing through the bulb would be of such magnitude that it would eventually be destroyed.

Ballasts also supply the correct starting voltage and provide circuit pro-tection. Each bulb uses its own special ballast. Fluorescent ballasts are rated as to preheat, instant-start or rapid-start circuit, wattage required, am-bient temperature, noise, and other special factors. HID ballasts are rated similarly.

Ballasts draw electrical current. When calculating the amount of electri-cal energy a system consumes, one must also calculate the energy that ballasts draw. In addition, particularly in the rapid-start systems, ballasts constantly draw electric power even when the lights are switched off or when the bulbs are removed. To stop this electricity consumption, ballasts must be disconnected.

Some ballasts will burn out if their bulbs are removed and they are not disconnected. Others will require at least two bulbs to work on the circuit. If one burns out, or if one is removed, the other bulb does not function. When one cycles on, the other cycles off. However, in an effort to save electrical energy in some facilities, one out of every two lights is turned off. In a two-bulb circuit this is impossible to do, unless a dummy fluorescent is installed, with special wiring to complete the circuit.

The National Electric Code requires that fluorescent and HID fixtures in indoor installation have ballast protection. The Underwriters Laboratories has standards for a ballast classification known as Class P, or protected. This means that these ballasts are equipped with thermal protectors that shut off if the temperature rises too high.

Some ballasts on the market are not Class P. Generally less expensive, they will continue to operate until they melt or explode if the temperature is too high. Used primarily for outdoor installations such as signboards, they can cause fires indoors. At the very least, they can melt, oozing a gooey black tar that drips down one end of the fixture. (Tar will form even on Class P ballasts that are about to fail.)

Ballasts are also rated for noise. The best ones, usually known as "A" ballasts, do have some vibration, but it should not be noticeable until toward the end of their lives. Unfortunately, the noise level of a ballast can be the function of the heat of the case, the fixture design, the cavity design, the ballast mounting, or even the resonant qualities of the room and the furnishings. Some ballasts buzz, and no attempt to quiet them is successful. Renovation may be necessary as a last resort. First, the ballast should be changed—it may have begun to fail. Next, the ballast rating should be checked—the wrong one may have been installed. Only if nothing else works should renovation be considered.

In comparison to bulbs, which last 5 to 6 years at the most, ballasts have a long life, many operating for 12 to 13 years.

Rated average life

All bulbs and ballasts have a rated average life, usually specified in a manufacturer's catalog. Incandescents have the shortest life spans. Some function for only a few hundred hours. There are long-lived fluorescents and HIDs that will burn for 24,000 hours or more. For fluorescents and HIDs, the rated average life generally depends on the number of hours per start. For example, one fluorescent may have a rated average life of 12,000 hours at 3 hours per start and 18,000 hours at 12 hours per start. Metal halides have a rated average life between 7,500 and 15,000 hours. It is important to know these facts when purchasing bulbs in the first place.

The rated average life is, as the name indicates, an average. If a bulb has, say, a rated average life of 1,000 hours, and 100 bulbs are installed, somewhere near 500 hours of operation some will burn out. One-half will burn out by 1,000 hours; the others will continue to operate on a downward curve. By about 1,500 hours, all the bulbs will have failed.

Most light bulbs darken with age and give less light as they grow older. In incandescents, almost the entire interior of the bulb appears dirty. Most fluorescents appear dirty near the edges, although there are some that stay bright to the end (but they usually have a shorter lamp life than bulbs that darken). HIDs also darken, but their light output decreases only slightly throughout their entire lives. As most bulbs age, they deliver less and less light per unit of energy. Therefore it pays to remove many of the bulbs before they completely burn out. Cost analysis favored by the lighting industry shows that it usually pays to remove all bulbs in a large facility after approximately 14 percent have ceased to function. Removing all bulbs also saves on maintenance time. Of course, for a small library, group relamping, as the wholesale replacement of the bulbs is called, may not be viable.

Lighting and the eyes

One of the most obvious changes that age makes in the human body occurs in the eye. These changes affect the eye's ability to deal with light intensity, contrast, and glare. Generally about middle age, the lenses of the eye begin to thicken, eventually making it difficult to focus clearly on objects close up or far away. At the same time, the lenses begin to turn yellow, causing certain colors to muddy. By old age, almost everyone has some eye difficulty, and the overwhelming majority of people wear glasses. Even though less than perfect eyesight is so common, and affects all age groups, there is really no such thing as a "seeing standard" for libraries.

Furthermore, lighting techniques go far beyond visual impact. People are attracted to light, a fact known to retail merchandisers. Some library areas can attract more people than others simply by lighting them with a trifle more care. In fact, light is to be viewed as an integral part of architectural and interior design. In more recent years, variety in the "look" of the light and the fixtures has become very important. At the same time, the era of cheap energy has ended. Architects, engineers, interior designers, and librarians, among others, have begun to take a hard look at lighting techniques, particularly those that appear wasteful, if for no other reason than that certain "standards" have been found to be unsuccessful and some are too costly to operate.

For a library, the best light is well diffused, or scattered about evenly. In the reading areas there should be no glare or sharp contrasts. In addition, where possible, it is best to vary the lighting for specific activities, known as "lighting for events." Instead of placing row upon row of fixtures at uniform intervals in the ceiling throughout the entire facility, it may be a good idea to consider the tasks that will take place in the particular spaces. Variety in lighting is an attractive interior design tool, and when handled correctly it is cost-effective. Corridors, for example, can have lower light levels than work areas, and can use decorative fixtures with dramatic techniques, out of place in other library spots. Book stacks, on the other hand, need fixtures that center light on the shelves.

However, the sharp contrasts and patterns formed by lighting variety can cause disorientation. In reading areas, for example, some experts state that a desk lamp should not light the printed page more than three times the level of the adjacent desk top or five times the level of the room.

Direct and indirect glare

There are two types of glare—direct and indirect. Both are annoying and can be temporarily blinding, whether a single light bulb is shining directly in someone's line of sight, or a person is attempting to read a book in full sunlight on a cloudless, clear day. The older people get, the more they are affected by problems of glare, yet the more they require higher intensities of light in order to see.

If a ceiling is high enough, it is rare that the light shines directly in the line of sight. Many ceiling-hung fixtures are designed so that the bulb is hidden by a diffusing panel or grills. Other fixtures are designed so that the light bulbs recess into the ceiling. However, direct glare from ceiling-hung fixtures is not often a major problem. Besides, the deeper the bulb and the fixture are recessed and the darker the interior of the housing (to prevent glare), the less light will be disseminated. Except for certain fixtures with mirrorlike interiors, bulbs in deeply recessed housings provide less light than surface-mounted ones. The main reason is that the light is absorbed by the ceiling.

For energy conservation, some facilities have experimented with unadorned light bulbs. In this example, the result obviously is glare. Little children rarely seem bothered by the effects of glare, but adults are. It would be difficult for some adults to work in this space. (Shown here is a daycare center in Anacostia, Washington, D.C.)

Indirect glare is caused by a light shining on a surface and then reflecting into the viewer's eyes. In the most extreme case, the light of a bulb is reflected by a mirror. However, on glossy printed surfaces, particularly glossy paper, a like situation often occurs. The glare on the page appears so bright that it seems as if a veil has been drawn across the eyes. Thus the effects of indirect glare are known as the veiling reflection—the apparent veil and "whiting out" of the letters prevents seeing.

Usually the veiling reflection is easier to deal with than the effects of direct glare. If one changes position, the printed matter is legible once again. (With direct glare, an architectural motif may be the villain.) However, in this day of specialized equipment, particularly computer terminals and microform machines, the veiling reflection is a common problem. Many viewing surfaces on these machines tend to be glossy and tilted in upward positions. They pick up the reflection of ceiling lights, sometimes 20 feet away. People find the screens difficult to read. Therefore, instead of placing these machines just anywhere in the facility, their positions should be thought out carefully. At times it is only a matter of facing them toward blank walls. If that is possible, a high partition may be constructed a few feet away to block the indirect glare of the lights. In certain cases, a ceiling-mounted baffle may do the job.

For reading printed matter, or hard copy as it is called in the computer industry, rather than viewing the screens, the best light is positioned in such

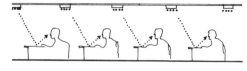

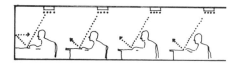

The top row illustrates a bad lighting condition. The angle of light hits the desk top and is reflected into the eyes of the reader. Indirect glare results and it is difficult to see the task. Lighting fixtures that scatter the light will minimize this effect, as will matte finishes on desk and table tops. The bottom row illustrates a good lighting condition. The light coming from behind the reader is reflected away from the eyes and the task can be comfortably seen. The only exception occurs when someone is seated close to a wall or in a carrel, where the light hits the desk top and bounces onto the back wall, causing a hot spot of light. The effect can be minimized by using matte or soft fabric finishes on the carrel back wall. Always avoid bright colors on that wall as the light will cast a strange glow over the task area.

a way as to shine over the shoulder and onto the page. In this manner, the viewer is protected from the effects of direct and indirect glare. The viewer cannot look directly at the light, and, at the same time, the angle of light reflects away from rather than toward the eyes. The only exception is when the reader faces a wall a few feet distant—exactly what happens when viewing a computer terminal or microform screen. In this case, there is a possibility that the light hitting the wall will reflect back at such an angle that it finds the reader's eyes. Occasionally this effect occurs on the back wall of a carrel.

As far as ceiling lights are concerned, a batwing fluorescent fixture has been designed. It looks just like any other fixture, but it sends the light sideways instead of straight down, easing direct and indirect glare. In fact, very little light is disseminated directly underneath. This lighting fixture is a good choice for large spaces, but because of such problems as reflection from vertical surfaces—the color of the light is severely affected by book bindings in book stacks and by walls in small rooms—it is not recommended for stack areas or small rooms.

Even carrel lights have problems. A small person may suffer the effects of direct glare by looking into the carrel light housing. A tall patron might have to sit at such an angle that light reflects onto the printed page and into the eyes.

There are two suggestions for the carrel lighting problem. Choose a carrel with an installed lighting fixture that "fits" most people. In the lighting industry, a visual comfort performance of 90 percent is excellent. (Librarians with similar facilities might be asked for opinions, or one of the carrels might be tried out in the library before buying in quantity.) The second possibility is to provide carrels with flexible or movable lamps, allowing the user more control. (Some librarians reject this because the lamps tend to be broken or easily stolen.)

The idea of the luminous ceiling was to create uniform light throughout the library. However, these installations are not recommended because they waste energy; not only are the task areas illuminated evenly, but so is the ceiling.

Diffused light

As we know, scattered, or diffused, light is easier on the eyes. Fluorescent bulbs tend to be more diffuse than incandescents or HIDs. The fluorescent bulb has no filament, or one point from which the light comes. Instead, the light emanates from the length of the tube. Fluorescents are fitted into fixtures that often feature panels, louvers, or grills at the base, which diffract or polarize the light to prevent glare. *Diffract* means to bend light. *Polarize* means to filter out certain rays and channel the rest in one way or direction.

Open-bottomed fixtures have become more popular of late. They allow more light to pass through than fixtures enclosed by panels. Some open-bottomed fixtures have light bulbs placed as high in the housing as possible. They depend upon mirrored surfaces to diffract and scatter the light. Some of them are also energy-efficient and, if built properly, maintenance-free.

Maintenance should be considered for any lighting fixture. In some instances a fixture with an open bottom or one with a grill or louvers is not as efficient as one with a panel. The panel tends to seal the fixture and keep the inside clean, although some efficient, open fixtures have a coating to alleviate this problem. (Some panels, grills, or louvers made of plastic do yellow with age, but many plastics on the market today do not yellow. Yellowing cuts down the light in the space.)

Visual comfort probability index

Most large lighting manufacturers can supply information on how efficient their fixtures will be—how they scatter light, how broadly the light is disseminated, even the optimum number of fixtures required for a room. They can also tell the client how many people will be comfortable with these fixtures in an area, using a numerical rating known as the visual comfort probability index (VCP). A VCP of 70 or better is considered good. That means that 70 out of 100 people are comfortable in the light broadcast by a particular fixture. A high VCP would be 90—90 out of 100 people are comfortable.

Light spill

The light spill, or the configuration light takes once it leaves the bulb and the fixture, is important. Each light bulb, fixture, grill, louver, panel, or mirror surface has a different spill. For example, an ordinary incandescent light is bulb-shaped and therefore tends to disseminate light in a circle. A fluorescent light is tubular and broadcasts light in a more elongated configuration. A recessed floodlamp will have a downward-directed circular beam pattern when pointed toward the floor. By slightly angling the fixture, an elliptical pattern can be obtained. The same elliptical pattern may be made by changing the lens mounted in front of the reflector housing and angling the lens somewhat.

Therefore it matters very much what general type of fixture, bulb, panel, louver, or grill is used to illuminate a space. The angle at which it throws out a beam is important also. Changing anything about the lighting system may change the spill.

One can learn about light spills by looking at manufacturers' specifications. In many instances they feature drawings showing the spill. Otherwise, the information can be obtained at a lighting supplier's showroom. By turn-

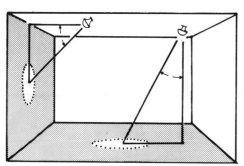

Each bulb and fixture has its own spill of light. By angling the light in any direction, the spill is changed. Walls can be washed with light, elliptical and circular light patterns created on the floors, bringing interest and drama to the design. But used incorrectly, light spill can increase glare.

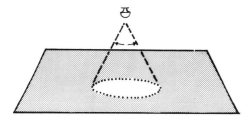

ing out all other lights, the spill from one light can be seen clearly in the room.

Spill can have a major impact on the electrical requirements of the library. For example, the recessed spotlamp, with its fairly constricted pattern, should not be used in the stack and reader areas, only in lobbies and corridors. Many more spots are needed to effect the same illumination as obtained from similarly mounted fluorescent fixtures. (Even surface-mounted incandescents are more energy-conserving.)

One of the chief problems with some fixtures in libraries is that sometime along the way the wrong bulb has been installed. This mainly pertains to incandescents (it is rather difficult to install the wrong-shaped bulb in a fluorescent fixture). The recessed fixtures that take floodlamps disseminate very little light when a regular frosted bulb is installed. (The same problem occurs with surface-mounted, can-type fixtures that are supposed to utilize only flood- or spotlamps.)

Besides variations in the light spill from one bulb to another, or one diffuser to another, there are also variations in the fixture design that can be categorized as up, down, and sideways. Upward-directed light shines upward, and the ceiling usually acts as a secondary light source to scatter and disseminate the illumination. That is why this system is known as indirect—the light indirectly reaches the surfaces where needed. Downward-directed light simply shines down. This system is often called direct. Sideways light—or semidirect—is the type one sees through the edge of certain fixtures and lamps. Some of the light goes sideways, some toward the ceiling, and some straight down.

Light distribution on walls, floor, and ceiling may differ substantially. Unwanted hot spots may occur. However, it is not uncommon to wash a back wall with light to keep it unshadowed.

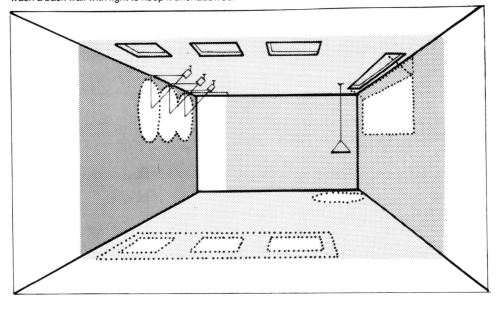

Psychological impressions can be created by light. Table lamps in this Biloxi, Mississippi, library provide a feeling of coziness. The lighting fixtures were used to heighten the aesthetic sense. Although shadows and glare may be a problem in this type of facility for some adult readers, the attractive design overcomes all drawbacks for others.

Often three spills are combined in one fixture, such as in the ordinary table lamp and shade. The shade allows some light to travel up, some down, and some through the shade itself, sideways. In other instances, two spills are combined. A batwing fixture usually sends most of the light sideways and a small portion directly downward. Other fixtures use an up-and-down spill; the majority of light is broadcast from beneath the fixture, but some light shines onto the ceiling and then reflects to the surfaces below.

A good installation always takes the light spill into consideration. For example, an up-down ceiling fixture can have its effectiveness reduced if it is put into a coffered ceiling that cannot utilize the upward-directed light. The light is trapped—sometimes 50 percent—and never finds its way into the areas below.

Shadowing

A downward-directed light that is not scattered will cause shadowing. So much light bathes the top of the object beneath the light and so little below that the absence of illumination causes shadows. By scattering the light, almost as much light strikes the top of the object as the bottom, and shadowing is all but eliminated.

Shadowing techniques are an important aspect of interior design. Light that is well scattered is often bland and flattens the three-dimensional space. Shadows, on the other hand, lend depth, mystery, and interest. How-

TABLE 1

Surface	Reflectance (pre-energy crisis)
Ceiling finishes (generally white)	80–90%
Walls (perhaps light buff)	40–60%
Furniture (perhaps light green)	25–45%
Office machines and equipment (perhaps light green)	25–45%
Floors (perhaps medium green)	20–40%

ever, except to highlight certain architectural or interior design points, or to heighten the visual impact of an artistic object, by and large, shadows do not belong in libraries. In the reading areas, in the stack areas, and in the staff work spaces, the light should be as well and as evenly diffused as possible. If a designer insists on shadowing for effect, make certain that he or she limits the technique to lobbies, hallways, high ceilings, plants, and such. Shadowing rarely belongs where people are expected to browse, read, or work.

Absorption/reflection

Absorption and reflection play a large part in how well a lighting system functions. Some fixtures use reflectors to disseminate light; others use dark sockets and baffles to cut the effects of direct glare.

Most people are aware that a mirrorlike finish will reflect all the light touching its surface, but it is not so generally known that a white ceiling does almost the same thing. A black ceiling absorbs nearly all the light pointed toward it. Light surfaces help to disseminate room illumination; dark surfaces absorb it. Thus the lighter the walls, floor, and ceiling, as well as the

Ceilings, walls, floors, furnishings, even clothing absorb light. The darker the surfaces, the more light is absorbed. The more spaces are subdivided, the more light is absorbed. Light colors reflect light and aid in its dissemination.

TABLE 2

Color	Reflectance	Color	Reflectance
White	80%	Salmon	53%
Ivory (light)	71%	Pale apple green	51%
Apricot beige	66%	Medium gray	43%
Lemon yellow	65%	Light green	41%
Ivory	59%	Pale blue	41%
Light buff	56%	Deep rose	12%
Peach	53%	Dark green	9%

furnishings, the more ambient light there will be, because light surfaces often act as secondary light sources.

When choosing the color of paint or furnishings for a library facility, it is important to consider whether it would be beneficial to aid the lighting system by choosing only light colors.

Before the energy crisis, the Illuminating Engineering Society, a group of engineers, manufacturers, and lighting consultants, recommended the reflectance levels for various surface finishes, shown in Table 1. The energy shortage has changed these levels to the extent that many libraries have turned away from dark green or black stacks and are using light colors to upgrade the lighting, at the same time avoiding glossy surfaces.

Whenever possible, objects should be chosen with matte finishes. Glossy surfaces, including marble on walls and glossy textured carpets, should be avoided. Some carpeting is so glossy that the color is reflected onto the ceiling and casts a strange glow throughout the entire facility. A library filled with glossy surfaces usually is also filled with glare.

Some libraries have taken the opposite tack and painted ceilings black to utilize open ceilings where the electrical raceways and duct work are easily reached for repair and maintenance. In such a case, the library can use a downward-directed lighting system only. Otherwise, not only would a good deal of light be absorbed by the ceiling but the light would be shaded to a definite degree.

Other libraries have tried indirect systems. Here the light is strongly dependent upon the color of the ceiling and upper walls; they must be off-white since pure white causes glaring hot spots.

Various colors have different absorption rates depending on how much white or black the particular color contains. (Color, concerning light bulbs and all library features, is discussed in detail in the next chapter.) Table 2 shows the reflectances of some paint colors as supplied by the National Paint and Coatings Association. Nearly all paint manufacturers will supply the consumer with the reflectances of their particular paints.

Certain building materials disseminate more light than others. New white plaster, because it tends to be glossy and very white, has a reflectance level as high as 92 percent, while red brick has a reflectance level between 10 and 20 percent. Dark walnut, one of the richer-looking woods,

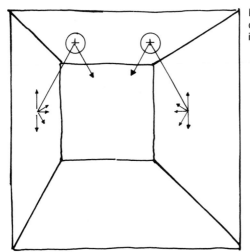

Low-reflectance room surfaces—dark colors on walls lower the apparent lighting level.

absorbs most of the light touching its surface; birch, a color used in many libraries, is fairly light and therefore falls somewhere in the medium range.

Because of the ability of the walls and other surfaces to absorb light, the smaller the room, the more light is needed. Stacks, in fact, tend to act like small rooms and need much more light than equivalent space in a larger room. In addition, because many book bindings are green, red, brown, or black, a good deal of light disappears by simple absorption (which is exactly why white stacks have become so popular—the idea is to counter the effect of the size of the stack area and the color of the books). Larger rooms need less light because there are fewer walls (which absorb light) and, in addition, the spill of one light tends to aid the spill of the next.

The cleanliness of the walls, ceilings, furnishings—in fact, everything in the room—has an effect upon light absorption. Repainting surfaces the

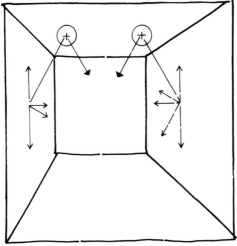

High-reflectance room surfaces—light colors heighten the apparent lighting level (may add glare unless light is diffused). The color of ceiling and upper walls will give a decided tint to a room if light reflects from them. That is why most rooms use white ceilings.

same color as before and cleaning bulbs and fixtures results in a noticeable increase in illumination, up to 20 percent. (That is because dirt either blocks or absorbs light.)

Air handling

Many lighting fixtures can be installed as part of the heating, ventilating, and air-conditioning system. The air may circulate through special holes in or around the light fixtures. Some fixtures have holes at either end. Paneled fixtures have small cracks around the periphery to do the same thing. In ceiling systems (a prefabricated ceiling assembled on the job), a barely noticeable crack among the acoustical tiles may handle the air and not involve the lighting fixtures, except indirectly.

It is a good idea, if at all possible, to make the lighting system a part of the overall heating/ventilating/air-conditioning complex, although special circumstances may require otherwise. (For example, in a renovation where duct work already exists, such a system may be too costly to install. In a small new building it may be too costly in terms of construction.) The reason is that all electricity consumed can be directly translated into heat. Although the heat that is formed comes in relatively small amounts, if allowed to build up, it can cause havoc with the air-conditioning system. Besides, it can blow lights; fluorescents, for example, are damaged unless they run relatively cool. That is why many fixtures are vented at the top, so as to remove the heat, provided, of course, the heat has someplace to go. (Usually it finds its way into the plenum above the false acoustical ceiling. In some instances, a fan may exhaust it from the space, or it may just sit there until it dissipates.)

Why waste heat in this energy-conserving age? Why not reuse it? Several libraries have done just that. The buildings are primarily heated and cooled by the waste heat generated by electrical equipment, such as the lights, and the body heat of the people using the facility.

If circumstances allow, it is always best to purchase fixtures that vent. As the heat tends to rise, a small draft will carry away the dirt that forms in and around the bulb and housing. In other words, the bulbs will be cleaner and thus will keep up their efficiency.

Measuring light

There are several ways to measure light. Even though a librarian may not become too heavily involved in these technical details, it may be helpful to understand some of the terms used in light measurement. (More complicated terms can be found in a standard lighting text.)

Current is the movement of electrons through a medium, often a copper wire surrounded by plastic or rubber insulating material.

Amperes measure the flow of electric current. As electrons flow through wire, they meet resistance, which causes friction. The friction translates into heat. If the heat is too great, the insulation will begin to melt, exposing live wire. In electrical circuits, the wires are protected by a fuse or a circuit breaker, which either melts or trips when an excessive amount of heat is present, thus protecting the wire and therefore the building from an electrical fire. In other words, the failing point for the fuse or circuit breaker is below that of the wire. That is why it is so dangerous to put a copper penny in a fuse box instead of the proper fuse. The melting point of the penny is *above* that of the electrical wires. A 30-amp fuse will melt when the heat of the flow of the electricity is above 30 amps. (Amp and *a* are abbreviations for amperes.)

Voltage is the measurement of the tendency of electrons to move. It can be likened to the force of water inside a pipe when the faucet is closed. Different incandescent bulbs and ballasts require different voltages, two of the most common being 120 v and 277 v. (For fluorescents and HIDs, the ballasts regulate the electrical voltage requirements.) Voltage is expressed in units known as volts and abbreviated as v.

Wattage is the rate at which electrical energy is changed into another form. In other words, it is the rate of electrical energy *consumed* by, say, a light bulb. Wattage is expressed in units known as watts and abbreviated as w (1 watt = $1/746$ horsepower).

Formula: Watts = Volts × Amperes
 w   = va
If a 30-amp fuse is protecting a lighting circuit, how many 100 w incandescents can be put on that circuit if the voltage equals 120?

w = $(120) \times (30)$
w = 3,600 total load possible; $3,600 \div 100 = 36$

36 incandescents total load possible

Lumens are the measurement of light emitted by the light source—the light bulb alone or the bulb and fixture together. Many people confuse lumens with watts, but they do not have any relationship, except to explain the cost of operating a particular light bulb. For example, a cool white fluorescent may need only 40 watts to achieve 2,960 lumens, whereas a frosted incandescent may require 150 watts (see Table 3). HID bulbs tend to be far more efficient, so that a high-pressure sodium may require 100 w to achieve 9,800 lumens. At 3 cents a kilowatt (1,000 watts) hour, the difference in cost is extraordinary. (Kilowatt is abbreviated as kw; kilowatt hour is kwh. Many areas of the country pay in excess of 3 cents per kwh. New York City, for example, pays 10 cents per kwh.)

Let us take, for example, the difference in cost to run two 100-bulb systems, one featuring 150 watts per bulb and the other 40 watts per bulb

TABLE 3

Lamp Type	Mean Lumens per Watt
Low-pressure sodium	183
High-pressure sodium	127
Metal halide	80
Fluorescent	66
Mercury vapor	48
Incandescent	23

TABLE 4

Incandescent	Fluorescent
150 w/hour	40 w/hour
× 100 bulbs	× 100 bulbs
15,000 w/hour = 15 kw	4,000 w/hour = 4 kw
15 kw/hour	4 kw/hour
× 10 hours/day	× 10 hours/day
150 kw/day	40 kw/day
150 kw/day	40 kw/day
× 30 days	× 30 days
4,500 kw/month	1,200 kw/month
4,500 kw/month	1,200 kw/month
× .03 (cost per kw)	× .03 (cost per kw)
$135.00	$36.00

There is a $99 difference per month at .03 cents per kw.

(incandescent versus fluorescent), in a library open 10 hours a day for 30 days. The cost of electricity is 3 cents per kwh (see Table 4).

Foot candles measure the ambient room lighting levels. A standard foot candle is equal to the amount of light produced by a plumber's candle at a distance of 1 foot. Thirty-foot candles are considered adequate for most library browsing areas; desk lamps are usually 100- to 150-foot candles. Foot candles do not take into consideration glare, shadowing, contrasts, or any other things that affect the ability to see. Thus they are raw lighting levels. Unfortunately, foot candles are often used as the standard. Foot candles are measured by a special light meter, available at stores selling professional lighting equipment.

TABLE 5

Area	Suggested ESI
Book stacks (active)	30 (foot candles)
Book stacks (inactive)	5 (foot candles)
Card files	100
Circulation desk	70
Conference	30
Corridors	20
Microform, files	70
Microform, viewing	30
Offices: accounting, business machines	150
Offices: reading handwriting in ink or medium pencil on good-quality paper	70
Offices: reading poor reproductions	150
Reading printed material	30
Reading—study and note taking	70
Washrooms	30

Foot lamberts, the opposite of foot candles, measure reflectivity of surfaces. A standard foot candle meter can be used to measure foot lamberts. (Directions should come with the meter.)

Equivalent sphere of illumination is a method of measuring room lighting levels to take into consideration not only foot candles but glare, reflection, absorption, shadowing, contrast—everything that affects the ability to see. The ESI, as it is known, is a very complicated procedure, although an ESI meter may soon be on the market (but quite costly). Given the spacing of fixtures, size and coloration of the room, furnishings, lumens being broadcast, and other important facts, large lighting suppliers and manufacturers can provide computerized figures to explain the ESI for various parts of the library. Obviously, ESI and foot candle figures are not interchangeable. However, although almost all standards given by various associations are in ESI, many people simply change the figures into foot candles. Except for book stack areas, all the figures in Table 5 are in ESI (figures supplied by the Illuminating Engineering Society).

An ESI of 30 is recommended for generalized lighting (except for corridors); 150 for certain office work; 70 for others. The difference can be accommodated by desk lamps. Overall lighting in the library can range between 30 and 50 ESI. (The lower number is probably best, but since most Americans prefer a great deal of light, general ambient light in the more energy-conserving libraries built in the past few years is about 50 ESI.)

Since the energy crisis, many people reject the standards in Table 5 as too high. Several lighting consultants use the ESI designations in Table 6.

Special lighting problems in the library

Most libraries have special areas of lighting concern, which may include stack lighting, office space, high ceilings, flexibility needs, use of daylight, and lighting for the visually impaired.

Stack lighting. Stacks are lighted in five general ways:

1. A grid pattern in the ceiling, very common because it is one of the

TABLE 6

Condition	ESI	Type of Illumination
Small detail, prolonged periods, high speed, extreme accuracy	100–200	General lighting plus desk lamps
Normal library work—staff and user areas	30–70 (50 preferred)	General lighting (desk lamps may be required for some people)
Recreational areas, including lounges, rest rooms, and cafeterias	10–30	General lighting
Corridors	5–20	General lighting
Storage	5–10	General or supplementary lighting

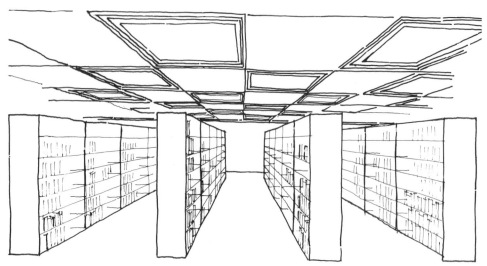

Fluorescent or HID fixtures affixed to ceiling in a grid pattern; minimum 3-foot clearance to ceiling required. This configuration offers the ultimate in flexibility. Stacks can be placed in any direction, and fixtures will be nearby to illuminate them. Especially good for high ceilings where HID or fluorescent batwing fixtures are used. However, pattern is energy wasteful in low ceilings as spaces are lit without regard to stack patterns. Not recommended for low ceilings.

Stack or ceiling-hung fluorescents, running parallel to stacks down the center of the aisle. No clearance above stacks required. This is the most energy-conserving configuration. Light is close to the stacks it must illuminate. No light is lost over the top of the stacks. Excellent for stack arrangements that are fixed in place. Not a flexible arrangement and not recommended where stacks are to be added or removed.

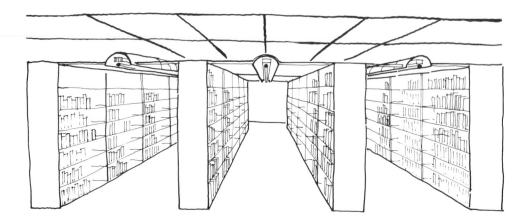

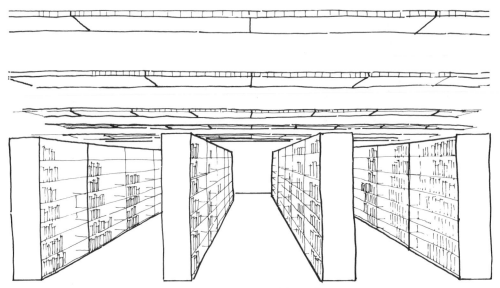

Ceiling-hung fluorescents perpendicular to library stacks, minimum 1 foot above stacks. Lighting fixture rows should be placed 4 feet 6 inches to 6 feet on center. This configuration allows good flexibility. Stacks can be added or removed without affecting light spill. Some light is lost over the top of the stacks, but the light over one single face helps to illuminate the opposite single face.

Ceiling-hung fluorescents in batwing fixtures running parallel to and directly above the stacks, about 1-foot minimum. This configuration is designed for stacks fixed in place. Batwing fixtures tend to be energy conserving. However, the majority of light is broadcast sideways rather than downward, so fixtures must be positioned on top of the stacks. The light from the fixture illuminates the face of the opposite stacks. But because the light is directed sideways, the reflected light from book bindings gives long runs of stacks a strange glow. For this reason, this pattern is not recommended for stack lighting. Batwing fixtures are highly recommended for wide area lighting in the rest of the facility.

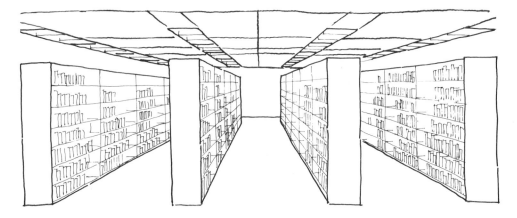

simplest to design. Sometimes grids are very successful in lighting stacks because there are so many lights. At other times they fail because ceilings are low and stacks are placed without regard to whether there is a fixture above.

    2. Ceiling- or stack-mounted parallel to the stacks, and running down the center of the aisle. This system is particularly good when the stacks are fixed and not expected to be moved. The light spill can be calculated so that the entire face of each stack is lighted from top to bottom. In addition, if the ceiling is very high, the lights can be hung on stems and brought down to the areas where needed, or attached to the cross ties, thus saving on electricity that might otherwise be wasted by lighting the ceiling, upper walls, and top of the stacks. However, this lighting has drawbacks. If it is installed incorrectly, the light spill may cast shadows. Even worse, such lights limit any change in size of the stack area. To move the stacks, one also has to move the lights. To change the stack area, one must change everything.

    3. Ceiling-mounted perpendicular to the stacks. In this case, some light is wasted over the top of the stacks, but because of the perpendicular configuration, the angle of the light covers the bottom to the top shelves. Another stack can be added or taken away, as the light spill does not have to be calculated exactly. This method is desirable when flexibility is an issue and when the ceiling is not extremely high, perhaps 9 feet (otherwise lights will have to be hung on stems or somehow dropped from the ceiling).

    4. Ceiling-mounted parallel to the stacks, placed directly above each stack. Here the lighting fixtures have to be mounted directly over the top of the stacks themselves because the batwing fixture is used. This system has

Fluorescents affixed to stack tops, which illuminate the ceiling. The ceiling acts as a secondary light source and illuminates the stacks. Minimum 3-foot clearance to the ceiling, otherwise the indirect system will not wash the ceiling properly. In this indirect lighting system, the light broadcast depends largely on color and texture of the ceiling. First developed in the 1930s, it is gaining popularity once again. Because light bulbs rest directly on stacks, the installation is relatively inexpensive and minimal fixtures can be used.

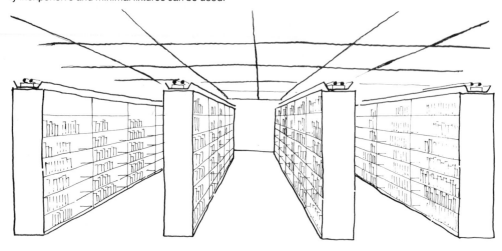

a definite drawback in that it is often installed incorrectly. In addition, because the light shines sideways from the batwing fixture, it reflects off the bookbindings, causing strange light in the stack area (the reflected light has an eerie blue color). It is not recommended.

5. Fixtures that are manufactured as an integral part of the book stacks themselves. The book stack is purchased with a light already installed somewhere along the top. Two different methods are used. The light emanates from the top of the stack and washes down the edge of a single face, the most common example. Or the light is attached in the center on the top of the stack and shines onto the ceiling, an indirect method that uses the ceiling as a secondary light source, disseminating the light to the stacks below. Usually, in the case of indirect lighting, the ceiling cannot be too far above the top of the stacks. The indirect lighting method has been in use since the 1930s, and works well in some instances. The problems with this type of lighting concern dirt. The bulbs usually sit on the top of the stacks unprotected. Also, it is important that the top of the stacks be either white or silvered, and the color of the upper walls and ceiling be white.

Office space or technical process area. Regular office lighting, usually in a grid pattern, is the most common and works well if care is taken to see that every desk receives proper light and that lights are set at proper levels to avoid glare.

A newer method is task-ambient lighting—indirect lighting set in kiosks that shine onto the ceiling. Each work station also has a desk lamp. Often

A grid of lighting fixtures in the ceiling is the simplest way to light a library —as long as the ceiling rises a minimum 3 feet above the stacks. But such an even, diffused lighting pattern flattens the architectural and interior design. It also tends to waste energy as all spaces do not have to be illuminated to the same degree. Wherever possible, it is best to vary the lighting in relation to the tasks to be performed in that space.

Lighting fixtures hang on pendants below the peaked ceiling. The juxtaposition between fixtures and ceiling heightens the aesthetic interest —during the day. At night, unless the light illuminates the ceiling, its height diminishes (it is in the dark). The lighting fixtures become the ceiling, and the aesthetic display is lost.

energy-conserving (because metal halide bulbs are used in the kiosks), the entire office lighting system may consume 1.8 to 2.5 watts per square foot, as opposed to 4 and 5 watts a few years ago. But such systems incorrectly installed often have "hot spots" on the ceiling and too many shadows on task areas.

Energy-conserving lighting can be set up in almost any method, provided the correct bulbs and fixtures are used. Task-ambient lighting is just one method. Care should be taken that whatever the lighting system, work spaces are adequately supplied.

High ceilings. Some libraries, particularly some academic, art, and public libraries, have extremely high ceilings in the reading rooms, perhaps five or six stories high. Sometimes a school library moves into a gym with a ceiling three stories tall. What to do? For generalized lighting, a few HID ceiling lights would help. In the stack area, the best method would be lighting that hangs above the top of the stacks, perhaps resting on cross bars. And for the rest of the facility, desk lamps can be used where necessary.

Flexibility needs. Many librarians are concerned with flexibility. They want to be able to move lights at will to cover all possible circumstances. In that case all lights can be hung on tracks. Some libraries have all fluorescents on individual tracks; others have done the same with HIDs. Such installations tend to be quite expensive.

Use of daylight. How can natural light be used effectively, especially as a way to save on electricity costs? It is important to remember that glass is not as good an insulator as other building materials. Thus a skylight or floor-

The glare from the window walls may bother users who face them. Blinds or some sun screening may be necessary.

to-ceiling window, although less costly in terms of electricity for lighting, may waste money for heating and cooling.

However, most people do not like to work in rooms without windows. Natural light shining in is attractive, too. Windows belong in libraries. But sunlight is very destructive to fabrics, furniture, and nearly all library materials. Sometimes it is difficult to study or work at a desk bathed in sunlight. The glare is impossible and the whole area is too warm.

Wherever possible, people, not book stacks, should be near windows. Most readers prefer an outdoor view. Also, sunlight, and even reflected daylight, can damage books.

Sunlight should be welcomed into the library in lobbies, walkways, lounges, or areas of relaxed reading. But it should be controlled on desk tops or where people are expected to work for long periods of time without interruption. A view of the outside is pleasant, but too much sun on a desk is not.

Lighting for the visually impaired patron. Lighting attracts people. They tend to move toward areas that are well lighted. Yet a number of libraries and other buildings make the lobby quite dim, for aesthetic reasons. This can pose a problem, especially for those with vision impairment. These people have trouble with adaptation, the ability of the eye to adjust from light to dark and back again. Especially on a bright day, the contrast from the out-of-doors to inside may be blinding. (Most people have had the experience of adjusting to a darkened movie theater; it is harder to adapt from light to dark than dark to light.)

The librarian should be aware of the problems that aesthetic lighting can cause. Lines of light may vibrate and cause confusion. Pools of light may lead where people should not walk. A common problem occurs around doorways and panels of clear glass. The glass should be marked in some way, perhaps with a piece of colored tape, especially if the area is not well lighted. Otherwise people may think the space is open and attempt to walk right through.

Indirect glare is another concern, especially for the elderly, who suffer greatly from its effects. Floors that are highly polished sometimes create the impression of depth. People feel there should be a step when there is none, or they feel that the floors are not level (especially true on marble stairs).

Changes in illumination should be gradual, at least where those changes are near walkways, doors, and steps. Because adaptation to light is often a problem, it may be useful to provide unobtrusive general illumination in all areas and work around that with a variety of lights. Where lights in areas are to be switched on and off, especially areas that are well used, illuminated wall plates may be a workable idea.

Patrons who wear bifocals and trifocals have special problems. Because the top glass aids in focusing on objects in the distance, people with these glasses often cannot see the titles of books on the top shelves of book stacks. They are standing too close. Occasionally, the same thing may happen when searching for a title on a bottom shelf. Now they are standing too far. There is no perfect solution here, except to limit books when possible to the middle four or five shelves. And perhaps add lights here and there that can be turned on and off.

People with bifocals also have problems with the screens of microform machines. Most microform viewing screens are tilted upward toward the far focusing glass. However, one type of machine throws a lighted picture onto the desk top, which is easy for a person wearing bifocals to see. These machines are not generally popular, but it might be a good idea for the library to have one or two for the visually handicapped patron.

Card catalogs often cause problems for wearers of bifocals and trifocals, because many of these people need high-intensity but well-diffused light to see fine print. And the lettering on catalog cards tends to be rather small. The catalogs should be positioned directly under fairly bright, very diffuse light. This means that if the major library lighting is in a grid pattern, the catalogs should be positioned under a particular light in the grid. If this is not possible, lights should be installed somewhere in the area to provide the proper illumination.

Power

In today's world of microforms, computer terminals, audiovisual equipment, closed-circuit television, mechanical retrievers, word-processing and copying machines, electrified compact shelving, and the like, libraries need power in ever-increasing amounts. Power in this context means electrical, telephone, and cables and wires that bring electricity from the local utility and disseminate it inside the building. Cables are made of individually insulated electrical wires that form a thick, ropelike structure. They are protected by flexible metal pipes known as conduits, which may run through the building in loose channels called raceways or closed channels called ducts. If the library is fairly old and the building has been renovated recently, most of the electrical equipment has probably been added to or substantially replaced. CRT (cathode ray tube) cables (for computer viewing screens), for instance, are much broader than ordinary telephone lines and need

Libraries increasingly depend on electrical/telephone/communication equipment. Without an adequate power supply, this media center could not function.

wider spaces in which to run. (Renovation of this sort may be required even in a new building if the electrical/telephone/communication requirements were badly under-estimated.)

In the not-too-distant future, optical fibers may replace all metal wires and cables. These fibers should substantially reduce cable size. At present, however, the up-to-date library must allocate ever more space to house one or another of the various systems.

Floor and ceiling systems

Electrical/telephone/communication cables can be hidden in walls, on columns underneath floors, or above the ceiling. If the library is large and has few walls in relation to the interior square footage, a wall system—the most common type found in older libraries—simply is not enough. There must be some other means to deliver electrical power to, say, the middle of the floor. This can be done with a power grid used in one of several ways: embedded in the concrete subfloor (if the library has one), resting just underneath the finished floor, or running across the plenum above the false acoustical ceiling. Another method is to use the columns to run cables and hide wires under finished surfaces such as carpeting. But in many libraries, columns are at least 20 feet apart, so that additional means are still required to get the

Headphones in this San Jose, California, library provide good clarity for those who wish to listen, and allow the rest of the library to remain quiet. However, the locations of electrical outlets limit areas that can be used for audiovisual equipment.

power to the center of a bay—the space formed by any four columns. This can be done by utilizing wall partitions or special furniture panels prewired by the manufacturer. By connecting one partition or panel to another, electrical/telephone/communication wires can be brought to any spot. However, one should be aware that various municipalities have their own electrical codes; in certain cities variations of this method are against the local law, although this does not imply that the practice is unsafe. The code may be out of date or union pressure may be such that it is necessary politically to keep the law intact.

For underfloor wiring, the most familiar method is the underfloor fixed conduit system, where prewired electrical/telephone/communication outlets are provided at regular intervals. But extension of power into places not served by an outlet can be sloppy, often accomplished by running wires from the closest outlet in full view along the floor or over equipment. At times, this is also dangerous; people can trip or fires can start from flammable surfaces in contact with frayed wires. Should more power be needed, new wiring and new circuitry are required, involving renovation.

Manufacturers have developed power systems that are flexible and prefabricated. Some of the systems integrate into the building superstructure; ducts or raceways help support floors. Others integrate with prefabricated acoustical and lighting ceiling systems, which at the same time handle heated, ventilated, or air-conditioned air.

One of the simplest and oldest of the prefabricated electrical floor systems is an underfloor grid embedded in the concrete, formed by a series of ducts holding cables and pierced at intervals by inserts meant for outlet fittings. The grid runs across the length and width of the entire building, and wherever the cuts meet—perhaps every 24 square feet—there is a junction box. This system is particularly good for large technical process areas where power requirements are constantly changing, and individual outlets can be accessed and wired whenever they are needed. Depending upon the cost of the system, there may be outlet fittings every 4 feet. (Obviously, the closer the grid, the more metal and cable required, and the more expensive the system.)

A more flexible system, also an integral part of the building superstructure and embedded in the concrete slab, allows floor fixtures to be located at any point along the run rather than at preset inserts. Access is obtained by drilling a hole through the concrete into the metal channel holding the cables, which are then spliced and fitted with the proper outlets.

Another system brings power into the building in a different way. Metallic sheets rather than wires do the conducting. Well insulated, these sheets are layered under standard carpeting throughout the facility. Whenever an outlet is required, it is plugged into the sheet by a simple tool. However, this method tends to be expensive, due to the cost of the sheets, and is not widely used in libraries. Within the library field, a similar application has been a low-voltage system that distributes radio transmissions picked up by earphones.

The cost of a power system involves the labor charges to install the system in a building, plus the materials. Wires, cables, and metal structures tend to be very costly. That is one of the reasons why engineers prefer ceiling rather than floor systems to run cables. Ceiling systems, because of their implied flexibility—they are easier to get at and therefore less expensive to install, renovate, and maintain—use less materials than those under the floor. The cost of installation is about one-third that of a floor system. To save even more money, some libraries forgo a finished ceiling below the race-

The height of the plenum running above the false acoustical ceiling and the ceiling slab may be more than 3 feet. Ducts for the air system and cables for electrical/telephone/communication equipment run in that space, as does the support system for both the ceiling slab and the false ceiling.

A cutaway of the ceiling for a typical loft-type building. Besides all the duct and electrical work in the ceiling, one can see that the entire structure is supported only by thin columns (only one is shown to the left in the back). The walls in the foreground to the right do not bear the weight of the ceiling slab. The mechanicals are installed on the roof. Columns required to support this weight are not shown, but it is obvious to see from the sketch how the concentrated weight of book stacks or file cabinets could collapse a floor.

ways, paint everything black, and depend upon light to direct the eye away. In some libraries, ceiling systems do double duty, serving not only the floor below but the one above as well.

If an acoustical ceiling is installed, the cables can be reached just by pushing up a few tiles. A system installed under the floor means furnishings have to be moved, carpeting cut, concrete drilled, wires snaked, and a patch job done at the end. Besides, ceilings are not required to bear the kind of weight that floors must, particularly in a library. Drilling done once too often can weaken a floor and even cause it to collapse.

Different types of cables may run in the ceiling. To bring that power to the floor or desk top height where it is needed, a connection must be made to the power supply. In this photo an extension wire connected to a ceiling outlet brings the power down through a hollow pole, known as a power pole, but the effect is unsightly.

However, ceiling systems do have some of the same limitations as floor systems. Both are regulated by a national electrical code and by local law. In addition, service must eventually be brought to where it can be utilized near the floor. This usually means a spot about 30 inches above the floor, or desk-top height. In a ceiling system, a power pole does the trick. This is a hollow pole or hose carrying electrical/telephone/communication wires. Much furniture, even book stacks, can be purchased with power poles already fitted and prewired. For the library, power poles can be integrated into a system where certain desks, worktables, and stacks contain the requisite wiring. The base of the furnishings may even conceal a junction box. Power poles can also be attached to wall partitions, planters, and up-lighting kiosks, and the cross ties above book stacks can function as horizontal power poles. But if such equipment is not available, a free-standing pole is the only answer. Many people object to them because they are unsightly. They look like the vertical struts of a self-supporting stack system.

Besides power poles, the other problem with ceiling systems has to do with the ability to deliver air conditioning or chilled water for cooling directly to telephone and computer equipment, especially in an eye-pleasing manner. (Maintenance people prefer to keep all services near each other for easy location and access.) Then, too, leaky pipes overhead have been known to damage wide areas, whereas those under floors can be better contained.

Just as an acoustical ceiling tends to hang 1 foot or more below the ceiling slab (sometimes 3 feet are needed to run duct work and cables between the false ceiling and slab—lost space for a library), a raised floor rides above the floor slab some 9 inches to 1 foot. Until recently, because of the weight such floors were required to bear, libraries avoided them, except in main computer areas where louvers could be installed in the raised floors to deliver cooled air. But new methods of construction promise to make these floors as strong and durable as any others, and, just as important, cost competitive especially in relation to subfloor grid systems. In one installation in the offices of a major banking company, mini air-conditioning units, power cables, and other paraphernalia are connected to electrical tethers that allow ultimate flexibility, bringing connections to where they are needed without renovation. (In offices, departments may often expand and contract, requiring many different kinds of installations.)

It should be noted that in addition to the systems examined, many buildings, upon construction, also install empty ducts or raceways as well as electrical closets and distribution boxes in the event that power needs increase in the future. Entrances to the raceways are available at various points. In the floors the access points are known as handholes and are located at intervals throughout the facility. If more power is required, cables are snaked through and connected to the distribution boxes and then to the primary service of the local utility. When furnishing the library, the interior designers must be informed of such a situation and keep the areas above the handholes empty for easy access. In addition, these areas tend to be soft spots in the concrete floor and can be punctured by heavy equipment. (In small special libraries located in office buildings not designed for library furniture loads, layout possibilities often are severely constricted by structural difficulties and access needs to the handholds.)

Also, in terms of interior design, especially if an underfloor system is to be installed, the layout of the carpeting must be examined as well. It is foolish to install expensive carpeting in areas where it will eventually have to be removed or at least cut. The solutions are many, such as the installation of carpet tile over access points, or strips of contrasting carpeting, perhaps only 3 feet wide, running on top of underground raceways, or pasting a piece of carpet the exact size of a hole above the handhole and blending it into the rest. There are many easy-release cements on the market that make any one of these possibilities viable.

Power distribution and costs

Besides interior power distribution, the librarian must also be aware of power coming from the utility to the building and the distribution of the system to cables in the building. Obviously, everyone would prefer the original installation to be large enough to take care of the library's needs for the next five if not ten years. But because the electronics industry moves forward so fast, this is not always possible.

First, the librarian must be careful with the original purchase. Some highly vaunted electronic equipment may require larger primary service and distribution within the building than the library already has available. To install additional power may be too expensive.

Second, there is the cost of operation. Some machinery requires an initial jolt of electricity to start and then needs less within a few seconds, settling to a much lower level. In effect, that is why home refrigerators or air conditioners dim lights. Instant fluorescents work this way. In a large installation the primary service as well as the distribution system has to be large enough to bear the initial jolt; otherwise wires can be damaged and circuit breakers tripped. In other systems, such as rapid-start fluorescent lighting installations, small amounts of electricity are being consumed all the time to keep the machinery warm and ready, avoiding the large initial jolt. Surprisingly, this system, although continuously consuming electricity, may be less costly in terms of local utility rates as well as the size of cables and primary service required. It is not uncommon for utilities to charge varying rates for differing usages. They often have varying rates for day- and nighttime use as well as high-low as against even use. Equipment and installation that at first appear to be cost-effective in terms of operation may be very different when compared with local rates—particularly true of high-low against even use. Thus, before proceeding with any major renovation or new building, it is wise to contact a representative of the local utility to discern possible rate and power variations.

There are many private telephone systems on the market that also appear to be less costly in terms of installation and operation than those supplied by the local telephone affiliate. But the telephone company may add a charge to bring power to a distribution point within the building to where the private system may hook up. In addition, some private systems are not well supplied with backup protection in case the electricity fails and the air-conditioning systems stop functioning (another electrical requirement). One insurance company had its telephone complex catch fire within three minutes after a power failure.

It must be made clear that the power is first brought by the local utility to the building, and if not enough power is available on its lines, the utility may charge the library extra to bring it. Next, that power is spliced and distributed in a distribution box, usually containing circuit breakers, to cables that in turn transmit the service along the walls, floor, or ceiling. If the library is large enough, not only will there be a main distribution box but several smaller ones on other floors that further divide the service. All this costs money. Anything that can minimize steps puts funds back into the library's budget.

Unfortunately, the tendency to minimize can be taken to an extreme. In many facilities, too few wall switches are installed in order to cut down on the cost of wiring and labor. The World Trade Center, New York City's mammoth twin towers, had only one switch installed to control each floor quadrant. Any person working on a floor after dark activated all the lights in the quadrant, no matter how much light was required. Cleaning the building at night cost a good deal just in terms of wasted electricity. Today, especially with the reemergence of desk lamps and individual lighting, individual switches are a necessity. Otherwise a large facility may find itself paying for the cost of operating many small lamps where no one is seated. In addition, library floors can be divided so that switches can be turned on in small areas without bothering the rest of the lights, or the switches may activate only half the lights in a given space, allowing different day- and nighttime illumination. Studies have shown that two identical buildings can use greatly differing amounts of electricity because one facility routinely turns off all lights when not in use, while the other allows them to burn. Computers can monitor electrical usage, switching lights at preset intervals or when daylight fades. In addition, an individual switch, a master switch—perhaps key-operated to prevent problems—should be installed so that the library can turn off everything at once at the end of the day.

When discussing power in terms of prefabricated integrated systems, union jurisdictions should be mentioned. Because so many of these systems have overlapping requirements—a carpenter, an electrician, perhaps a plasterer or a metalworker—there are times when the library may find itself in a strike situation. These problems should be worked out in advance, particularly when there is no general contractor involved and the librarian is overseeing the work. Probably the best bet is to find out where such a system was used locally and discover what that facility did about any problems.

Energy

Once considered cheap and available, the cost and quantity of energy supplies are a major concern in late twentieth-century America. And yet libraries and other buildings are still being constructed without taking into consideration climatic variations from one part of the nation to another. All across the country buildings go up using glass as the major exterior component. Glass is a poor insulator, and because windows in glass buildings rarely open or close, many of these facilities must depend on mechanical means

A building of glass appears as a three-dimensional sculpture at night.
The light welcomes people, but, unfortunately, too much glass
wastes considerable energy.

to warm, cool, or ventilate, even on those days when the outside temperatures remain within comfort levels.

Passive conservation

Building with the climate in mind is not a new idea. Air-conditioning systems
are a relatively modern invention. Even fuel for heating was difficult to find in
various parts of the nation. Indian pueblos in the Southwest were built of
adobe, a material particularly suited to desert conditions where temperatures are apt to rise and fall 70° F in one day. The exterior materials of the
pueblo kept out the heat of the summer sun, but slowly absorbed the warmth
to reradiate it into the interiors at night. The Seminole Indians, living in a hot,
humid climate, raised large gabled roofs well insulated with grass, and built
their villages in such a manner as to allow free air movement. This encouraged the evaporation of humid air. The same idea was later translated by
plantation owners into large homes, magnificent white edifices three stories
high with wide windows shaded by verandas. On the northeast coast, colonial architects also used wood, a plentiful material that is a first-rate insulator, to fashion more economical houses, still copied today. In the coldest
regions, the "colonials" burrowed into hillsides, exposing only one story to
fierce northern winds, while the southern facade was open to the sun. (This
idea has been appropriated and used in several libraries to construct
"underground" facilities with only the south side above ground.)

These techniques were, and are, passive methods of energy conservation. The manner in which the sun's rays are taken in or avoided does a
major part of the job. Most passive systems depend upon the fact that in all
parts of the continental United States the sun rides high in the sky in the
summer and at a much lower angle in the winter, allowing solar radiation to
be avoided in warm months and captured in cool periods. Even in this tech-

nological age, passive solar systems are possible and can cut energy usage from building to building. To design a passive system, one must take into account:

1. Site selection. Some building sites are better than others. Obviously if an area is plagued by freezing winds, the library should not be constructed on the highest hill.

2. Orientation. Certain facades are better than others. Too much glass facing due west in a hot climate overwhelms even the best air-conditioning system; too much glass facing due north in a cold climate forces the heating system to work harder and harder.

3. Building shapes. Exterior style influences interior comfort. A long, rangy building is out of place in a northern mountain climate because it offers too much surface to freezing winds. An "A"-frame construction is out of place in a southern desert because it collects the heat at the top and does not let it dissipate.

4. Building materials. The insulation and even the color of exterior materials influence indoor temperatures. Single-pane glass abutting a black asphalt parking lot and facing due south builds up heat in adjacent interior spaces.

The ultimate design of a new library building should take climate into consideration. The best methods of building often are updated variations of indigenous older structures.

Humidity and temperature factors

To understand energy conservation and, for that matter, how some systems are expected to work, it is important to understand conditions that affect

An old church in Portland, Maine, makes a charming library. But inside, the high ceilings create a large cubic volume that must be heated, ventilated, and possibly air conditioned. It is also difficult to bring light into the central space. Energy-related operating expenses may be high.

human comfort. We all know that relative humidity is very important to comfort, and that during a good portion of the year, for example, the deserts of California tend to be more comfortable than the bayous of Louisiana. Actual temperatures in the two areas may be identical during the day, but in a hot, *dry* climate, people feel more comfortable than in a hot, *humid* climate. Body perspiration tends to evaporate in the former and not at all in the latter.

However, a too-dry climate is not beneficial either. In northern homes during the winter, the indoor relative humidity can drop to below 10 percent, causing the skin to dry and the membranes of the nose and throat to crack and allowing harmful microbes to enter (one of the chief causes of the common cold). Spraying a fine mist of water into the air is a good way to raise the relative humidity, and the comfort and health of the inhabitants as well.

Relative humidity depends upon the temperature. Warm air holds more water than cold air, warm air is less dense, and therefore has a larger volume capacity. That explains why it gets so dry indoors during the winter; cold air with, say, 40 percent humidity is brought indoors and heated. The humidity level drops. That is also why it rains when warm air meets cold air. The colder air cannot hold as much water as the warm, and it shakes the excess out of the sky.

For the interior of a building, the relative humidity is best when it is about 45 percent, 30 to 65 percent being outer limits (although, as noted, in northern climates it is not uncommon to find extremely low relative humidity in the winter inside a building). For a library, it is best to keep relative humidity as close as possible to the 45 percent mark. Above 60 percent, mold starts to grow on certain papers and bindings; below 45 percent some papers— particularly those stretched on frames—tear from the effects of shrinkage. Above 60 percent, film tends to become soft and sticky; below 30 percent relative humidity, it tends to become quite brittle. (Some film must be kept between 30 and 40 percent humidity, a fact noted on the packaging box.)

Humidity also plays a role in keeping down static electricity. The colder it is, the more likely one is to pick up static electricity while walking along the floor, even with antistatic agents in the carpeting. A higher relative humidity helps to keep the problem within manageable levels, as humidity dissipates the electrical charge.

In the United States, the temperature comfort zone ranges between 65° and 80° F, with the indoor average somewhere between 72° and 74° F. This is substantially different in most other nations. The British, for example, have a comfort zone between 58° and 70° F for winter (many homes in Great Britain do not have central heat) and a much higher one for summer. Many office buildings in Europe are not air conditioned, nor are many public meeting places. A visit to a Parisian restaurant on a hot day can be a very trying experience for an American. The heat of the ovens along with the heat of the street makes the restaurant unbearable—but the Parisians don't seem to notice!

Obviously, differences in comfort zones are generally cultural. The British and Germans expect to wear much warmer clothes indoors in the winter than Americans. Such heavy textiles are not commonly sold on the American market because they are perceived as too warm for indoor use even in the winter.

Temperature transmission

The mechanics of temperature transmission help to explain energy conservation to a degree. Temperature changes are transmitted through three basic processes: radiation, convection, and conduction.

Radiation works in a manner similar to light. As a matter of fact, most heat is only a variation of light, long waves as opposed to the shorter visible waves of the same electromagnetic energy. As in the case of sunlight, as long as one is somewhere within its radius, one can feel the heat. Move away and the warmth will disappear. That explains why it is warmer in the sun—all things being equal—than in the shade. That also explains why someone standing in front of a blazing fire can still feel a chill on the back.

Building materials can absorb and reradiate the sun's heat. Adobe, cinder block, brick, and masonry walls can absorb solar heat and reradiate it into the interior space. In some geographical areas, such as deserts where temperatures vary greatly, that property is very beneficial, but not in others. For example, in a hot, humid climate, one would not want the interior of the building to stay warm at night because the outside temperature does not cool down. In a cold climate, uninsulated masonry absorbs the heat manufactured by the heating system and eventually dissipates it out of doors, obviously not beneficial in this age of expensive fuel.

Radiation can be helped by the color of the building material. Dark-colored objects absorb heat; light-colored objects reflect it. On many buildings in the sun belt, reflective glass facades have been erected so that very little of the sun's radiation can make its way indoors. (That explains why people feel better wearing dark-colored clothes in winter and light-colored ones in summer, to maximize the heat-absorbing/heat-reflecting effects of clothing.)

Radiation with *convection* is one of the chief causes of wind on the earth's surface. Solar radiation warms pockets of air, which then move upward, leaving space for cooler air to sweep in at lower levels. (Hot air rises, cold air falls.) In a library, heat vents are placed near the floor and air-conditioning vents closer to the ceiling to take advantage of this natural movement of air. (In a forced air system, it is not uncommon to have ducts installed in a ceiling. Then the heated air must be pushed down to the floor by means of fans installed in the ducts.) Sometimes convection currents cause drafts when the heated air starts to rise toward the ceiling and the cold air flows in along the floor. This is particularly so in large libraries designed with many atriums and mezzanines. Convection currents caused by the heating/ventilating/air-conditioning systems move unimpeded from one floor to another. In addition, infiltration of air through cracks around windows or entrance doors that remain open often compounds the problem, especially on days when the air pressure outside is either much higher or lower than inside the building. In other words, air of different temperatures is always flowing in or out.

It should be noted that with a forced air system in particular, the interior of a building may have an air pressure much different from that of the exterior. If the air pressure is much lower inside than out, hinged entrance doors become very hard to open; the outside air, in an attempt to gain entry, forces the doors shut. If the air pressure indoors is much higher, entrance doors have a tendency to blow open all day, especially if not attached by a strong door closer, because the interior air is trying to get out.

Annoying convection currents may be blocked and their flow stopped. Floor-to-ceiling walls do the best job, as do doors at the end of especially long halls between two large open areas. If the library building has been planned as an open loft with no interior walls, panels can be used to deflect the drafts. Open atriums may be enclosed with glass, as can balconies and mezzanines. However, in any renovation where convection currents in particular are the target, it is wise to retain a mechanical engineer. In many facilities the return vents are in one place while the rest of the system is somewhere else. Floor-to-ceiling walls may block certain vents, while closing off balconies may block others.

To prevent air from seeping in or out of the building, windows and doors should be weather-stripped and well sealed. Revolving doors do a good job of preventing air inflow/outflow and solve the sticking or blowing open entrance door problems. They do a much better job of keeping the interior

Heating/ventilating/air-conditioning ducts can be expressed as part of the building decor, as in the Acorn School, New York City. This is a favorite technique of hi-tech design.

draft free, whereas the more popular treadle-operated doors often stay open much too long during busy times. Unfortunately, revolving doors are impossible for wheelchair users (and difficult for someone with an armload of books). Therefore an alternate means of access is necessary.

The third method by which variations in temperature are transmitted is through *conduction,* the process in which materials transmit changes by touch. For instance, a frying pan with a metal handle may be very hot after sitting on an open fire for any length of time and will burn the unprotected hand that touches it. The metal handle picks up heat from the rest of the pan and transmits it to the edge. A wooden handle, on the other hand, insulates; it can be touched even after the pan becomes hot.

A similar situation takes place on the frame of a window. Metal frames do not rot and for that reason are often the preferred frame for institutional buildings. But metal frames transmit outdoor temperatures inside. If the outdoor temperature is much colder, the metal frame will become quite cold, and water condensates and ice even may form, particularly if the indoor humidity is high. Although wooden frames do not last as long and need more maintenance, they are far better insulators and especially good in cold climates.

Window glass conducts temperature changes as easily as metal frames. When the outside temperature is 0° F, a single pane of normal window glass may be only 17° F on the interior surface. Heated air broadcast by the heating system will be cooled down considerably by freezing window surfaces. That is the reason many buildings use storm windows. The air trapped between the two window surfaces stops the conduction problem of the glass and frame. However, storm windows require maintenance and must be removed and stored away. For that reason, many librarians have purchased double-glazed windows. A window that is double-glazed contains two glass pieces separated by an air space. In very cold climates, triple-glazed windows are now specified.

Surprisingly, even double-glazed windows do not solve all problems. On a very cold day, the inside surface of a doubled-glazed window may be only 35° to 40° F. Therefore blinds, screens, and/or draperies are decorative means to insulate windows further, especially if people are expected to sit nearby. It should be noted that the warmth manufactured by the human body is attracted to adjacent cold surfaces. (Molecules move from areas of high concentration to areas of low concentration.) Although the air temperature in a library may be more than a comfortable 72° F, people seated next to cold windows will feel chilled. Thus a neutral or insulating surface is necessary.

Of course, window glass transmits heat as well as cold. A very warm window heats up air-conditioned air and wastes more energy dollars in terms of fuel costs than does a cold window. It is important to locate heated and air-conditioned air vents in such a way that the "conditioned" air does not hit the window surface first, but is pointed toward the interior of the building. This is not always easy to do. Most systems run around the periphery of the building. The first priority of any heating/cooling system is to take care of the area of greatest outside air infiltration, which is the periphery of the building, particularly near the windows.

Whenever possible, ducts or pipes delivering heated or cooled air should be insulated. Sometimes ducts or pipes run right up against window glass, particularly in buildings using glass-curtain walls. If the pipes or ducts run in an area less than $3^1/_2$ feet from the floor, or more than $6^1/_2$ feet above the floor, the adjacent window areas can be blocked, possibly with decorative insulating materials. This will save a certain percentage of "conditioned" air and will not block the view out of doors. The normal viewing range of the windows will not be affected.

On the other hand, in many cases window treatments that insulate are hung incorrectly; they capture the "conditioned" air. Draperies, blinds, and screens are hung in such a way that the heated or cooled air coming out of adjacent vents is caught between the window treatment and the glass. Great savings in fuel costs can be effected by a little bit of commonsense rearrangement.

Another difficulty caused by conduction is the transfer of cold temperatures through concrete floors. This may be a problem for staff members whose offices are located in basement areas constructed slab on grade— the concrete, in other words, rests directly on the dirt, and the dirt may get quite cold through the winter. One of the best methods to ease the problem is to build a false floor several inches above the first one so that an air space is created between the two. Carpet is then placed upon the false floor as added insulation. Unfortunately, the technique is expensive, and therefore not as popular as simply laying carpeting with an underlay or foam backing directly onto the concrete floor. Here there is a possibility that water condensates may form underneath the carpet. For that reason synthetic carpets are suggested, particularly nylon or polypropelene. Jute as an underlay should be avoided, as natural fibers have a tendency to rot.

Insulation

As indicated, any material will impede the flow of heated or cooled air to some extent, even decorative fabrics or books. (Books are first-rate insulators, but they tend to fall apart after several years of temperature extremes.) For special building insulation purposes, certain materials do better jobs than others. Six inches of fiberglass, for instance, is as effective an insulator as a brick wall more than 8 feet thick. The ability of a material to retard the flow of temperature is measured by the R or resistance value (see Table 7). The higher the R, the better the insulating properties. Six inches of fiberglass has an R value of 19, the preferred insulation for ordinary house roof construction.

R values are additive. Two batts of insulation, each rated R-19, together yield R-38. Therefore, in adding up the R value of, say, the roof of the library building, all components have to be taken into consideration: the subroof, the insulation, and the roofing material. An uninsulated library attic in an old wooden frame building may have an R of 4. Adding to that 6 inches of fiberglass, the total may rise to R-23.

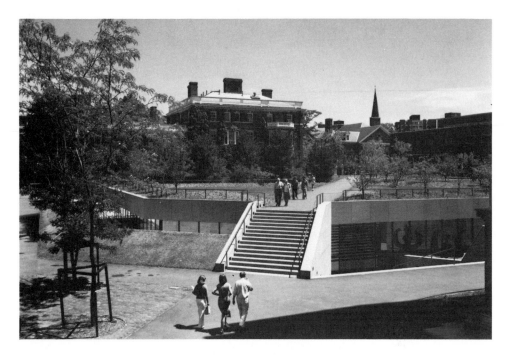

The Pusey Library at Harvard University was built under the quad, more for aesthetic than energy conservation reasons. An engineering marvel, it is difficult to believe there is a major facility under the landscaped walk. A central atrium brings daylight to all spaces underground.

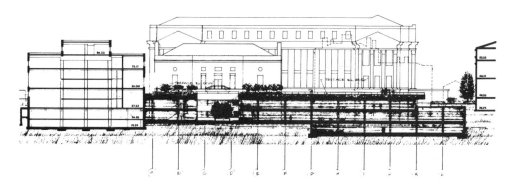

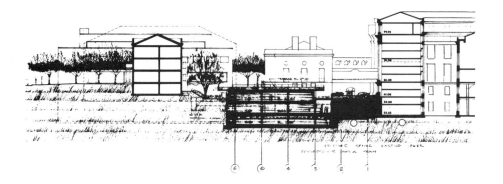

TABLE 7 R VALUE FOR EQUIVALENT 1-INCH THICKNESS OF INSULATING MATERIALS*

Material	R Value
Urethane sheathing (isocyanate and isocyanurate)	R-8.0
Extruded plystyrene foam board	R-5.0
Urea formaldehyde	R-4.8
Expanded polystyrene foam board	R-3.9
Cellulose	R-3.7[†]
Mineral fibers	R-3.3[†]
Glassfiber batts	R-3.2[†]

*Data from the Mobay Chemical Corporation, Polyurethane Division, Pittsburgh, Pa. 15205.
†These three insulation materials are usually applied in thicknesses larger than 1 inch.

There are four basic types of insulation:

1. Batts and blankets. Included here are fiberglass or mineral wool made in standard thicknesses, generally yielding total R values of 11, 13, 19, and 22. The varying widths are meant to fit between wall studs and floor joists. This type of insulation is the most common for home use. It is also the most common on the market.

2. Loose fill, including cellulose, mineral wool, perlite, fiberglass, and vermiculite. Cellulose was once fairly common, but is avoided today because of the extreme fire hazard; it is made out of reprocessed paper. Loose fill can be poured or blown into place behind finished walls, although it can be used for new construction also. Unfortunately, it may settle in time, thus lowering the R value substantially.

3. Foam. Urea formaldehyde is the chemical used, basically suitable behind finished walls only. It is not economically competitive for new buildings with other forms of insulation. Foam does have some serious drawbacks. It can deteriorate under the effects of high temperature and high humidity. Proper installation is essential, as the chemicals must be mixed with care before application. Then, too, the temperature range for application is very narrow. Injection holes must be left open to allow water to evaporate and the foam to cure. Care should be taken in the choice of the contractor, and the work guaranteed with a firm contract.

4. Plastic foam boards. Urethane, polystyrene, and beadboard are types of insulation boards on the market. They are used as exterior sheathing or to cover finished walls. Easy to apply because they are rigid, they are, however, combustible and must be covered with fire-retardant material. Some building codes may ban their use, particularly on institutional buildings.

The enemy of insulation is water. Nearly all insulation is applied with a vapor barrier, a sheet of foil, plastic, or treated paper facing inside the building to prevent moisture condensation, which could soak the insulation and lower the R value. Too much moisture causes construction elements such as studs, joists, and sheathing to rot. Exterior paint can blister if too much water gets underneath. Therefore, besides a vapor barrier, it is often important to allow moisture to vent.

The reciprocal of R value is U, or the coefficient of heat transmission. The smaller the U, the less the transmission. Most insulating materials are explained in terms of R values, but building materials are explained in terms of their U factor. An 8-inch-thick masonry wall has a U of about .70; in other words, it transmits changes in temperatures with ease (although, as explained, this transmission may take time, perhaps 8 to 12 hours). But the same wall covered by metal lath and plaster, inside of which flexible insulation has been placed, will have a U of .23. Wood siding covered by $\frac{1}{2}$-inch gypsum sheathing, onto which metal lath and plaster are placed as an interior finish, has a U of .33. The same wood siding sheathed by a 1-inch thick insulating board with an interior finish of 1-inch insulating board and plaster has a U of .12. Here is confirmation that wood is a better insulator than masonry, brick, or stone. That is because wood is less dense and its cellular structure is made up of many pockets of air.

However, masonry, brick, or stone construction is more durable and certainly more fireproof than wood. For that reason they are the preferred materials for institutional and office buildings, although many smaller public libraries are housed in wooden frame structures. Techniques have been developed to make masonry, brick, or stone as insulating as wood, and almost all of these techniques incorporate insulating materials as well as pockets of air within the basic construction. For example, 8 inches of hollow concrete block made of lightweight aggregate has a U of .36. By adding a 1-inch furring space filled wtih insulation and finished with metal, lath, and plaster, the U drops to .18. Even better insulation can be afforded by other techniques to drop the U to .12.

A great energy conserver is the deciduous tree. In the summer, the leafy shade cools the Hamilton-Kirkland Colleges Library in Clinton, New York. In the winter, the tree is without leaves and allows the warming rays of the sun to pass through.

How much insulation is enough? Buildings vary from one climate to another, as do standards. There are 8 basic heat-insulating zones (12 for solar heating systems), ranging from mild to very cold climates. There is also one zone in which it is unnecessary to insulate for heating purposes at all. For cooling, there are three basic zones. For a particular library's area, standards can be supplied by local code or the U.S. Department of Energy.

Cooling methods and keeping cool

Surprisingly, perhaps, it is far more expensive to heat, cool, and ventilate a library building in Houston, Texas, than the same size facility in Minneapolis, Minnesota. The reason is that Houston depends upon air conditioning most of the year, and air conditioning uses electricity. Minneapolis depends upon heating, using such more economical fuels as oil and gas (see Table 8).

Electricity is the most expensive form of regularly used energy, far more so than oil and gas. The major reason is that there is a great deal of energy loss in electrical transmission. Electricity generated somewhere else is transformed, stepped up, and transmitted on long lines to its ultimate destination, where it is stepped down and transformed once again. During the transformation, transmission, and final transformation, a great deal of electricity is lost. The line transmission and distribution alone account for 10 percent. Some estimates indicate that of all the energy stored in a lump of coal, only 3 percent eventually is supplied to the consumer (4 to 6 percent for oil or gas).

Obviously, then, except for instances where electricity is especially cheap—at locations where most of it comes from hydroelectric power or other "free" sources—or where other types of fuel are difficult to procure (in isolated areas or where snows are high), electric heat should be avoided.

TABLE 8 ESTIMATED ANNUAL HOURS OF OPERATION FOR PROPERLY SIZED AIR-CONDITIONING EQUIPMENT IN TYPICAL CITIES DURING NORMAL COOLING SEASON*

City	Hours
Atlanta, Ga.	750
Boston, Mass.	200
Chicago, Ill.	400
Cleveland, Ohio	450
Dallas, Tex.	1,400
Fresno, Calif.	900
Jacksonville, Fla.	1,600
Minneapolis, Minn.	350
New Orleans, La.	1,500
New York, N.Y.	350
St. Louis, Mo.	1,000
Washington, D.C.	800

*From *ASHRAE Guide and Data Book—Systems—1973* (New York: American Society of Heating, Refrigerating and Air Conditioning Engineers, 1973).

But air-conditioning systems are dependent upon electrical energy. Because of this, librarians should pay a great deal of attention to the methods of keeping their facilities cool in the summer, especially those in warmer climates. Unfortunately, the reverse is easier to do. Cold drafts are felt immediately, partly because there is such a difference on a really cold day between inside and outside temperatures—as much as 70° F or more. On the other hand, warm drafts are less noticeable. The difference between inside and outside temperatures may be only 15° F. (To test this, put a hand near a known air leak on a cold day. The inflow of cold air is immediately noticeable. Try the same thing in the summer. The inflow is less apparent, and in some cases not noticeable at all.)

Some libraries buy individual room air-conditioning systems and some buy central systems. On the whole, the central systems are more efficient, but for the smaller facility, they are too expensive. When buying individual units, the EER, or energy efficiency ratio, is of utmost importance. The EER is a measure of the amount of cooling an air conditioner can accomplish relative to the amount of electricity it uses. Air conditioners with the same cooling capacity (as measured in Btu—British thermal units—per hour) may vary greatly in efficiency. Some use more electricity to achieve the same cooling. The higher the EER, the more efficient the air conditioner. For example, 7,500 to 8,500 Btu per hour, 115-volt window models may have an EER range of 5.4 to 9.9. The more effective models—those near 9.9—are almost twice as efficient as the least effective.

Besides buying equipment wisely, it is also important to plan well for a new library. One of the easiest methods to effect both warm and cold climate energy conservation is to orient the facility so that the major facades face north-south rather than east-west. Such buildings use one-third less electricity to run cooling equipment than those facing directly into the paths of the morning and afternoon sun. This is especially important for libraries in warm areas of the country. The same facility also tends to be warmer in the winter. On the southern exposure, the angle of the sun is high overhead in the summer and low in the sky in the winter. Shaded by the roof during the warm seasons and shining directly through windows in cold ones, the sun helps to maintain the indoor temperature most of the year around. In warm climates, buildings are designed with overhanging roof lines or colonnades angled in the right directions. Buildings in warm areas need shaded walkways to encourage cool breezes and protect exterior surfaces.

Another method of keeping cool is to avoid large expanses of glass, particularly on western exposures, which suffer the worst heat gain. As the sun moves across the sky, in any time of year, the angle becomes very low in the late afternoon, during the hottest period of the day, shining directly into west-facing windows—at least into those not protected by sun screens, glass, or foliage. The same thing occurs in the early morning when the angle of the sun is quite low just after dawn. But at that time few buildings are open, and the heat outside has only begun to build up. Therefore the eastern exposure is of less importance than the western in terms of heat, but obviously can be a problem several weeks each year.

Glass is a handsome architectural element (as shown in the University of Massachusetts Library). It appears to bring the outside in and saves energy to the extent that artificial light is unnecessary most of the day. On the other hand, glass has poor insulating characteristics. Too much glass allows heat to build up in the summer and cold to build up in the winter, which can overwhelm the mechanical system. The Department of Energy limits the use of glass to 30 percent of the building exterior. A lobby area, as shown, is one of the places where glass can be used for maximum aesthetic impact but little functional dislocation.

Reflective glass is one way to reduce solar heat gain. Placed on the worst exposures, or for that matter on all exposures, it prevents the heat or the reflected heat of the sun from entering the building. But reflective glass is decidedly not beneficial in extremely cold climates. As a matter of fact, it is even questionable if it is beneficial in climates where there are more than 200 days a year in which heat is required and perhaps another 60 to 90 days in which the outside temperature is comfortable. It prevents much needed solar heat from getting inside, when the interior needs help to maintain comfortable temperatures.

Some energy conservationists believe that there is nothing better than a deciduous (leafy) tree, especially next to a western exposure. In the summer, the leaves of a deciduous tree are in full foliage, shading the library building; in winter, when the facility needs heat, the tree is without leaves, allowing the full force of the sun to shine through. If trees are not possible, some shrubbery should be placed close to the building.

Another favorite is operable windows, although many architects and engineers do not like them. Such windows are considered not as attractive as fixed glass. They also cost more, and they tend to form cracks or open spaces in areas where the windows meet the frame or the wall. There is more maintenance on an operable window than on one that is permanently shut. But in a study of 86 high-rise office buildings in New York City, it was found that those built between 1950 and 1955 averaged only half the energy consumption of those built between 1965 and 1970. One of the major reasons was the amount of sealed window glass in the newer buildings, forcing complete dependence on mechanical means to heat, cool, and ventilate interior spaces. Sealed structures for the most part are more energy hungry.

This too-great dependence on mechanical means has vast implica-

Wherever possible, windows should be operable. The small windows adjacent to the desks are operable in this library, as are the vents above the lighting fixtures (Williams College Library, Massachusetts).

tions. In the modern world, the weakest link is the availability of electricity. Without it, everything comes to a halt. Even oil burners fail; most are electrically fired. Think of the library with sealed windows in a hot climate in the summer when the power goes out. If it is hot out of doors, it is worse inside. Not only do people suffer but machines as well. Under particularly warm conditions, the inner workings of computer terminals stick together, while some fancier telephone systems have been known to catch on fire! Then, too, microfiche and microfilm melt, ruining precious records.

Ventilation

Architect Richard Stein determined that 53 percent of all energy consumed by the average school in a major northern city was used for space heating, and two-thirds of that energy was required to heat outside replacement air made necessary because of ventilation requirements and/or codes.

A local code may require an air change of 15 cubic feet per minute per occupant in a sealed building. The engineer designing the library building may design into the ventilation system capacity to handle the maximum number of occupants. In other words, the ventilation system may change on a basis of 100 people when only 20 may be in the building at any given moment, except under very special circumstances. Obviously, energy waste will be the result. A simple solution is to fit the mechanical system with several different fan speeds that can vary depending upon conditions.

It is also important to know exactly where the heated or cooled air is flowing. Besides "conditioned" air trapped by window treatments, there are even more common incidents where people place desks, couches, book stacks, and other large objects against walls without checking to see what they are blocking. Vents or radiators may be shut off. Cooled or heated air trapped between furnishings and walls does little to make the interior spaces comfortable.

In a large facility, there are often exhaust fans in the ceiling to remove heat produced by the electric lights, machinery, and equipment, and even the heat generated by human bodies. Most often this heat is exhausted to the outside, no matter how cold it is on that particular day. In recent years, because of the demands of energy conservation, systems have been developed that reuse this heat, either by the application of heat exchangers or heat pumps. The exhausted heat may be pumped back or may be used to run machinery that can cool the building. There are several major buildings that have only peripheral heating/ventilating/cooling systems and depend upon reused heat to keep the rest of the facility comfortable.

Energy audit

Libraries should audit building energy use on a regular basis. When correctly carried out, by an architect, electrical or mechanical engineer, or a special consultant, the audit can tell the librarian how much money is being spent on fuel and energy the year round on a square-foot basis, and how much should be spent by like buildings in the same geographical area. (These latter figures are available from standard sources, such as local utilities.)

In certain circumstances, an energy audit can point out areas in which no special capital outlay is required to upgrade energy use: changing filters, regularly turning off lights, shutting down machines when not in use, and resetting thermostats. Electric light generation, for example, accounts for about 40 to 50 percent of a library's energy use. Anything that can be done to cut usage will substantially save the library money. Dirt blocking the combustion in the furnace is another way energy is lost. Warmth escapes up the flue in the form of soot. If the library uses forced air, it is often easy to tell if this is happening: dirt forms around vents and on ceiling tile near them. The furnace, ducts, and vents should be cleaned. But if the library depends upon a steam heat system, all that is noticeable may be a strange rumble from the furnace, a vibration in the radiator, or soot blowing out of the flue on the roof. A good ear or a quick eye is necessary to catch the problem. Air-conditioning condensors also have to be cleaned on a regular basis; otherwise they tend to function poorly.

An even more common problem is the loss of heat or cooled air through uninsulated pipes and ducts. Usually there is a contract for keeping the existing HVAC (heating/ventilating/air-conditioning) system clean, but no contract to spot the inefficiencies the same system contains. All too often uninsulated pipes run through unheated areas—basement crawl spaces and parking garages. Hot water pipes tend to be less insulated than most others. But heated or cooled air from the HVAC system lost directly through pipes or duct walls via conduction and leaks around connections finds its way into all sorts of unused nooks and crannies—inside walls, under floors, in the plenum above the false ceiling, and even in closets.

Many people are under the impression that this unattached warmth or cold is beneficial, that it lingers in the facility, keeping temperatures within comfortable ranges. But generally the "conditioned" air dissipates wherever it comes to rest, and, in effect, gets lost. A hot water pipe $1^{1}/_{2}$ inches wide, transporting water at 160° F, loses 13 million Btu for each 10 feet of length per year—a very large amount. Methods to keep the "conditioned" air or water where needed can be effected by insulating valves and joints, removing leaks in steam traps, and wrapping pipes or ducts with some insulating fireproof material such as fiberglass.

An energy audit can also spot oversized equipment. Usually installed in buildings because of mistaken engineering, oversized heating and cooling equipment may function at only 15 to 30 percent efficiency. An audit also can point out areas in which thermostats do or do not belong. A thermostat located on a wall at the periphery of the building is bound to call for more "conditioned" air year-round than the same thermostat on an interior wall. That is because it is less insulated from changes in outside temperatures. Thermostats directly across from an entrance door also work harder than those enclosed in interior rooms.

If the library is fairly large, it pays to have more than one zone on the

HVAC system, so that different rooms can have different reactions for the system. The cut in energy usage pays for itself in short order.

In light of the fact that energy supplies, for various reasons, are becoming hard to obtain at times, it may pay for the library to install dual fuel burners, so that more than one kind of fuel is compatible with the HVAC system, such as oil and gas or oil and coal. (In this relation, a separate solar energy system may be feasible indeed.)

Besides finding inefficiencies in mechanical systems, an energy audit can pinpoint other difficulties. In one library building, a soft-drink machine was found to be using more energy than three electrical heaters combined. The cooler was right in front of one of the heaters and had to cycle on and off constantly to keep the soda cool. (See Table 9 for typical energy audit.)

In a similar circumstance, a library in Connecticut saved $25,000 on a $3,000 energy audit in the first year. In this rather large facility, some very silly—and very normal—things were happening. Outside the furnace room, for instance, an air-conditioning thermostat was in year-round operation. Whenever the heat went on in the furnace and the temperature rose, the temperature rose in the adjoining room, triggering the thermostat. The cooling cycle functioned even on the coldest days of the year in this basement room that nobody occupied. (Table 10 shows typical annual electrical usage for a sample library.)

Some aspects of life-cycle costing can also be explained by an energy audit where initial expenditures, energy, and operational/maintenance costs are weighed against each other. Some systems do seem to offer great savings in energy, but their operational or maintenance costs in the short run are far too expensive. For instance, suppose the initial expenditure for Sys-

TABLE 9

Electrical Equipment	Estimated Weekly kwh of Energy Used
Back door heater	202.0
Front door heater	116.0
Soft-drink machine	112.0
Rear floor heater	47.9
Upstairs floor heater	40.5
Downstairs floor heater	40.4
Office floor heater	36.6
Circulation desk floor heater	33.2
Copy machine	11.2
Electric typewriters (3)	3.0
Coffeepots (2)	2.8
Battery chargers, emergency lights (2)	2.0
Clock	2.0
Microfiche readers (3)	1.8
Adding machines (2)	1.6

TABLE 10
PUBLIC LIBRARY X ANNUAL ELECTRICAL USAGE
Approximate Average in Kilowatt Hours[a]

Use	Approx. kw-Connected Load	Hours of Use and Computed kwh												
		Jan.	Feb.	Mar.	Apr.	May	June	July	Aug.	Sept.	Oct.	Nov.	Dec.	Total kwh
Receptacles	16	20[b]	20	20	20	20	20	20	20	20	20	20	20	
		320[c]	320	320	320	320	320	320	320	320	320	320	320	3,840
Lights	14.9	210[b]	190	210	205	210	210	210	210	205	210	210	215	
		3,129[c]	2,831	3,129	3,055	3,129	3,129	3,129	3,129	3,055	3,129	3,129	3,204	37,177
Heating	44.25	260[b]	420	120	50	20	0	0	0	20	70	170	220	
		11,505[c]	18,585	5,310	2,213	885	0	0	0	885	3,098	7,523	9,735	59,739
Hot water	6	10[b]	10	10	10	10	10	10	10	10	10	10	10	
		60[c]	60	60	60	60	60	60	60	60	60	60	60	720
Air conditioning, library	12.5	20[b]	20	120	130	180	220	250	250	200	150	100	29	
		250[c]	250	1,500	1,625	2,250	2,750	3,125	3,125	2,500	1,875	1,250	363	20,863
Air conditioning, multi-purpose room	5	10[b]	10	50	50	100	150	150	150	100	80	30	10	
		50[c]	50	250	250	500	750	750	750	500	400	150	50	4,450
Total kwh per month		15,314	22,096	10,569	7,523	7,144	7,009	7,384	7,384	7,320	8,882	12,432	13,732	126,789

Total annual electrical usage = 126,789

[a]This is an all-electric building. The table reconstructs the energy use requiring estimation of the connected load and a varying monthly pattern usage.
[b]Hours per month of 100 percent usage.
[c]Kilowatt hours per month (the kw-connected load multiplied by hours of use).

tem A was $1,000, and for System B, $2,000. System A costs $700 per year for energy use, System B costs $200. But operational/maintenance costs per year for System A are $100 and for System B, $600.

So, even though System B has less energy use costs, System A, because of lower operational/maintenance costs, is the less expensive system. All things being equal, the cheaper one is the one to buy. The operational/maintenance costs indicate either extra service or more personnel time, and both are bound to rise at nearly the same rate of inflation as energy.

Solar energy

As the costs of fossil fuels escalate, there is more and more talk of solar energy. Proponents view solar energy as the "free" source to provide heat in the winter and, when collection systems improve, energy to run air-conditioning systems in the summer. There are several well-known solar buildings in existence today, and more are planned. However, the majority are private residences, not institutional or office buildings. Solar energy seems to have its greatest application in small-scale structures. But because many libraries are housed in small buildings, solar energy may hold promise for certain facilities.

Although some people claim that solar energy can do anything, the more conservative contend that it looks most promising in areas of the United States where cloud cover is sparse most of the year; in other words, in the deserts of the Southwest. It looks less promising in the Northeast, where some clouds cover the sky 60 percent of the time. That is because, as the name implies, solar energy needs uninterrupted supplies of sunshine most of the day.

The most common solar systems have collectors positioned on roofs to catch maximum sunlight, although the collectors can be erected in backyards at equally suitable angles or even attached to walls. It is important that the collectors be positioned to catch the most solar radiation, but at the same time they must be pitched properly so that any liquids inside the collectors have a positive flow.

There are two types of collectors—air and water. In an air collector, the captured heat often is stored in a reservoir of stone (nothing more than a large pile of rocks) in the basement of the building. When needed, it is circulated throughout the building in a system almost identical to that of forced air. But more people are familiar with water collectors. The most common, the flat-plate collector, consists of five basic parts: a transparent cover plate, which may be one or more sheets of glass or plastic; an absorption plate such as copper or aluminum coated with a blackened surface; tubes or fins that circulate the hot water away from the collector's surfaces; insulation to prevent heat loss; and a container that protects the whole thing. In one variation, the heated water is gravity-fed into a very large and heavily insulated cistern in a basement or close-by underground storage area. When required somewhere in the building, the heat is transferred to pipes somewhat similar to those in a steam heat system.

In any event, the storage of heat can last for several days, but if the heat becomes exhausted, as over several cloudy or cold days, a supplementary source of heating may have to be used. That is one of the main reasons why solar heating is still considered so expensive. In many locations, a solar system is not enough to provide proper heating year-round, and a backup system with conventional fuels must be installed. Two separate and perhaps incompatible systems may be needed, although some solar systems work with more conventional ones (and this may be where the future lies). But as yet the up-front costs are quite overwhelming, and in certain areas of the country it takes between 14 and 20 years to pay back an initial installation.

In the near future the widest application for solar energy will be to provide hot water. Easily connected to a conventional hot water system, solar hot water heaters are quite practical. Many countries have used them for decades, Israel, for example.

If the library does decide to purchase a solar system, there are several important points to consider.

1. Durability. How long is the system expected to last? What about the guarantee or warranty?

2. Leaks. With many pipe junctions, water systems always have the possibilities of leaks. Remember that roof areas holding collectors may have to be specially supported. Water is heavy. One flat-plate collector usually weighs about 200 pounds. A sagging roof can cause even the best collectors to leak.

3. Corrosion. Metals such as copper, steel, or aluminum used in the collectors may be subject to corrosion. This obviously shortens the life span of a system, and, even worse, could possibly cause a health hazard. Inhibitors must be maintained.

4. Weatherproofing. How well is the system protected from freezing or overheating? Is antifreeze necessary? Even in a hot, dry climate, a freak cold wave could cause major damage. There have been complaints that the black paint at the bottom of the boxes has boiled off from too much heat, making the collectors inoperable.

5. Insulation. With ducts, pipes, and collectors, adequate insulation inside and out must be installed.

6. Ease of repair. Who fixes the system when something goes wrong? In fact, will the system be installed with repair in mind? Collectors, pipes, cisterns, or reservoirs installed in inaccessible places cause great difficulty when things go wrong. Are parts obtainable locally?

7. The view. The collectors are put on the south side of the building because that is where the sun is all day long. But is that where the view is as well? Collectors usually take up the entire south wall, although windows are possible if planned for carefully.

COLOR
AND
SIGNAGE

When arranging library space, two highly important factors (yet sometimes largely ignored) are color and signage. Color in the library is not merely a question of "I like yellow and gold," or "the university colors are blue and white." Color can attract, detract, gladden the spirits, or depress them. A library signage system plays much the same role. It invites readers into the library by its clearly stated directions or information. It can also confuse and discourage them. No library design or space planning can be successful without careful attention to both color and signage.

Color

Most people at some time were taught so-called rules of color harmony: "Certain colors go together, others do not." These rules were so enforced that even today many people reject certain combinations because the colors seem to clash.

Years ago, colors were said to affect our lives. People wore red on their underclothes to "ward off the evil eye." Red was also the passionate hue, causing hearts to pound and blood pressure to rise. In anger, we "see red." Green was the soothing hue, considered so calming that the army still uses it to paint barracks and clothe soldiers. Hospital walls were at one time usually painted green as a calming effect on patients, especially those confined to bed.

Most rules and tales about color have little meaning today, although color still plays an important part in certain psychological testing. For the most part, color preferences or uses can be attributed to cultural differences, regional upbringing, and personal idiosyncrasies (some of which have a physical basis). For example, in Western Europe and the United States, black is generally the color of mourning, while in Japan, it is white. (Technically, black and white are not colors, but are referred to as such here.) In the United States, yellow is often a bright and cheery kitchen color, but on the highway it suggests caution.

In truth, there is no such thing as standard or universal color harmony. What is seen as harmonious by people can be divided into:

1 Color combinations that are recognized and are familiar, and therefore enjoyed, and

2 Color combinations that are not recognized, are seen as new, different, and exciting, and therefore enjoyed.

The psychology of color

In the field of library design, as in most other areas, there are "color fads," crazes for particular combinations—from the dark woods and white ceilings of the early twentieth century, to the buff walls, medium-toned furnishings, and almost colorless libraries of the late 1940s through the early 1960s, then into a short period of earth tones, and on to the bright, vivid colors so often found today. In some newer facilities, cinder-block buildings often sport fuchsia or vibrating blue interior walls. Bright chromium lighting fixtures light up the circulation desk, while colorful flags and tapestries hang overhead. In other facilities, all the furnishings are white, accented by lively green plants and carpeting of brilliant oranges.

Interior color tends to give that interior an identity. Law libraries offer the sedate, prosperous look of deep reds, dark leathers and woods, promising

The same color may look entirely different depending upon the background. The smaller the color area, the more pronounced the effect.

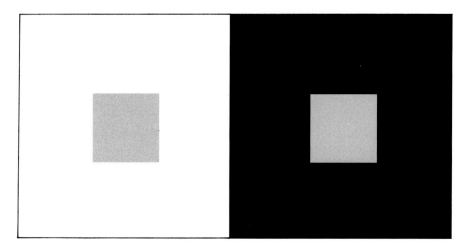

The brain attempts to heighten contrast. A medium gray on a white background will appear dark, and on a black background appear light.

Very bright colors next to one another set up optical vibrations, which are difficult to look at. Stripes are the worst offenders. Avoid bright colors on desk and table tops or on the back inside wall of carrels and work stations.

Three color schemes: monochromatic—variations of only one color; related—colors adjacent to one another on the color wheel; contrasting—colors opposite one another on the color wheel.

A 75 percent contrast between lettering and background is best, and the smaller the letter, the more contrast required (top two rows). Highway signs use color for legibility. All federal highway signs use white on green; state highways use white on blue. White on red is used for STOP signs. Note legibility of the three combinations.

Bright primary colors cause visual impact at Chula Vista Public Library in California. The architecture provides a neutral background for the colorful interior design.

success and stability. These same "wealthy" colors were used in the studies of upper-class gentlemen of the nineteenth century. Many small New England towns still furnish public libraries in colonial motifs, reflecting a sense of history and stability. That may also be why so many libraries prefer wood tables, chairs, and shelving. They give a traditional "library look." But in places such as California, where many people are relatively young and on the go, one often finds library buildings with furnishings in brilliant hues. These people see themselves as breaking new ground and pushing down old barriers.

Understanding subtle differences in color psychology is of major importance to the librarian. People are attracted to, and sometimes repelled by, color. They are generally drawn to bright colorful places, although some will leave immediately if they feel that the colors "jump out" and annoy them. Obviously, if the library is to attract users to certain areas and away from others, color should help to do so. If the library is to be an information center, upon first entering the facility, the user should see a well-lighted and colorfully displayed information area. The circulation desk should be less visible, not as brightly lighted, and colored with more subdued shades.

Some people are more affected by color than others. Being strongly affected by color has nothing to do with artistic ability, although the great artists probably do react strongly to color. Some people simply see color less well than others. Certain colors, particularly blues and greens, appear somewhat muddy to the elderly. Some people cannot see color as most do because of similar physical differences in the eye. But all kinds of people use a library, and in some way they all react to color.

Using color

Understanding colors differently pervades the ability to use color well. There are only a dozen or so specific color names, but over 10,000 variations. Trying to match one manufacturer's named color against another's is impossible. Exactly what is sky blue, powder blue, or baby blue? One scientist's red is another's magenta. Color language is indefinite.

Without light, there is no color. What we see on the surface of a material is the portion of "white" light that is reflected. That is why a building painted white may look brilliant in the noon sunshine and dirty before a rain; the light absorbed by the painted surface has changed from slightly blue-white at noon on a cloudless day to strong blue-white just before rain.

When light strikes the surface of a material, part of the color spectrum is absorbed and part is reflected. In leaves, the red portion is absorbed and the visible radiation that is reflected creates the impression of green. If a surface absorbs nearly all the light striking it, the color we see is black. If it reflects nearly all the light, we see white.

As we can see, the lighting in a library will have a major effect on the colors used. The color of the light coming from the bulbs and the fixture is very important. Incandescent bulbs tend to have a yellow-orange glow (discernible through a window at night), whereas cool white fluorescents and ordinary mercury bulbs are on the blue side. It matters very much what color is emanating from a particular system. One special library, for example, used warm white deluxe bulbs, with a strong pink color, over rows of brightly painted orange file cabinets in a small room. The light was of a color almost "too hot to handle." Actually, the maintenance people had inserted the wrong bulbs. Cool white bulbs belonged in the space.

Similarly, cool whites should not be used in areas decorated with deep blues, purples, or greens. They should be avoided in rooms facing north; north light tends to be blue.

Because different bulbs give different color light, it is important to choose paints, fabrics, wall coverings, and carpeting under the type of lighting that will be in the building. That means if the library is using cool white fluorescents, incandescent light in a furnishings showroom will give colors a different look. It is not uncommon to find that certain colors look dreadful in the library, even though they looked terrific in the showroom. Many showrooms use incandescent flood-, spot-, and pinlights to make furnishings look better and give them certain highlights. Most libraries find this lighting too expensive to operate.

Then, too, it is important to view all fabrics, materials, and paints in the same positions they will be in the library. A tweed carpeting on the floor and expected to be carried up a wall may reflect one way in a horizontal position and an entirely different way in a vertical position because of the texture. A chair fabric may darken considerably in one room and lighten in another. And certain fabrics are severely affected by daylight. Nylon carpeting may have a brilliant appearance under artificial light, but may appear washed out in natural light broadcast in a glass-enclosed lobby.

Because color is a function of light, once a dye lot is run, the exact same color can never be created again. The slight variations in chemical composition change the color. What can be created are colors that appear identical under the same light. Have you ever tried to match clothing, and then walked into another room to find that the two colors didn't match at all? Originally they did, but when the light changed, the colors changed. Therefore, if getting an exact match is especially important, do the matching under the same conditions to be used in the library.

Because the reflectance of light is so important, it is best to view fabrics in as large samples as possible. This is true of paints as well. The smaller the swatch or paint sample, the better the color will appear, but flaws begin to show up as the color gets larger. In the case of fabrics, it is not uncommon for the weave to differ ever so slightly as it runs along the width or length, changing the reflectance. Some fabrics appear water-stained because the pile gets crushed in the wrong direction. In the case of paints, some wall surfaces absorb color and change the hue considerably. Cinder block or any porous surface often has an adverse effect upon the color of paints.

Unfortunately, it is often difficult for small libraries to get large samples of fabric. Fabric houses often are less than generous in giving away swatches. Obviously, if a library can offer the possibility of a large order, there should be little problem. Most fabric companies will be glad to offer as much service as needed. But for the small order, this indeed may be a problem. The only advice is to stand ground and try to get something bigger than a 1-inch square!

Red, yellow, and blue are the subtractive primary colors from which all others are made. In the subtractive process, the "white" light containing all colors of the spectrum strikes a surface, and the surface absorbs or subtracts part of the light. We see what is reflected. But light has different primaries. Mixing one light with another is known as the additive process. Here one light adds to another to form a third. A television picture tube consists of the three additive primaries—red, green, and blue. By adding green light to red, yellow light is formed. In the subtractive process, adding green to red makes black.

Normally the additive process is unimportant to the designer of an interior space, except in the case of actually choosing the lighting system to light the space. A light that is strongly yellow may muddy certain blues and greens. Occasionally the lighting system can be used to color correct surface colors, or the proper choice of surface colors may be an aid in seeing a task properly. Operating rooms in hospitals are still painted green. Organs can be better seen under their covering of blood.

Color correction of light is important in certain other circumstances. If a room faces north, it is best to avoid a blue color scheme in the area. The reason is that the color of light streaming in from a northern exposure tends to be blue. The same holds true, as mentioned before, in areas that tend to have too many overcast days. The color of the daylight is just too blue. On the other hand, when the sun rises and sets, its color is deep red, causing the daylight to be red as well. Few people are in the library at dawn, but many may be in the facility as the sun goes down in the late afternoon. It is wise to avoid red color schemes in western exposures, otherwise the entire area will take on a deep red glow.

When decorating a library, first choose the color of the area that will make the greatest impact. Generally, it is best to select the color of the largest areas first and proceed down to the smallest. Obviously, the larger the area, the greater the impact. Unfortunately, too many people tend to get fixed on a special thing and literally design the library around it. But the color that enhances one little table or chair may be wrong for the rest of the space.

If the library is a loft, essentially featuring just so many furnishings and equipment, the colors of the ceiling and floor are the most important decorative aspects. Usually the ceiling is the largest single unbroken expanse, for the furnishings and equipment block the floor and do not allow a clear view from one end of the building to the other. Because of the expanse across the ceiling, many architects embellish library ceilings with architectural niceties that show off their artistic talents. Here the problem has less to do with color than with the juxtaposition of lines running to and fro, creating vibrations that cause what is described as temporary astigmatism by users and staff. Another sensation may be the feeling that the ceiling is very heavy. For that reason the color of the ceiling should be carefully thought out. Most likely,

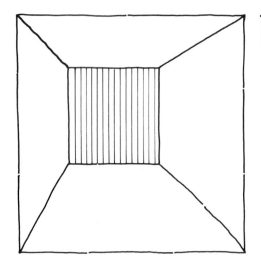

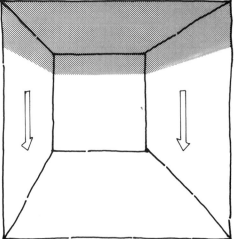

Vertical lines make short walls look taller. Horizontal lines make tall walls look shorter. Unfortunately, lines or stripes are difficult to apply and often create poor optical effects. They should be avoided in the library.

Dark ceilings appear to cut the height of the room. Light ceilings appear to increase the height. If a dark ceiling is used, only downward-directed lighting fixtures are recommended.

lighter and whiter colors are best. Neutral carpeting colors work well in such situations.

On the other hand, ceilings just as often are white, flat, uninteresting expanses, dictated by acoustical tiles and lighting fixtures. If this is the case, the color of the carpeting is the first thing that should be chosen. It may be bright and lively to offset the flat ceiling.

In a third variation, the ceiling is painted black to hide open raceways for plumbing and wiring. Ceilings may be painted black if the room height is out of proportion to the rest of the library facility. By painting the ceiling black, an optical illusion is created. The height is shortened into a more normal configuration. In any case, if this is the technique that is used, it is of utmost importance not to shine any light upon the ceiling surfaces, otherwise the room will take on a strange color. Only downward-directed lights can be used. The carpeting may be neutral or bright. Much depends upon the configuration of the space and the particular lighting techniques. (A too bright carpeting color may bring the floor upward, causing the horizontal space to squeeze together optically. On the other hand, a too neutral color may make the space appear cold and lifeless.)

If the library is divided into small rooms, the largest expanses are the walls. These elements should be the first dealt with. More than likely the ceilings will be painted white for no other reason than that acoustical tile is used. The color of the carpet should be chosen next.

Architects and designers on color

When it comes to color, we find a major delineation between the work of architects and interior designers. Although any generalization does not hold

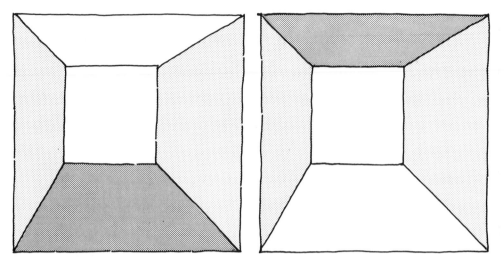

Two variations on a theme: left, the traditional look of dark floor color, medium tone walls, and light ceiling; right, dark ceiling color, medium tone walls, and light floor. Either color use can be attractive, but to save energy and aid dissemination of light, many libraries are using medium color carpeting, and light wall, ceiling, and furnishing colors.

true for every member of these professions, both architects and interior designers understand themselves to be artists. Architects, on the whole, use less color than interior designers; one of the reasons is that color can destroy architectural form. Painting a column with candy stripes infringes upon the column's "integrity." Then, too, many architects have been trained as disciples of the Bauhaus school, a system of design that glorifies the natural look of objects. Wood should always look like wood, and stone, like stone. That is why so many library buildings built in the 1960s are devoid of color; the best and finest materials were used in their natural state. The color was supposed to come from the books. But few architects realized that, without paper jackets, books have very little color. Bindings tend to be uninteresting and rather uniform—dark red, green, brown, black.

Architectural design has not always been devoid of color. Byzantine architecture, for example, welcomed the interplay between form and hue. The three-dimensional surfaces were forced to compete with two-dimensional paint. Ancient Greeks also adorned their palaces and temples with polychromatic designs. The pure white marble edifices we see in ruins today have been washed clean of color by centuries of erosion, but if one looks closely, a dab of red or a spot of gold may still exist.

A small steady trend toward colorful interior architecture as a variation of interior design has begun, and several buildings are quite striking in both form and color. But the librarian must be aware of the consequences. By allowing a building to be striking, embellished with all sorts of architectural insignia that cannot be removed without harming the structure, the possi-

Architects tend to use less color than interior designers. Contemporary architecture depends upon shades and shadows to heighten building form. (This is a model for Lake County Public Library, Merrilville, Indiana.)

Paint can create spatial areas that do not exist. It is all in the eye of the viewer. Paint can lend interest to a fairly mundane space with very little cost. The only thing that is required is a bit of creativity, a fresh approach.

bilities of interior change become limited. One would certainly think twice before hiding a barrel-vaulted ceiling adorned with frescoes by floor-to-ceiling stacks. Of course, there are times when it is in a library's best interest to be housed in such a building. In an academic facility where alumni funds are important, the library may be the one building clearly remembered from college days, while in a large city the library may stand for the strength and riches of the area. In other words, such buildings are erected as landmarks, but librarians must be aware that the building's ultimate flexibility may be severely constricted, and that in 20 or 30 years the structure will have to be relegated as a rare book depository, while the more active collection resides in a less handsome structure down the street.

As far as interior designers are concerned, color is their "meat and potatoes." While architects tend to speak of the spatial qualities of the masses and voids of the building elements, and are concerned whether or not the whole structure "works," an interior designer expresses the same sentiments for the smaller spaces and the juxtaposition of surfaces, planes, and especially colors. There is nothing wrong in either approach, but it does cause conflict for many a librarian. The architects may feel that the interior designers are destroying the space they have created with too many little things, especially too many "little" colors. The interior designers just as strongly may believe that the facility is too sterile and lacking in warmth. As far as the users and staff are concerned, the most important thing is the general ambience and the functional aspects of the facility.

If the architecture is designed as particularly vibrant, the work of the interior designers should become relatively modest. If the architecture is subdued and sedate, interior designers may bring life to the facility. Colorful walls and vibrant furnishings rarely mix. Buildings that are handsomely adorned tend to overshadow the furnishings. Yet some of the most colorful library buildings in the United States are all glass and white walls. The color comes from the furnishings, for which the interior architectural form provides a backdrop.

Designs such as supergraphics, logos, or even large random patterns work well on large walls but quite poorly on smaller ones. This may sound like common sense to some, but too many librarians ignore it. A large bold pattern on a small wall overwhelms the wall and causes problems for the viewer. The only instance in which this works is when the small wall is only one of many little partitions in a large space, and the viewer actually sees a long vista. The unexpected splash of color can be exciting.

Unexpected color use is almost always attractive. At the end of long corridors and at the end of book stacks, a splash of color is a fine idea. Murals on partitions—there are extremely attractive photo murals on the market—is another possibility. Trompe l'oeil, the technique of painting a scene as if it really exists, is popular. In New York City, trompe l'oeil is sometimes used on the outside of buildings, making facades that do not exist. In an interior space, a large painting of the out-of-doors may be a good idea, especially if it is well lighted.

Another color effect is to paint coffers, moldings, door frames, and all sorts of interior details different colors so that they stand out. This is a very

Some artists prefer to use walls as their canvases—trees can grow out of concrete.

tricky technique and requires the guidance of a first-rate colorist, otherwise too many colors next to one another can be annoying. But under expert guidance, satisfactory results can be obtained, and especially for the library with money only for paint, not for refurbishing. By and large, such techniques are applied to long interior corridors and big interior rooms. In other cases, instead of hiding the open raceways on the ceiling by painting them black, every pipe is painted a bright color. Free-standing radiators are colored so that they stand out.

Beware of stripes. Nondirectional patterns are far easier to apply. Stripes that run along long walls, or from one end of the building to another across the floor or ceiling, require exacting care in application. Nondirectional patterns, on the other hand, hide small mistakes. Stripes tend to lengthen or shorten walls, depending upon whether they are horizontal or vertical. Decorating an interior with color can be likened to outfitting a person with clothing. Vertical lines make low ceilings appear higher and shorter walls taller. Clothing that accentuates the vertical makes short people look taller and fat people skinnier. Horizontal lines make tall walls shorter and thin walls wider.

Stripes in a carpet, especially in long vistas such as lounge areas, can cause optical illusions. Vibrations appear. However, it might be a good idea to carpet different areas with different colors, especially areas of high traffic. The reason is that carpeting is hard to patch; color variations between new carpeting and old are readily noticeable. But if the carpeting is different in areas of high traffic, where it is likely to wear out in five to ten years, no one will notice that the carpeting in the rest of the facility has not been removed and replaced.

Another good idea is to color code the library. Color coding can be done simply by painting columns different colors so that the person at the information desk can say, "The 800s are near the blue columns," or color coding can be effected by changing the color of the furnishings in entire areas—fiction, for example, would have furnishings in blue, history in orange. Here the problem is to pick color schemes that are not too jumbled. For example, if the library is rather large and the vistas are long, it would be wise if one area was done in brighter hues and the adjacent area in more pastel hues.

On the whole, lighter color schemes aid in the dissemination of light. That is one reason why black or dark green metal shelving is being replaced in so many facilities. White shelving requires less light. But wherever white is used as a furnishings or equipment color, it is essential to avoid glossy surfaces (and to dim the lighting system). Otherwise the bright glare reflected into the eyes will make it annoying to read or browse.

It is wise to be careful about glossy surfaces, no matter what color, although primitive colors have special problems. After staring at shocking pink or a very bright yellow for any length of time, one is liable to see spots in the eyes after turning away. Glossy carpeting has the tendency to reflect color onto the ceiling, causing a strange glow. Bright fabrics, particularly oranges, reds, yellows, blues, and greens, set against carrel desk tops or work station desk tops also reflect and modify light, but in this instance it is the light upon the desk that is modified. People get headaches; productivity is decreased. (This does not mean that a bright fabric should not be used on a carrel or work station partition, but very bright colors should not be put next to a desk top or any place that people will face for any length of time.) Too highly polished table tops cause annoying reflection problems, as do highly polished floors. Certain people, especially those with poor sight, have trouble walking on highly polished floors.

As a general rule, white and light colors tend to make spaces appear spacious and cleaner. A white ceiling raises the apparent height of a room. Dark and bright furnishings stand out better against white backgrounds. So do paintings, antique chairs, and displays. Dark and medium colors tend to make rooms appear smaller and, depending upon which colors are used, richer. Dark and medium tones make things look cozy, but beware of dark woods under dim light. They appear grim. Dark colors are excellent to conceal flaws in walls or ceiling surfaces. A dark brown wall with many doors will appear more solid than one painted white. That is because the shadow lines around the doors are not seen. Light furnishings stand out against dark backgrounds, and a particularly stunning look is white furnishings against dark walnut walls (although most libraries avoid such combinations because the contrasts are just too strong).

Light and medium colors, such as buff, beige, and gray, are institutional tones, the easiest with which to work. All of them tend to hide dirt and they

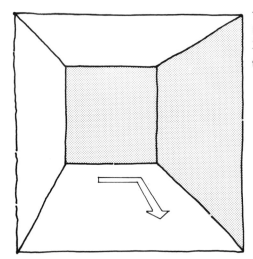

The darker the wall, the more likely apparent imperfections will disappear. Shadow lines blend in with the color. Two walls can be unified by painting them the same dark color.

are perfect foils for stronger, more vibrant hues. Buff as a wall color hides finger marks, as does beige as a furniture and carpet color. Gray and beige on the floor hide white lint and dark dirt spots. Tweeds and nondirectional patterns and prints also hide dirt well and can be found in many libraries for this reason.

Cool colors such as light blues and greens appear to recede. Used on a far wall of a short, squat room, they help to make the space appear larger and seem to push the walls away. However, blue tends to be unflattering to most skin tones, and if blue is used, the light should be warm and inviting.

Warm colors such as reds, oranges, and strong yellows appear to advance. Used on the far wall of a long, narrow room, they will make the area appear shorter and seem to bring the wall forward. Because such colors are associated with the sun, they are fine in areas that receive little or no natural light, especially interior rooms. Warm colors are particularly in favor, and many libraries have installed the same red-orange carpet; that is because warm colors are good foils against large neutral backgrounds. Therefore the color of the architectural elements in such buildings may be quite staid, and the "oomph" comes from the carpeting running throughout the facility.

The more primitive, or the brighter and purer, a color is, the more it seems to advance, move forward, whether it is one of the cool or warm colors. On the other hand, the more pastel, the softer, and paler it is, the more that color seems to recede. Colors can be played with, and some of them can be made to look purer by separating them from one another, perhaps by a white band. If less glare is desired, a black band should be used.

When designing any interior, one must be careful about eye vibrations. These are caused by using one particularly bright color against another. Especially true of colors that are opposite one another on the color wheel, the effect occurs because the eye—or rather the brain—tries, and fails, to make sense out of what it sees in terms of reflection and absorption. Confusion follows. A red pigment, for example, absorbs the exact opposite of

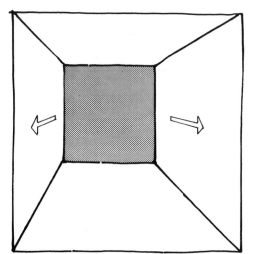

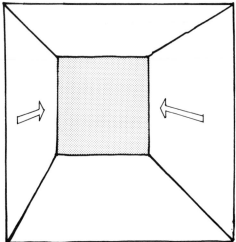

Warm colors—reds, yellows, oranges—advance. The illusion is that they move toward the viewer. Bright and dark colors also seem to advance; they make spaces appear smaller. An extremely bright yellow wall will appear to jump forward, foreshortening the space.

The cool colors—blues, greens, purples—retreat. The illusion is that they move away from the viewer. Pale colors also retreat; they make spaces appear larger. A pale blue wall will appear to move farther away, lengthening the space.

the spectrum absorbed by a green pigment. Bright red and green set one against the other causes the brain to vacillate in terms of what it sees, trying to contrast the colors properly.

Because of the tendency to contrast colors, identical colors appear different on different backgrounds. A dull blue will appear more bluish against green and more greenish against blue. Dark colors will appear darker against a light background, while a light color will appear lighter against a dark background. This is particularly true if the colored area is small and the background large. The same spot of gray will be nearly black against white and nearly white against black. This is another reason why it is so essential to get as large a swatch as possible. It is just too easy to be fooled in a well-decorated showroom. Colors can change dramatically once brought into the library.

Color schemes

There are four basic color schemes: colorless, monochromatic, related, and contrasting. In a colorless scheme, only black and white are used, although we would also classify as colorless some of the more neutral architectural designs in which only the "natural" colors of the building elements are used. Here the carpet may be gray, the ceiling white, and the walls either the color of the natural elements or simply white. Libraries are moving away from the colorless scheme, once considered quite elegant.

In a monochromatic scheme, only one color is used, either alone or in combination with black and white. In many libraries, the only "real" color may be the bright carpeting. Wood shelving, wood tables, and wood chairs of natural color make up the rest of the color scheme. This is a variation of the colorless scheme and is also going out of favor.

A related color scheme is one using colors that are close together on the color wheel. Earth tones are one favorite variation—the rusts, oranges, browns, and yellows. A livelier variation uses orange as a central color, and yellows and reds complement it. Here the problem may be too much color, and a large dash of white or "institutional buff" may be necessary to cool things off. For example, the ceiling and walls may be white, while the "hot" colors come from the carpeting, furnishings, and end panels of the stacks.

A contrasting color scheme can be as lively as a related color scheme, but here the colors used are opposite each other on the color wheel. Red and green may be the central colors, or one may use blue and yellow. The chief problem here may be the color blindness of some users or staff members. If the colors are too vibrant, a large dash of white or some other neutral may be required to give the eyes a rest. The walls and ceiling may have to be painted in neutrals or pastels.

Today, color schemes that depend upon natural plants for design are in great favor. There are quite a few companies that specialize in the field. They landscape the facility and will maintain the plants as well. Often, the plants are rotated from the greenhouse to the library and back again so that those that remain in the facility always look healthy. There are several obvious problems, the primary one being possible water damage to floors and furnishings. A secondary problem may be allergic reactions to specific plants by members of the staff or by some users. And then there is the cost of maintaining the plants. In some cases this can be quite expensive. But, by and large, decorating with plants is a handsome technique and may be worth the few difficulties.

As far as color schemes are concerned, when in doubt, use fewer colors. Accents can always be added. Accents can come from carpeting, fabrics, paints, paintings, tapestries, and even flags. Signs can brighten space also.

It is important for one person to coordinate the color scheme. Many people have different, and conflicting, tastes; color design by committee rarely turns out well. In the case of a small facility, an interior designer may be retained for this aspect of the work. On a larger commission, the architectural firm may request the job, although color selection is not traditionally an architect's field. (Unless so specified in the contract, many expect extra compensation for this service.) Architects often use interior designers to select the colors. In certain situations, particularly in small facilities, knowledgeable salespeople help make the choice; in others, the librarian does it.

If the librarian is to choose the scheme alone and must prepare a presentation, it is a good idea to follow the tactics used by many designers. Photos or catalog pictures of the furnishings and equipment are pasted on 12-inch by 18-inch boards. Each area or room has its own separate board. The paint chips, samples, and swatches are clipped beneath the photos. Samples for the largest colors should be bigger than those for the smaller ones. In other words, the sample of the carpeting should be much larger than the swatch for the fabric end panels of the stacks. Once the presentation is completed and the colors are accepted, a floor plan is obtained on which the colors and fabrics of each area are stapled. In that manner the librarian can follow the installation as it proceeds. Obviously, if the library can afford it, an even better method is to build a model. But this is often very expensive (although models are excellent teaching devices).

If an interior designer or architect is handling the color, it is a wise idea to get duplicate copies of the presentation boards and the floor plans with the colors attached. It is always beneficial to have records, and even better to be able to follow a job—even when one is not intimately involved in the process. In the end, no matter who does the work of choosing the colors, it is the library staff that will see the results day after day.

Signage

Not surprisingly, libraries tend to depend upon systems of signage more than most other service organizations. Except for a few—libraries with closed stacks relying on pages to retrieve the books—most libraries expect users to find materials by themselves (perhaps with a bit of advice from the librarian). Without good graphics to guide them in and around the facility, it is often difficult for users to find their way. There are just too many books, periodicals, or microforms stored all over the place.

Most librarians are avidly interested in the construction of good signs, if for no other reason than to make their own work a little less difficult. Pointing out the rest room all day can be enough to drive anyone mad.

Ironically, the people who design library buildings do not seem to understand the librarians' need for good signage systems. Many architects and interior designers seem to feel that a new library should be unencumbered by graphics of any sort. That is why a traveler to different library facilities across the country may find the most exciting, iconoclastic buildings depending upon small pieces of paper pasted here and there to point out, say, the differences between the 600s and the 800s. Even stacks with beautiful end panels may be ordered without slots to hold identifying numbers—a necessity if there ever was one.

When queried about signs, architects more than likely talk about them with great distaste, seeming to believe they are so much cultural junk and bring a note of disharmony into an otherwise well-functioning library facility. Certainly most signage systems are designed after the fact—usually long after a new facility is opened and the obvious need becomes desperate.

No matter how good the building design, most librarians will readily admit that libraries need signs and that the system should be planned along with the interior design. Provisions must be made for certain inflexible constructions. In many cases, the system of signage should be a part of the interior design contract. For one thing, signs that depend on electricity, such as lighted directories or neon signs (some libraries have used neon effectively indoors to point out the information desk or young adult areas), must have the proper electrical wires available. Once the wiring has been put in place and the walls, floor, and ceiling closed up, it is expensive to decide that new outlets are needed for a lighted sign. Then, too, although

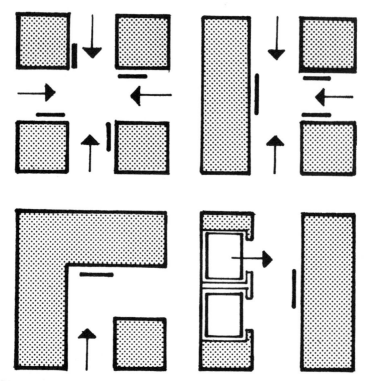

Placement of signs should be noted on the floor plan.

there are many companies that sell nicely packaged signs, often they are very costly, and a librarian who is aware of the building's proper require- ments may be able to have the work contracted elsewhere or done in-house for a good deal less.

Some signs, particularly those to be hung from the ceilings or especially heavy constructions to be hung from walls, may need special supports. This is another good reason to decide upon the system long before the library is completed. Why hire carpenters after the fact when good carpenters are already working on the job?

Have the sign designer or graphic artist in charge make several mock- ups. Everything may look good on paper, but the opposite is all too often the case. If the librarian in charge believes that the same design should be used throughout the entire library, is that design visible from all angles, under all lighting conditions, and, for that matter, to all age groups? For example, under dimly lit conditions, light lettering on dark background is more visible; under brightly illuminated conditions, dark lettering on light background is more visible. The same sign that is supposed to be visible during the day next to a window wall facing south, and therefore illuminated by the sun, may not be particularly visible at night with only a few small lights nearby and none directly overhead.

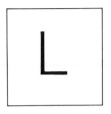 

In bright illumination, dark letters against light backgrounds are best. In dim illumination, light letters against dark backgrounds are best.

Two-way and three-way contrast

The most common types of signs use either a two-way or a three-way contrast. In a two-way contrast, the letters (usually pasted on, but they may be painted on as well) are affixed directly to a wall, book stack end panel, equipment, or whatever. The contrast is between the wall surface and the lettering. In a three-way contrast, the letters are first affixed to a background and then the background is placed on the wall. The contrast is three ways: lettering to background to wall.

Most people in the design field prefer the two-way contrast simply because it is less jarring and calls less attention to itself. A two-way contrast is considered more elegant and more often than not is affixed to the exterior of the building (often in the form of, say, gray letters on gray granite; this "camouflage technique" is hard to find and even harder to read).

For important messages, a three-way contrast is generally preferred, or at times mandated by law. The most common example is the exit sign, which is either always lit or formed by some phosphorescent substance so that it always stands out, particularly under darkened conditions. Not only does the message bring attention to itself but the signboard gets attention as well (which may be the reason why so many architects and interior designers dislike this type of sign).

Light as an attraction

Under darkened conditions, a white speck, particularly a lighted white speck, is much easier to see than a dark line under bright conditions. Light makes objects appear brighter. For example, some stars appear larger to us than others, even though all are great distances away. That is because the brighter they are, the bigger they seem. Not only do they appear bigger, but our eyes seem to be drawn to the brightness.

Just as light attracts an insect to a flame, so does a light that shines on a message draw our eyes to it. People just naturally look at the brighter things. This was shown forcefully on a visit to a library in Washington, D.C. A large academic facility, the library was designed so that a small information desk and a large circulation desk were close to the front door. However, the architects used an arcade principle, and the area near the door was dimly lit in comparison to the rest of the facility (a fad of the late 1960s and early 1970s in library design).

On the other hand, more than 50 feet away, at the far end of the facility (but directly in view of those entering the building), was a reference desk,

A lighted sign must not be too bright or a halo effect will occur around the letters. The message will be difficult to read, as in the waiting room sign. But the interior lighted information sign is very visible.

brightly illuminated. Many first-time visitors walked directly past the information desk, past the circulation desk, right to the reference librarian to ask the location of the elevators or stairwells. Ironically, those building elements were in the dimly lit arcade, immediately adjacent to circulation. The bright lights in the rear attracted most people.

When using light to illuminate signs, it is important to know that a too bright sign lit from behind can cause a halo effect around the letters, making them difficult to read. If the sign is lit from the front to an outstanding degree, the glare may be too great, so that again the sign cannot be read. (Designers of outdoor signs know that a dimmer switch has to be used at night to tone down the glare. During the day, the sign has to fight the sunlight, but at night a too bright sign loses its advertising effect.) For most indoor messages, if the overall ambient light in the building is, say, about 50 foot candles, there is little necessity to light above 150 foot candles, or three times the ambient light. (We are talking here of building signs as opposed to those used in retailing.)

Indoor signs

Most indoor signs fall into one of five categories. The first is identification: Is this the library? Is this the circulation desk? The second is direction: Where is the copying machine? How do I get to the meeting room? The third is warning or prohibition: Out of order! This is not an exit! The fourth is information: This library was erected in 1810. To use the microform machine, turn on the switch. And the fifth category is status, which may be in the form of larger or prettier lettering or special wall plaques.

Of course, some of these categories can be handled architecturally as well as with a system of signage. For example, to a person entering a build-

Five basic library signs (left to right): Directions—How do I get to the reference department? Identification—Where am I? What building is this? Prohibition and warning—Do not enter; Information—Hours 8:00 A.M. to 6:00 P.M.; Status—Office of the Director.

ing, the staircase is visible immediately because it is directly ahead; therefore it is not necessary to place a sign that says, "This way to the second floor." Prohibition is even easier to display architecturally. A locked door functions better than the best-made sign and says "Do not enter" in no uncertain terms. Similarly, status can be defined architecturally. By building an expensive structure surrounded by gardens, the library's worth to the community can be made known. However, information is rather hard to define architecturally. The only way one may know that a library was erected on this spot in 1810 is to say so. Even preserving the old building will not do; too many new structures imitate the old.

No matter how well the building is planned, a system of signage is necessary to aid the first-time visitor and the regular user. To plan such a system, one must first start with the exterior or the boundary. Is more than one sign necessary? Perhaps a sign should be placed on the periphery of the facility so that it can be seen from far away and another sign right over the front door. What is the first thing that should be seen upon entering the library? Perhaps it is the information desk and sign. One library consultant believes that the information desk is the key to the entire facility, so that in buildings on which he works, the desk is not only directly in view as one enters but it is lit to a higher degree than the surroundings. The desk and the large information sign above it act as a beacon. In smaller libraries, the sign is visible from nearly all access points.

After entering the library (and perhaps stopping to ask a question), the next step is to follow the paths that lead to the major areas. In small libraries, directional signs are not always necessary because everything is

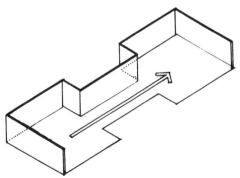

The feeling of direction can be imparted architecturally. A narrow environment gives the feeling of congestion and accelerates action forward. Most people are uncomfortable waiting in corridors.

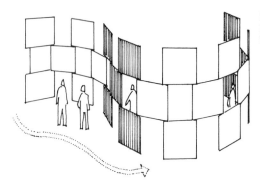

Movement in space can be controlled by walls, partitions, displays, and furniture.

in full view—orientation can be handled architecturally. But in larger facilities, directories and several directional signs are often of major importance.

Directional signs, as well as those indicating warning or prohibition, may have to be repeated. As someone walks down a hall, takes a turn in a corridor or two, the original directional message may be lost. In an elevator, for example, not only do most of us depend upon getting off at the proper floor by seeing a lighted number on the elevator wall in front of us but once

Information should be located in a central zone, easy to see from all access points. This holds true for libraries as well as train stations (Grand Central Station, New York City, shown in this photo) and airports.

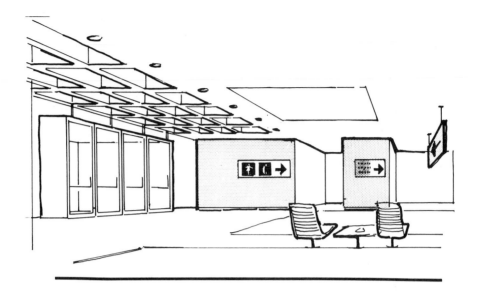

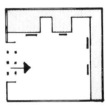

A good sign should be visible at access points as one moves into the space. The height of the message should be keyed to the speed of travel. It takes a minimum of 5 seconds and sometimes as long as 10 seconds to understand a simple phrase. The height of the message should be large enough to take this into consideration.

the door opens, we depend upon seeing the same message somewhere on the corridor wall. Or for that matter, many librarians handle the same problem unconsciously by cross-referencing the stacks. At the end panels on either side of a given range, the same information usually is repeated: 785–801.

Once the paths through the facility have been located, the next step is to identify particular areas, such as Audiovisuals or Microforms, as well as some prohibitions, No Exit, Up Only. Usually if there is only one access point, only one legend is necessary. However, for several pathways, particularly in larger libraries, obviously more than one sign should be placed at points of major access. (In the very large libraries, supergraphics may be used because of the viewing distances involved. They may cut down on the need for smaller signs.)

The last signs to be constructed are for information: Push Button for

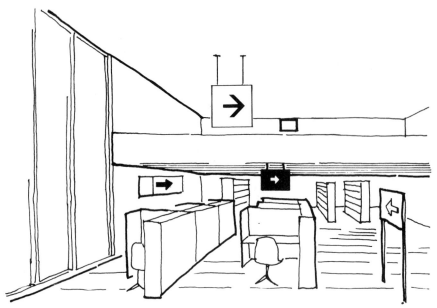

Signs can be wall hung, ceiling hung, or freestanding. Too many signs compete with one another and create a feeling of visual noise.

Page, as well as some information prohibitions: Taking Off Outer Panel Will Result in Electrical Shock. These signs are very specific and are not expected to be read from afar; one usually has to be almost on top of the sign to read it.

Sign locations

The first consideration is whether the sign should be hanging on a wall, directly in view as one walks down a corridor; freestanding, so that it can be moved easily; or hanging from the cross ties of the stacks (a supermarket technique often adaptable to the library) or from the ceiling. (Floors are rarely used for messages. When they are, the signs are more in keeping with the interior decor.)

The average eye level horizontal for an American is about 5 feet 3 inches (actually about 5 feet for women and 5 feet 6 inches for men). Although we all have peripheral vision, most of our viewing is done in a 60 degree sweep of the eyes. Thus, from the eye level horizontal, the maximum acceptable height of a sign should be about 30 degrees to that horizontal, with a 10 degree angle as the optimum. That is why many signs hang 10, 15, or even 20 feet above a floor and can be seen adequately. If a sign is to be about 5 feet away from an intended viewer, the optimum center of interest should be about 6 feet above the floor. At 10 feet away, the optimum center is about 7 feet, and at 20 feet, it is 8 feet 8 inches.

The American Institute of Graphic Arts (AIGA) suggests indoor signs not be placed more than 155 feet from an intended viewer. After that range,

Ceiling-hung sign systems can be attractive as well as easy to read.

either the sign has to become much too big for indoor use or else it becomes part of the woodwork (even though it is very large, a viewer doesn't notice it unless it is illuminated to a very high degree).

Not only are placement heights and distances important but so are the heights, configurations, and colors of the messages. The audiovisual industry has developed a set of letter heights for use in viewing films. At these distances, words can be discerned, but just barely—they are viewing maximums. To read a message adequately from these distances, the figures should be doubled, and to make the messages really stand out, they should be quadrupled (the AIGA uses only one standard for federal government work; triple the figures). See the table on Viewing Distances.

VIEWING DISTANCES

Distance	Message Barely Visible	Message Not Jarring	Message Stands Out
8 feet	1/4 inch	1/2 inch	1 inch (and beyond)
16 feet	1/2 inch	1 inch	2 inches (and beyond)
32 feet	1 inch	2 inches	4 inches (and beyond)
64 feet	2 inches	4 inches	8 inches (and beyond)

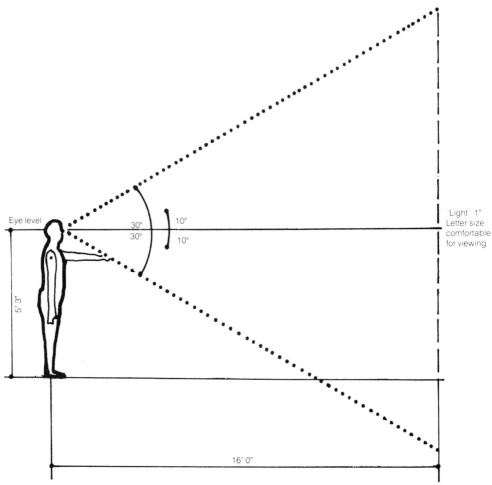

People see in a 60-degree sweep of the eyes. Average eye level is 10 degrees above or below a 5 foot 3 inch horizontal. From 16 feet, a 1-inch letter height will impart a "comfortable" message, adequate for most building signs. A 2-inch height will impart a message that appears to "jump out"—good for emergency signs.

Lettering

Concerning the configuration of the letters, simple block lettering is easier to comprehend than lettering that is either tall and skinny or very fat and short. Some sign makers believe that the easiest lettering to understand is that in which the width of the letters is not less than three-fifths the height (counting the ascender and descender: the parts of the letters that rise above the body—such as in a "b"—and the parts that fall below—such as in a "p"). Furthermore, the spacing between the letters should be about 15 percent, although white lettering on dark background requires slightly more letter spacing than does black on white. (Here one must allow for letter equalization. In other words, an "M" needs more space than an "i.")

When we talk of letter configuration, we are really talking of how people

```
┌─────────────────────────────────────────┐
│  L                              B         │
│  easiest                        hardest   │
│                                           │
│                                           │
│  b  d  p  q                    n  u       │
│                rotate                     │
│                                           │
│  was — saw                    no — on     │
│             backwards                     │
│                                           │
│                                           │
│  Entrance                     ENTRANCE    │
└─────────────────────────────────────────┘
```

The configuration of a letter (or word) makes it easy or hard to read. L is the easiest capital letter to read; B is the hardest. Poor eyesight and visibility can make a B look like an E or an 8. Dyslexic people tend to rotate and transpose letters—b, d, p, and q turn and appear to be the same, so do n and u. *Was* is read as *saw*, *no* as *on*. It is always best to use upper and lowercase letters. Beyond three or four words, avoid using only capitals.

read. Not only do many people have poor eyesight and thus confuse numbers such as "3" and "8," but some letters have inherent reading difficulties. About 10 to 15 percent of the population suffer from some form of dyslexia, a problem of perception. They often confuse the direction in which letters and words must be read; "was" is confused with "saw," "no" with "on." In the lowercase, p–q, n–u, and b–d cause a great deal of trouble. In the uppercase, a "W" may be seen as an "M." Thus, for these people it is especially essential that all "important" messages—notably direction and prohibition—be written as straightforward as possible. There should be no superfluous lines and no visual noise that competes with the message. Visual noise can be a problem for those with poor eyesight as well; they have a problem making out which words are on the sign and which are not. For this reason, the federal highways use Helvetica Medium. It is legible, has good compatibility with symbols, and is fairly aesthetic (according to current taste).

A great deal of research has been done on how the majority of the population comprehends the written word. Most of us seem to be keyed into the meaning of a word by seeing the first letter and the last simultaneously. In other words, to comprehend the word LIBRARY, the L and the Y should be visible at the same time. It is very difficult for people to read words that have been broken into fragments, such as IN FOR MA TION, although research has shown that some people read words by sounding out the spelling sections. But you can see that INFORMATION is much easier to read in this sentence than in the one above. That is probably due to the fact that schooling has

Letterstyle	Microgramma Extended
Americana	**Microgramma Bold Extended**
Broadway	MODERNE
CHATHAM	MOHAWK
Coronet Script	Old English
Craw Clarendon Book	Optima
Craw Clarendon	**Optima Semi Bold**
Craw Clarendon Condensed	Palatino
CRAW CLAREDON PROFILE	**Palatino Semi Bold**
DEEP BLOCK CONDENSED	**PRISMATIC**
DEEP RIBBON	RIBBON
Folio Medium Extended	ROMAN CLASSIC
Futura	ROMAN CLASSIC CONDENSED
Garamond	ROMAN CLASSIC OVAL FACE
Garamond Bold	SANS SERIF
GOTHIC	Stymie Light
GOTHIC BLOCK	Stymie Medium
HELLENIC	Univers 55
Helvetica Regular	**Univers 65**
Helvetica Medium	**Univers 67**

Popular lettering styles, some more legible than others. Lettering with good contrast to the background and strokes that appear heavy in relation to their heights are most legible.

taught us to key into words only as they are commonly written. (The implication here is that words that are hyphenated, written sideways, diagonally, or in any fancy way may look attractive, but are not good to convey messages.)

In addition, messages of any length should be written in a combination of upper- and lowercase letters, for the very same reason—we have been taught how the written word should look. Any message with more than three words probably should not be written in uppercase alone. (That is something learned from the computer age. Researchers have found that even highly educated people have difficulties with computer printouts written only in uppercase.) Therefore a message such as PLEASE KEEP OUT can be written in uppercase to emphasize the prohibition, but once past the three-word stage, messages such as PLEASE KEEP OUT OF THE FLOWER GARDEN BECAUSE IT HAS JUST BEEN SEEDED AND FERTILIZED are more difficult to comprehend.

The same is true of lowercase only; the poet e.e. cummings is well known and easily recognized, but without capital letters to begin sentences and without proper commas and periods, long messages in particular are very difficult to understand. Note the difficulty of reading the following: this

The closer to the horizontal that words are written, the easier they are to read. Note the difference in readability of the signs in these illustrations.

library was erected during the term of abraham lincoln as part of a campaign promise in 1870 it was partially destroyed by fire

In addition, use simple words to convey a message. Granted, many librarians think of their facility as a vast information center, but most users think of the building as a library. (An exception may be the word "Exit," although "Out" is often used successfully; even small children understand the notation of exit on a sign.)

Symbols

Symbols are good at indicating certain types of messages. Certainly they were used long before the alphabet. But perhaps the best solution is to use symbols and words simultaneously. For example, an arrow does, indeed, show direction better than the legend To The Community Room, but a sign with an arrow and The Community Room is even better. Furthermore, symbols tend to go out of style faster than words and may not convey a clear message. For example, the original telephone looks little like today's instrument, and some libraries use a microfilm reader instead of a standard card catalog.

Then, too, without an identifying legend, some commonly used symbols are not too clear. (Think of all those rest rooms where one cannot make out the identifying description. Is it a mens room or a ladies room?)

The AIGA, as a project for the federal government, developed a sign with three people confined to a box, above which are two arrows, one pointing up, one pointing down. Many people seem to have difficulty comprehending that this is an elevator unless an identifying legend is written below.

Wherever possible, signs should contain both print and symbols. Messages are unclear in the top row of symbols, but easily recognized in the bottom row.

No Entry   Restaurant

Another reason for combining words and symbols is that some people seem to be much more visual and comprehend symbols with ease; others seem more oriented to print.

Many people are interested in the shape of the sign. But unless the signboard actually disturbs the visual message, shape in library signage does not seem particularly important, except to give a unity of design to the whole program.

Sign colors

More important than the shape of the sign is the color. A colorful sign seems more visible.

Although most librarians are conditioned to black print on a white background (the type most often found in books), this is not actually the most visible combination. The easiest color to see is yellow. But yellow leaves an aftervision (spots in the eye long after looking away), even though some suggest black on yellow is more visible than any other combination.

Color, as discussed earlier in this chapter, is totally dependent on light. As the light changes, some people see certain colors better than others. Therefore it is important that there be a good contrast between the background and the message—75 percent contrast is the very minimum; otherwise, the colors may blend much too well. (One should also be concerned about the light reflectivity of the background. Certain glossy backgrounds make a message difficult to read, and for some reason most manufacturers seem to like glossy backgrounds. Matte finishes are the best.)

The graphic design can overwhelm the information it is supposed to impart. In this photo, the eye centers on the stenciled hand and may miss the word below.

But color contrasts and colors seen alone are not one and the same thing. One researcher believes that after black on yellow, the most legible combinations are green on white, red on white, blue on white, and brown on white. For outdoor use or in areas where the sign background is apt to get dirty, white is not the best choice. On highways, the federal government uses white on green for major messages (they are more interested in night-time rather than daytime visibility).

When designing a sign, care must be taken to avoid color vibrations. Just as stray lines affect those who have problems with their eyes, so do certain colors. When two colors are opposites on the color wheel and they are of the same intensity and saturation, the eyes may suffer from vibrating effects, a shifting from one color to the other. The message on a sign could become undecipherable.

And remember that it takes time to read a message. Usually in building design, the time it takes is unimportant, because the visitor can stand in place for a few seconds. However, there are times when it matters very much. For example, in an academic library during exams, when students come racing through the front door, a user may not be able to read a directional sign before being catapulted to the stairway. In this case the sign may have to be made a little bigger, so that it can be read from a greater distance.

Sign materials

Do not overlook the durability of sign materials. One of the most important questions to ask is how well the sign will withstand vandalization. Even the best-made signs can be destroyed in no time by a few creative mustache artists.

When thinking in terms of the material for signs, it is best to consider durability, washability, and replacement. Will a sign tear or shatter? Can it be cleaned periodically? Is it prone to rust? Can the letters be peeled off with ease? (That is at times a plus rather than a minus factor. Sometimes it is best that the lettering can come off easily so that the message can be changed.) Is the particular material suitable for the whole system of signage, or only suitable in one instance?

There are many sources that deal with various construction techniques. Remember that the graphic arts department at the local university may be able to supply the library with many handsome signs, perhaps as a class project. Call around and know your options.

Sign checklist

If you are planning a new library signage system, or rating your present one, ask yourself the following questions:

1 Is the message simple; can the whole thing be taken in at once?

2 Are the symbols straightforward and clear?

3 Is the sign hanging in an area with competing visual noise; can it hang elsewhere?

4 Is the sign directly in view?

5 Is it big enough from the viewing distances required?

6 Are there poor viewing angles that interfere with comprehension?

7 Does one have enough time to read it?

8 Is the sign well contrasted against its background; for important signs, has a three-way contrast been used?

9 Is the sign visible during all times of the day and night under normal conditions?

10 Does it have to be illuminated?

11 Does it have color?

12 If colors have been used, do they dovetail with the rest of the interior decor?

13 Is the sign reasonably vandalproof?

14 Are there any dangerous conditions attached to the sign (sharp corners, etc.)?

ACOUSTICS

Should a library be a place of complete and total silence? Certainly, complaints about noise are among the most common for librarians. For some people, trying to concentrate in a noisy facility is not merely difficult, but impossible.

Few rules govern library acoustics, for no other reason than that there are so many different types of facilities. Each library has a different acoustical demand. An elementary school learning resource center may tolerate, or even desire, a certain busy hum; a corporate law facility may demand absolute quiet in and around study spaces. To formulate any rules, one must have an idea of the service aspects of the particular library, as well as individual requirements of users and staff.

Studies indicate that Americans do not mind a certain level of noise, about the buzz of a whisper—somewhere between 40 and 50 decibels (see Decibel Ranges table). Noises that grate on the nerves are intermittent sounds—the tap, tapping of a typewriter, the constant ringing of the telephone, the whirr of a copying machine, loud conversations, and recurring footsteps. When not part of an overall steady hum, these sounds impinge upon the consciousness, so that those trying to concentrate are forced, instead, to listen.

However, most of these annoying noises can be masked. Some libraries and many offices use electronic random noise generators to disseminate sound and hide intermittent noises. The "white sound" or "white noise" created by these systems distributes a constant hiss, usually loud enough to

Decibel Ranges	Examples	Auditory Effect
140+		Extreme pain; hearing destruction
140	Jet engine nearby	
130	(Pain begins)	Deafening
120	Rock band	
110		
100	Auto horn, 10 ft. away	Very loud
90*	Noisy city street	
80	School cafeteria, untreated surfaces	Loud
70†	Typing pool	
60†		Moderate
50†	Large office	
40		Faint
30	Average residence	
20	Average whisper	
10	Leaves rustling	Very faint
5	Human breathing	
0	Threshold of human audibility	
−0		Inaudible

*Continuous noise above this level will probably be harmful to hearing.
†Normal speech range.

cover private conversations held in normal voice tones less than 20 feet away. White noise can be too loud. Above 50 decibels, people tend to raise their voices to make themselves heard. A white noise over 50 decibels is loud enough to force its way into the consciousness; it becomes noticeable in its own right.

The white noise created by electronic systems can be likened to the sounds from a heating/ventilating/air-conditioning (HVAC) system. Planners prefer electronic systems because the white noise from the HVAC is not reliable; it tends to cycle on and off in relation to ventilation and temperature needs, causing a noticeable sound pattern rather than a constant hum. Besides, sounds from the HVAC are difficult to control.

Whether one uses an electronic system or depends upon the HVAC, the ambient sound level for the small library should be between 40 and 45 decibels, and for a larger library, between 45 and 50. Because there is less noise in a smaller library, obviously, there is less noise to mask.

Decibels

In the science of acoustics, the "bel" unit, named for Alexander Graham Bell, relates the intensity of sound to a level corresponding to the human hearing experience. The decibel, or db, is a simple logarithmic function multiplied by 10 ("deci" means 10). And it is that decibel level we use to rate sound, as can be seen in the table on Decibel Ranges.

Decibels are measured by a sound meter, which can be purchased in most stores that sell sound engineering equipment. The meter uses a microphone to transform sound pressure variations in the air into corresponding electrical signals measured on a decibel scale. The most popular decibel scale is the A scale, which tends to disregard low-frequency sounds. Decibel readings taken on such a scale are abbreviated dbA.

By clustering people together, the sound levels do not increase arithmetically, but by gradual degrees. That is why it is best to group activity areas close to one another; areas of sound can be defined and isolated from the rest of the library.

As indicated by the example of the sound meter, sound depends on air pressure variations. Actually, sound is formed by the vibration of molecules hitting against each other, causing air compressions and rarefractions, which are then picked up by the human ear and transcribed by the brain as sound. The number of times a molecule vibrates determines the frequency of the sound. The more it vibrates, the higher the frequency, measured in Hertz, or Hz.

Most young people are capable of hearing sounds from 20 to 20,000 Hz. The upper limit diminishes with age. In other words, we all tend to become hard of hearing as we grow older, although generally men suffer more hearing loss than women. (Prolonged exposure to loud sounds can cause hearing loss even for the young and healthy. Highly amplified music, no matter how good, is as harmful as anything else.) At any rate, human speech contains energy from 125 to 8,000 Hz. However, certain frequencies contribute more to speech intelligibility than others. The component of speech at 2,000 Hz is more important for intelligibility than the component at 500 Hz. That is why the shaping of the white noise emanating from the sound-masking systems can be so important.

Sound absorption

Sound can be absorbed by soft materials. Most soft materials tend to have holes that are interconnected and mazelike. Sound passes through and cannot get back out. What actually happens is that sound energy is transformed into thermal energy. (The heat buildup in most cases is minimal. However, in some circumstances, when sound waves are carefully concentrated, the heat generated can be enormous.)

The amount of absorption of any given material can be measured in

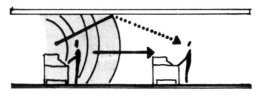

Ceiling dimensions affect noise levels. *Top:* Rooms with low ceilings have higher noise levels. Sound bounces off ceiling and directly into path of next user or staff member. Space people and equipment farther apart. *Bottom:* Rooms with high ceilings have lower noise levels. Sound is more likely to get lost in the space. Space people and equipment closer together.

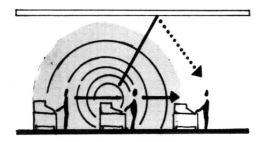

terms of its thickness, density, porosity, and fiber orientation. This measurement is expressed by an NRC, or noise reduction coefficient (see Sound Absorption table). The higher the coefficient, the more sound is absorbed. If an acoustical tile has an NRC of 0.95 (as do some open landscape partitions), it means that 95 percent of the airborne sound striking its surface is absorbed.

Although not technically sound absorption, high ceilings aid the dispersal of sound. Quite simply, the higher the ceiling, the more likely the sound will get lost in the upper reaches of the space, never to return—even if most surfaces are hard and reflective. (Unfortunately, a balcony overhead may collect all the sound.) On the other hand, high ceilings in small, narrow

SOUND ABSORPTION (Common Building and Furnishing Materials)

Materials	NRC*
Walls	
Brick, unglazed	0.00
Glass, typical window	0.15
Concrete block, painted	0.05
Gypsum board, $1/2$ inch	0.05
Marble or glazed tile	0.00
Plaster or brick or lath	0.05
Plywood, $3/8$-inch paneling	0.15
Wood, $1/4$-inch paneling with air space behind	0.10
Cork, 1-inch air space behind	0.30
Coarse concrete block	0.35
Material, lightweight (10 ounces per square yard, stretched flat on wall)	0.15
Mediumweight drapery (14 ounces per square yard, concentrated to half area)	0.55
Fiberglass drapery ($8^{1}/2$ ounces per square yard, concentrated to half area)	0.55
Heavyweight drapery (18 ounces per square yard, concentrated to half area)	0.60
Shredded wood fiberboard (2 inches thick on concrete)	0.75
Thick, porous, sound-abosrbing material, open facing	0.75
Carpet, heavy on $5/8$-inch perforated mineral fiberboard; air space behind	0.70
Floors	
Concrete, terrazzo, marble, or glazed tile	0.00
Wood	0.10
Cork, rubber, linoleum, asphalt tile, or parquet wood floors on concrete	0.05
Carpet, on concrete (no underlay)	0.30
Carpet, on foam rubber	0.55
Carpet, latex backing	0.35
Ceilings	
Concrete	0.00
Plaster on lath	0.05
Suspended acoustical tile, $3/4$ inch thick	0.95
Sprayed cellulose fibers, 1 inch thick directly on concrete	0.75

*Noise reduction coefficient. The higher the coefficient, the more noise absorbed. An NRC of 0.95 means 95 percent of the noise is absorbed.

Acoustically, a long narrow room is the most difficult to handle. Sound can reflect back and forth along the walls.

rooms are not beneficial. That is because if the walls are hard, the sound waves bounce back and forth.

Reflection, reverberation, diffusion, diffraction

Sound is a wave, and like a wave it can hit something and bounce back. A reflection, then, is the return of the sound wave from the surface. If the reflected sound is nearly identical to the original (different surfaces absorb varying frequencies) and loud enough, one hears an echo. If that sound continues to bounce over the area, reflected from one surface to another, one is in an echo chamber. (A whole series of sounds at varying frequencies reflecting around a library makes for a very noisy facility!)

Eventually, any sound will decay and the noise will stop. The time it takes to decay is known as the reverberant time. For a space to have some pleasant acoustical qualities, some reverberation is necessary. Otherwise the space will be acoustically dead. (Some places should be acoustically dead. A broadcast studio, for example, requires a reverberant time of no more than 0.4 to 0.6 seconds at 500 to 1,000 Hz. The walls, floors, ceilings, and even furniture coverings should not be any more reflective. Additional reverberations will be picked up by the microphones and may cause broadcasting problems.)

The shape of the space, and even adjacent surfaces of equipment and furnishings, as indicated, can be important when it comes to noise reflection. Concave sound-reflecting surfaces tend to focus noise; convex surfaces scatter it. However, noise can be scattered and then refocused in the wrong direction. This is a common problem in libraries with architectural embellishments attached to the ceilings. Sound from, say, a copying machine may hit a decoration on the ceiling, which may in turn refocus it and send it to an area 20 feet away. Enough similar situations, and the library can be extremely noisy. Acoustical renovation is necessary, which may take the form of adding acoustical tiles on the ceiling, acoustical baffles, or actually changing the ceiling shape to diffuse and diffract the sound waves.

Sound waves cannot be broken, as the word "diffusion" suggests. Rather, they can be scattered in new and different directions. In addition, they can be bent—or diffracted—entirely to other areas. Most of us are subconsciously aware that sound can be diffracted. We all know that we can hear noise from adjacent areas that are not completely enclosed, for example, from cubicles whose partitions rise only 5 or 6 feet high. That is because the sound traveling up and over the top or around the side is reflected and bent, finding its way into our ears. This is the major objection to office landscape systems—the lack of acoustical privacy. However, properly planned, open landscape systems can be very quiet.

Sound can be directed at will. As it emanates from the source in a cone-shaped fashion—somewhat like a pebble dropped near the edge of a lake—most of the sound travels forward. Outdoors, where sound energy can travel in any direction (because of the lack of absorbing and reflecting surfaces nearby), sound is 9 db less a few feet behind a speaker than in front. The obvious implication is that if two staff members constantly disturb each other while using the phone, they will be less disturbed if they simply face away, directing their speech in different directions.

Ceiling tile versus carpeting

The most effective way to absorb unwanted noises in most libraries is to carpet the floor and use acoustical tile on the ceilings. If the library has limited funds, carpeting should be the first choice because most of the noise in libraries comes from foot traffic. Carpeting absorbs up to 10 times more noise than most other flooring, and a carpet over a separate pad will absorb 55 percent of the airborne noise striking its surface. Glue-down carpeting

A library without carpeting is, not surprisingly, noisier than one that is carpeted, and the maintenance of a tile floor (seen here in a library reference section) may exceed that of carpeting. Tile floors have to be washed and polished often; carpeting has to be vacuumed, but washed perhaps once a year—and they cost about the same to buy.

will absorb less, but even this smaller amount is substantial as far as library acoustics are concerned.

Library public areas tend to be short on people and long on books, equipment, and furnishings, most of which absorb sound from one space to another. However, if the library is densely packed with seated people, as in certain special libraries, ceiling tile should be installed first. Noise stems from people who are speaking to one another, answering telephones, and using machines. Sound has the freest access across the ceiling in such a case, not across the floor. This is also true of the technical process area.

If the library has many walls with many little rooms or offices, the walls may have to be treated simply because they take up so much surface. This is especially true where the walls are of cheap construction and not acoustical at all. The simplest thing to do is to line the walls with books. However, bulletin boards, fabric-covered fiberglass, and even deep-clipped pile rugs affixed to such surfaces absorb a great deal of sound. Do not use acoustical ceiling tile on these walls; such tiles are not very durable. When installed in areas where they can be touched, poked, or somehow reached by passers-by, sooner or later the tiles begin to fall apart. Certain inexpensive types of pressed cork are equally as fragile and should also be avoided.

Ceiling tile can be painted, but one must be careful always to observe the manufacturer's recommendations. Water-based paints may make some

In an office where most of the floor is blocked by furnishings and equipment (as seen here in a library catalog section), the most important area to treat acoustically is the ceiling.

tiles swell. In other circumstances, oil-based paints may produce a chemical reaction. Usually the thinnest coat of paint is specified.

Lighting fixtures

The type and amount of lighting fixtures can change the properties of the acoustical ceiling. Ceilings made up entirely of lighting fixtures, such as luminous ceilings featuring translucent flat plastic panels lit from above, make for noisy facilities. The entire ceiling tends to be a hard, reflective surface.

Fixtures with any kind of flat lens diffusers tend to reflect more sound than those with plastic fins or open-bottomed parabolic reflectors. (Recessed, lens-type fixtures in false ceilings seem to circumvent this problem.) However, if these fixtures are to be used, it is suggested that the ceiling should not be more than 15 percent fixture to tile. In addition, some experts suggest that they be hung in a 2-foot by 2-foot configuration, rather than 2-foot by 4-foot, to minimize sound vibration.

Another point to note is that wherever small partitions are to be used,

Books are first-rate sound insulators. The noise gets trapped in the mass of paper.

particularly in office landscape systems, they should not be placed directly underneath lighting fixtures. That is because the sounds will travel across the space, up to the ceiling, and be reflected to the other side of the partition by the fixture, rather than be absorbed by the tile. All spaces should be formed so that the lighting fixtures hang either to one side or another of the partitions.

Windows

Windows add to the acoustical difficulties in a library. Many librarians seem to believe, falsely, that noise travels directly through the glass and outside the building, bothering no one. Windows are very sound-reflective surfaces; they are hard and flat. In addition, if not installed properly, some windows vibrate and creak with every change of the wind or the rumble of nearby traffic. Obviously, for those windows that do rumble and creak, a refitting may be necessary, if for no other reason than they may eventually break their seals and allow too much outside air in during the worst part of the winter or the hottest part of the summer.

Wherever possible, enclose noisy equipment in carrels made of sound-absorbing materials. Avoid desks or tables that project from panels as supports for noise equipment. These furnishings tend to vibrate; it is better to use desks or tables that are supported firmly on the floor by four legs.

There are several ways the librarian can try to alleviate sound reflection problems. Draperies can help to some extent, although they have to be heavy to do any good at all. Some vertical blinds also deaden sound, and there are a few on the market that are filled with as much as $5/8$ inch of sound-absorbing material. In addition, sound-deadening screens can be placed near the areas of the greatest trouble. And if the library has extra funds, certain portions of the glass can be tilted so that unwanted noise is deflected either toward the ceiling tile or carpeted floor, rather than horizontally across the facility.

Sound isolation

Acoustical tiles tend to be poor sound isolators. They are porous, so in order to isolate or stop sound, they have to be backed to decrease the ability of sound to pass through.

Indeed, any holes, cracks, or crevices will allow sound to travel from one side of a wall to another. A 1-inch square hole in 100 square feet of gypsum board will allow as much sound through as can be transmitted by the rest of the partition. Thus one should avoid back-to-back electrical outlets, ventilation ducts, or even open plenums above partitions. In fact, to isolate noise, the entire space has to be sealed when the door is shut. The door then should feature stripping and gaskets that seal it tight, otherwise it will be the weakest acoustical link. (For this reason, ventilation ducts allow noise to travel freely, unless acoustically treated on the inside in the form of baffles or acoustical lining.)

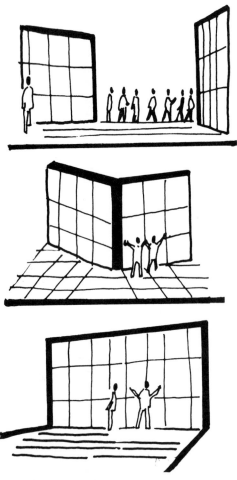

Sound can be isolated. *Top:* Noisy space, open, free movement of sound. *Middle:* Quieter space, partially enclosed, sound deadened. *Bottom:* Quietest, completely enclosed space, sound contained.

Below: Any holes in a wall will allow sound to travel from one side to another. (Community Learning Center, Washington, D.C.).

Sound transmission

As many an apartment dweller knows, sound can be transmitted directly through an object, such as a wall. The more surface weight a wall has, the less sound is transmitted. Actually, by doubling the surface weight, the transmission will decrease. It is the first doubling that is the most important acoustically. Each successive doubling produces proportionally less improvement per unit of weight, along with a great increase in cost.

The most effective walls absorb some of the sound that strikes them with the addition of acoustically absorbent materials on their surfaces; impede the flow of sound around, under, and above by sealing all cracks, crevices, and holes; and stop transmission by adding enough surface weight (often this is effected by fitting the interior with a core of honeycombed acoustical material, perhaps fiberglass, divided by hardboard or aluminum foil at the center). However, should a weaker element be fitted into a wall, such as a door, the composite sound transmission usually is closer to that of the weaker element than to the stronger partition. For example, if a loudspeaker disseminating noise 100 db strong is focused on a brick wall, 50 db may manage to pass through. If the wall is constructed of three-quarters brick and one-quarter single-pane glass, 74 db may get to the other side. Single-pane glass transmits 80 db. For this reason, single-pane windows or nonacoustical metal doors, both of which transmit sound with ease, should be avoided in areas that require first-rate soundproofing. In addition, heavy machinery, particularly heating, ventilating, and air-conditioning equipment, should not be located near spaces where concentration is expected.

Unfortunately, in too many public and academic libraries, the technical process area seems to wind up next to the boiler room. The result is that staff members constantly hear the booming of compressors all day, or the screeching of poorly oiled machinery, or the whining of the fans. (There are noises and there are noises; high-pitched frequencies seem to bother people more than low-pitched ones.) Those sounds are enough to drive anyone mad.

Walls can transmit some sound, although less than in an open area. The more surface weight the wall has, the less sound will be transmitted.

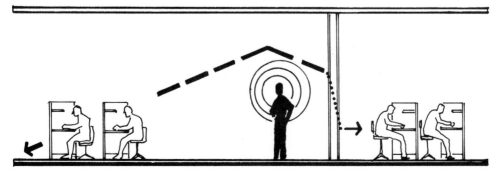

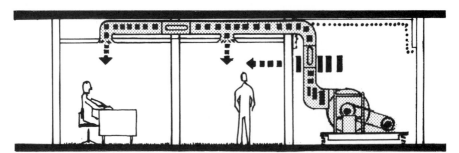

Mechanical system noises can be prevented by lining the mechanical rooms with sound-absorbing materials, sealing around mechanical room openings, placing machinery on resilient mounts, or lining ducts with sound-attenuating mufflers.

Heavy machinery, particularly the heating, ventilating, and air-conditioning equipment, should be suspended on resilient mounts and located as close as possible to structural columns to minimize floor vibrations. In addition, to avoid vibrations that cause furniture to reverberate, wherever machines are nearby, it is best to avoid tables and desks that are cantilevered or hung from simple partitions. To support any library machinery that vibrates, free-standing tables are best.

Sound transmission class

The Sound Transmission Class (STC) is a number rating of a structure's sound transmission performance. The higher the STC, the more efficient the construction as far as blocking sound transmission is concerned (see the table on Sound Transmission Class). For example, a louvered door with up to 30 percent open area will have an STC of 12; a 6-foot open landscape partition composed of two layers of fiberglass as a core divided by a septum of aluminum foil may have an STC of 20 or 25; a 1³/₄-inch hollow 16-gauge steel door, filled with fiberglass and complete with the proper gaskets and seals, will have an STC rating of 38.

Space arrangements

As we move away from a noise, the sound gets fainter and fainter. It simply gets lost in the space. Sound levels decrease approximately 6 db each time the distance between the source and the listener is doubled. At 3 feet one hears the sound of an ordinary voice at about 60 db, a raised voice at 66 db, and a loud voice at 72 db.

For an acoustically designed open plan, usually 80 square feet of space is sufficient for normal sound privacy; that is, some sound makes its way into the partition, but little is understood or heard. For confidential privacy, 200 square feet is considered necessary. In most typical open plan office facilities, the distance between staff members ranges from 9 to about 12 feet.

In a loft-type library, the overall ambient sound level, as mentioned previously, should be between 40 and 50 db, depending upon the size and

SOUND TRANSMISSION CLASS (STC) FOR SAMPLE BUILDING MATERIALS

Materials	STC Rating*
Exterior walls	
4$^1/_2$-inch brick with $^1/_2$-inch plaster each side	42
9-inch brick with $^1/_2$-inch plaster each side	52
6-inch concrete with $^1/_2$-inch plaster both sides	53
Interior walls	
2 × 4 wood studs, 16 inches on center, $^1/_2$-inch gypsum board both sides	32
2 × 4 staggered wood studs, 16 inches on center, $^1/_2$-inch gypsum board	
both sides, 1$^1/_2$-inch fiberglass insulation in cavity	49
6-inch concrete block, painted	44
8-inch concrete block with $^3/_4$-inch wood furring, gypsum lath	
and plaster on both sides	52
Floors and ceilings	
2 × 10 wood joists, 16 inches on center with $^1/_2$-inch plywood subfloor,	
$^{25}/_{32}$-inch oak on floor side, $^5/_8$-inch gypsum board on ceiling side	37
4-inch thick reinforced concrete slab	44
6-inch thick reinforced concrete slab with $^3/_4$-inch wood flooring on	
1$^1/_2$-inch × 2-inch wooden battens on 1-inch thick glasswool quilt	55
18-inch steel joists, 16 inches on center, with 1$^5/_8$-inch concrete; $^5/_8$-inch	
plywood nailed to joists and heavy carpet on underlay; on ceiling	
side $^5/_8$-inch gypsum board nailed to joists	47
Doors and windows	
1$^3/_4$-inch hollow wood core door, no closures; air gap at sill	19
1$^3/_4$-inch solid wood core door with gaskets and drop seal	34
1$^3/_4$-inch hollow 16-gauge steel door with glassfiber-filled core;	
gaskets and drop seal	38
$^1/_8$-inch single-pane glass window	26
$^1/_4$-inch + $^1/_8$-inch double-plate glass window with 2-inch air space	39

*The higher the rating, the less sound is transmitted.

traffic patterns. Here the average conversation cannot be understood beyond 18 feet in an open space and 12 feet in a space blocked by partitions.

Common sense says that those areas generating the most traffic, and therefore the most noise, should be as close to the central core and main entranceways as possible. This includes all main elevators, escalators, stairwells, corridors, and walkways. In other words, a central core should exist that is accessible to major departments via a central corridor or walkway. One should not have to weave in and out of other areas.

Because the main entrance/exit is the central point of reference for nearly everyone entering the facility, it should be located as close as possible to the center of the library. In addition, rest rooms, lounges, copy centers, and other popular locations should not be placed at extremes of the facility; otherwise traffic will move continually from one end to the other.

Wherever possible, major departments should be separate and have their own access to the central corridor. There is no reason why one should

In a totally open plan, sound has free access. It is essential to use acoustical tile on the ceiling, carpeting on the floor, and absorbent materials on the walls.

have to walk from one major department through another to get to the central corridor. Departments that have a great deal of communication with each other should not be separated by great distances either. The same is true for staff members; if they work together, they should be located close together.

The noisiest departments should be located closest to the central core, for they are least likely to be bothered by the noise of the library traffic. Obviously, the quietest departments should be located farthest away, for they are the most likely to be annoyed. (What this means is that the bound periodicals should not be put next to the main entrance, while the new periodicals are located upstairs and to the back. The other way around makes for a better allocation of space, and a much quieter facility.)

Should the library lack corridors in a formal sense, those running through the furnishings can be viewed as a system instead. Similarly, that system should get even smaller as it works its way through the facility so as to minimize noise. The most popular areas should be placed closest to the entranceways.

If one is talking about an entire building, the design is most important if one is interested in quiet. Even attractive, central atriums are detrimental. The noise travels freely from one level to another (although the first floor may be very quiet; as pointed out, the noise often collects above). The same is true of mezzanines. They either disseminate noise or collect it. Grand staircases are another problem. All of these open features also cause problems with the heating, ventilating, and air-conditioning systems, especially in the form of drafts.

Exterior courtyards can be a source of considerable racket. Hard-surfaced parallel walls sometimes cause annoying echoes, which manage to seep through nooks and crannies or directly through the windows into the facility. The courtyard can be formed by staggering the walls and orienting the noise away from the upper stories.

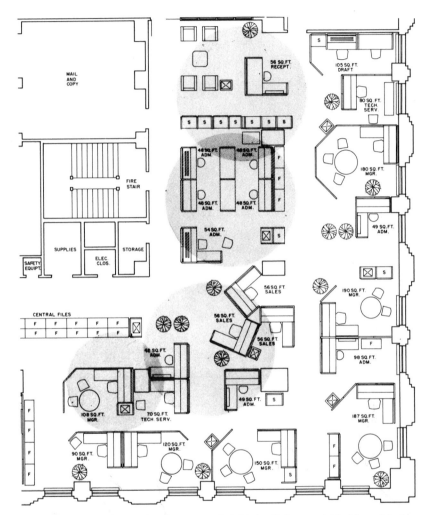

Some departments need quiet; in others, a comfortable bustle is acceptable. The noisiest departments (shaded areas) should be located closest to the central core and major walkways. When possible, save the perimeter for quiet departments.

Architectural elements such as open stairways and atriums allow sound to travel from one level to another. The spaces near these elements may be very quiet on the first floor, but extremely noisy on the top floor. Sound usually collects at the top. (Photos show Countway Library of Medicine, Harvard University.)

Site orientation

A particular noise problem occurs when a library is located next to a busy highway, or in an urban environment right next to a firehouse. Usually there is little that can be done, short of spending money in the construction process (see next section). But if the library is part of a larger facility and has not yet moved into the space, perhaps the designers can block the library from the most offending sounds. By reallocating the space, a janitor's closet or even a lavatory can be put at the very worst noise spots.

In addition, a noise barrier can be formed by shielding the building with, say, an earth berm, and then dropping the most critical library areas below the level of the source of the noise. (In the case of a busy highway, the library would be placed one or two levels below the roadbed; the choice here is between less natural light or less noise.)

Trees and bushes are not particularly effective as sound barriers. Dense planting of 100 feet deep provides only 7 to 11 db of sound blockage. Of course, if there is nothing else to be done, plantings provide some relief. (Although deciduous trees are first-rate energy conservation aids, they offer poor acoustical help during their leafless months. For noise blockage, the best bet is to use plantings made up of trees or bushes that keep their leaves year-round.)

Exterior wall construction

Whenever possible, a building should be constructed of materials that offer mass and the layered effect. For example, 9-inch brick with 1/2-inch plaster on each side has an STC rating of 52.

An exterior wall made up of two or more layers separated by an air space is always better than a single-layered one. In fact, if the layers are separated by a considerable distance, they are in effect forming two independent walls, each of which acts on its own to block noise. Here rigid ties between the walls should be avoided; otherwise the ties will transmit noise vibrations from one wall to another. In addition, by filling the cavity formed by the walls with sound-absorbing material such as fiberglass, even more sound will be blocked. (The density of the cavity insulation has very little effect on the wall's STC rating. In other words, a lightly filled cavity is about as effective as a densely filled one.)

Single-pane glass is a poor acoustical isolator. Windows should be formed by two separate panes of glass, each of a different thickness to avoid resonance effects. The panes should be separated by an air space and sealed to block all cracks and crevices.

Library acoustics

As already mentioned, although most users and staff members do not mind ordinary library bustle, there are areas where noise of any kind is not welcome. Such spaces usually include study areas, particularly out-of-the-way carrels, where people go to work and, in effect, hide. In law libraries, for

The acoustics of an auditorium-type space must be different from the rest of the library. An auditorium needs "live" acoustics where sound can be easily heard.

example, it is not uncommon to find users camping out for days, even weeks, at a time researching a project. For these people, absolute silence may be necessary.

In addition, certain staff members, particularly directors, need a special degree of privacy in their offices to carry on library business, financing, and employee relations. Such offices must allow for better acoustical privacy than that in other administrative areas.

In most libraries, there are several places where users and staff speak in anything but quiet tones. Near the circulation desk or in the lobby, raised voices are common. Louder voices may filter out of community rooms, especially when discussions get hot and heavy. And wherever working machinery raises a clatter, people project their speech in order to be heard.

Therefore, in order to make the library especially quiet, the acoustical engineer or architect (if one is retained) must understand which areas need more acoustical treatment than others. An acoustical engineer or architect does not need to be called in on every project. In most cases, the designer (architect, engineer, or interior designer) can do the work—perhaps just a simple rearrangement of space. However, on some large jobs where quiet is a special problem, an acoustician may be needed.

Among other things, to calculate the amount of acoustical privacy required, one will have to know the floor area. This is important because it has a direct effect on the noise levels. In a small room with all hard surfaces, there is a greater degree of noise buildup than in a large room. In the larger room, the sound tends to spread out and dissipate.

One will need to know also indications of how the building has been or will be built. For example, a structure possessing only a 4- to 8-inch structural slab with no provision for sound-deadening material above or below will be inherently noisy. Footfalls and thuds will be transmitted from the floor directly to the ceiling below. In addition, the ceiling will reflect almost all sounds back into the space. Should fans be bolted directly to the concrete slab, vibrations will be transmitted everywhere in the structure. Certain changes will be required to effect a quieter facility.

In the case described above, the simplest thing to do is to place a good carpet on a foam rubber or hairfelt underlay directly on the slab and below it to allow a 6-inch air space, and then hang a resiliently suspended plaster ceiling upon which is affixed ceiling tile. The fans would then be supported by resilient mounts and placed as close to the structural columns as possible to reduce structure-borne sound.

In addition, one will have to know whether or not walls stretch beyond the suspended ceilings and directly to the structural slab so as to isolate noise, and the types of noise absorbers in the form of baffles and linings in the ventilation ducts. Next, one will have to obtain the figures for the NRC and STC, as well as the seals around the walls, floor, ceiling, partitions, and furnishings.

If the building has not been constructed, "guesstimates" will be required for the number of people inside the building at any one time to calculate the ambient sound levels coming from that source, as well as the

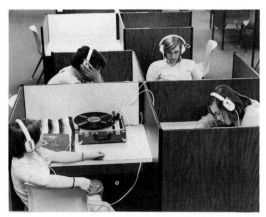

Acoustical environments are often created with sets of earphones, even in the most crowded areas (Kearsarge Regional High School, Sutton, New Hampshire).

ambient sound levels emanating from the HVAC system. At times these sounds alone will be great enough to mask individual noises. At other times, especially if hard surfaces are used, the din may be enormous and acoustical materials may have to replace certain building elements.

Finally, in the reference area, the constant jangling of phones is annoying to many, as well as the constant conversations of the reference librarians answering questions. First, if at all possible, the tone of the bell should be muted; today there are many different types of phone equipment on the market for this exact purpose. In addition, the phone should be fitted with an acoustical mouthpiece. If at all possible, the librarian's desk should be moved to an area that is less disturbing to concentrating users, and if that is not possible, perhaps the librarian should have some means to direct his or her voice into some acoustically absorbent surface when speaking either on the phone or to a user.

MOVING

Although reality usually falls somewhere between, moving a library
can be an overwhelmingly awe-
some business or, as in the following
examples, actually fun. To move
their library, 400 volunteers (old,
young, tall, short) in a small New En-

gland town lined up single file across a busy intersection. The line stretched from the old library to the brand new building across the street. Books were passed down the line until the old library was empty and the new one filled up. Although it was a cold day in mid-January, the process took only 2½ hours, and when the last book was passed down the line, a cheer came from the line of volunteers. The public library could have received funds to move, but this method was considered good public relations. And it was.

In a large university chronically short of funds, the director of the library enlisted the basketball and track teams to move the collection. Reasoning that the athletes were strong and could lift heavy loads, he suggested that they use plywood boxes (made in-house), each exactly one shelf long, so that packing and unpacking could be kept to a minimum. (They did, and it was.) The collection was placed in two tractor trailers borrowed from a local trucker for a two-day stay. Then the collection was fumigated and moved in good order to the new facility.

Everyone in a medium-sized town was asked to check out books from the local public library for a few days' stay. The books were given out in alphabetical order according to people's last names. During that time period, the library furnishings and equipment were moved to a new building. Then everyone was asked to return the books in alphabetical order. Every book was returned.

Unfortunately, for varied reasons, most libraries cannot use such "fun" methods when faced with moving. But following are some ways in which those in charge of moving a library can keep the frustrations and hassles to a minimum.

Retaining a moving company

Some companies specialize in moving library collections. A few have special book truck equipment that reduces or eliminates cartons—and such costs—entirely. Obviously, their services may be expensive, but the savings they afford elsewhere (including time and worry) often are worth it.

Moving companies range from small nonunion truckers to large unionized movers regulated by the Interstate Commerce Commission. Although generalizations always have exceptions, the small company tends to do the job for the least cost because of low overhead. However, some of them may be unreliable. The large movers, because they are regulated by state and federal laws, tend to be reliable and expensive.

Most moving companies work on an hourly rate. They will prepare a written estimate in advance for the time they *think* the job will take, including costs that can be eliminated if the library staff takes over certain aspects such as packing. But if things do not go as planned and it takes more than the estimated time, the library usually is responsible for the extra fee. If possible, an upset price (a top-limit dollar amount) should be negotiated before the contract is signed, so that the library can be protected from unforeseen developments (such as an elevator breakdown). For the larger libraries, moving companies will enter into competitive bidding for a set fee. It does not make sense for a major university library to pay an hourly rate; such an estimated price might be more than a million dollars!

When negotiating, it is essential to have everything in writing. In that way there is no misunderstanding as to what the contract includes. Extras added to the job in progress can be an expensive decision.

If a moving consultant is to be retained, it is imperative that the scope of the consultant's work is understood. *Exactly* what is the consultant to do? Is a contract necessary? Will the consultant work directly for the library and act, in effect, as the owner's agent on the job, supervising the work? Or will the moving company retain the consultant and pay him or her out of its fee? If legal difficulties crop up, the point may become important.

Weeding the library

Before the actual move, it is necessary to weed out the unwanted in the collection and furnishings and equipment. It makes no sense to relocate useless material in a brand new space. Because not everyone is given ample time to get ready for a move, it is wise for all librarians to keep an inventory of the collection, furnishings, and equipment. The list should note what is to be kept or eventually discarded. In this way a quick move will not cause havoc.

The collection

Weeding the collection may take several days or months, depending upon the size. So it is essential to think ahead. Possibly the staff may be able to do the job, or it may be necessary to turn to outside help. Some people weed collections for a living. Usually, they are located in the larger cities where there is more call for their specialty.

Weeding is not as simple as it sounds. Some of the discarded paper may have to be transferred to computer or micrograph form, and someone who is knowledgeable must do the job. If the library does not have the funds to hire expensive help, the nearest school of library science may be able to suggest students who will work at an hourly rate.

Furniture and equipment

Weeding the equipment and furnishings might be handled by the architect, interior designer, or contractor. It is also possible that all new furnishings and equipment will be installed in the new facility. But if anything is to be saved, somewhere along the line the responsibility will fall upon the librarian. (The hardest move of all is to buy only a few new pieces while the whole facility is being renovated. There is no room in which to pack and unpack, and spaces are cramped. Besides, stacks, desks, and machinery often are relocated temporarily from one side to another as the renovation proceeds, causing all sorts of problems.)

To weed furnishings and equipment, a master list (see sample Master

MASTER LIST   Department _____
                               Date _____

Item	Num-ber	Dimensions (height × width × depth)			Disposition*	Library Location		Refurbish†	Comments
						Old	New		
Newspaper rack	1	31"	36"	26"	Keep	Lounge	Lounge	—	—
Armchairs	3	30³/₄"	20¹/₂"	20¹/₄"	Keep 2 Add 1 (discard 1)	Lounge	Lounge	Upholster backs	1 broken

*For disposition, use the following terms: Keep, Discard, Store, Remove (show department), Add.
†For refurbish, use the following terms: Paint, Upholster, Carpentry, etc.

List) must be prepared, showing the location and dimensions (height, width, depth) of every piece in the library. It is important to find out if the pieces are too large to go through doors, corridors, and elevators, and it is important to know if the pieces are the right size for their new locations. The list should clearly indicate which furnishings and equipment are to be kept, discarded, moved elsewhere, or added (bought new). Certain items may have to be repainted, reupholstered, or repaired, which should also be indicated.

Preparing for the move

In preparation for the actual move, the person in charge should make up a list of questions to be answered before moving day. The more questions answered, the smoother the move will be. Following are examples of questions that are important to answer before the actual move.

1   If a moving consultant or company is to be used, will in-house staff be available to guide them?

2   Is extra space, such as a work station or office, even an extra desk, needed for weeding the collection, furniture, and equipment?

3   How long will the weeding take?

4   How long will packing, moving, and unpacking take? What is the time frame?

5   Are clearances needed from any of the following: police/fire departments, building owners (old and new), other lease holders or neighbors?

6   Have the following points been checked: must floors or walls be protected from moving damage; is someone else moving in or out of either building at the same time; what is to be done in the event of a union jurisdictional dispute?

7   Is special permission, possibly written, needed to obtain use of elevators and/or stairs for specified periods (both old and new buildings); remove doors from hinges or windows from

frames if necessary (old and new buildings); obtain a special route for moving during any part of the day?

8 Have extra costs been considered—more cartons, the services of a carpenter?

9 As boxes are packed, where will they be stored until they can be moved? Will they have to be moved a second time in the library? Is it essential that they are stored in order that they can be moved in order?

10 Is special equipment needed to move cartons down the elevators/stairwells/windows? How will fragile or special equipment be moved? Are maintenance people needed?

11 If the library is using a truck, how will cartons and equipment be staged in front of it?

12 In the new facility, where will cartons be stored until final destination? Will each department have a specific storage place? Are maintenance people available?

13 Who will remove the trash (old and new facilities)?

Packing and unpacking

When the actual packing takes place, at least one staff member may be needed to aid each group of packers. One of the biggest mistakes packers make is packing books in "reverse order by handfuls." One packer removes books from the shelf, turns around, and hands them to another packer, who places the books in the box. This is done again and again. The books become reversed by handfuls.

It is unwise to pack the contents of two shelves into one box without careful labeling. It is also unwise to pack the contents of two desks together.

Some unions forbid their workers to pick up dead weights that are more than 50 pounds. Depending upon the depth of a file drawer, one carton may be able to take only half the contents. The same thing is true of a book stack shelf.

Labeling

If the job is large, departments may be labeled separately. "A" may stand for Government Documents, "B" for History, and so on. The large letters can

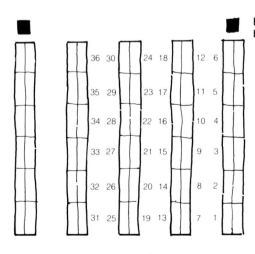

Book stack sections should be numbered in serpentine fashion.

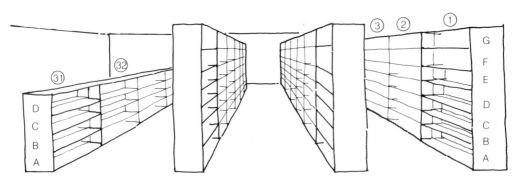

Label book stack shelves with letters, starting at the bottom.

be hung from walls or ceiling tiles. Letters rather than whole words are easier to read at a quick glance.

Cartons should be labeled on at least two sides; three sides are better (two sides and the top). Fragile items must be clearly marked on all sides and top.

Book stacks can be labeled with each single-faced stack numbered and every shelf lettered. "Stack 1, Shelf C" can mean only one place.

The stacks are labeled in a serpentine manner, first along one run of a double-faced range and then along the other side. If the library is very large, the stacks can be divided among departments so that a stack may bear the following legend, A21c, meaning Department A, Stack 21, Shelf c. (It is best to save numbers for the stacks, as there are often many stacks—larger libraries may have thousands. If a demarcation has to be made between departmental lettering and shelf lettering, use lowercase letters for shelves.)

The numbers and letters can be affixed to the shelves by pressure-sensitive tape for easy removal. Here the major problem may be caused by rearranging the collection. For example, Shelf Q18b may be moved to P12d. In such a case, a notation must be made on old Shelf Q18b that all material is to go to P12d. On the new shelf P12d, a notation must be made that all material will be coming from Q18b. Split-shelving can be handled in a similar manner.

New shelving

For new shelving arrangements, it is important to calculate the current linear feet and the new linear feet to make a simple ratio. For example, if 100 linear feet now exists in a section and the new shelving will allow the section to grow to 200 linear feet, the simple ratio is 1:2. Therefore, depending upon whether the collection will grow by intershelving, as in fiction, or by addition, as in serials, the new shelving will be filled only 50 percent on each shelf, or compacted to allow a 50 percent growth at the end of the collection.

Obviously, different segments of the collection may grow at substantially different rates. It is up to the library staff to determine which segments will show almost no growth, which will grow slowly, and which will grow faster than others. Some will need a 1 : 2 ratio, others a 2:3, and so on.

Once these calculations are done, mark off a "fill" line at the end of the old shelves, as well as the new ones, with pressure-sensitive tape. In other words, current shelf A51a will be divided into two segments. Two pieces of tape will show the segments. On the new shelves A51a and A51b, a tape will show that they are to be filled only two-thirds.

BIBLIOGRAPHY

Albers, Josef. *Interaction of Color*. New Haven: Yale University Press, 1975.

Alexander, Mary Jean. *Designing Interior Environment*. New York: Harcourt Brace Jovanovich, 1972.

Arnheim, Rudolf. *Art and Visual Perception: A Psychology of the Creative Eye . . . the New Version*. Berkeley: University of California Press, 1974.

————. *Toward a Psychology of Art*. Berkeley: University of California Press, 1972.

————. *Visual Thinking*. Berkeley: University of California Press, 1969.

Blake, Peter. *Form Follows Fiasco*. Boston: Little, Brown, 1974.

Bloomer, Kent C., and Moore, Charles W. *Body, Memory and Architecture*. New Haven: Yale University Press, 1977.

Brawne, Michael. *Libraries, Architecture and Equipment*. New York: Praeger, 1970.

Callender, John Hancock, ed. *Time Saver Standards for Architectural Design Data*. New York: McGraw-Hill, 1974.

Cohen, Elaine, and Cohen, Aaron. "Architectural Considerations." *LJ Special Report #7: Strategies for Survival*, pp. 44–51. New York: R. R. Bowker, 1979.

Conran, Terrance. *The House Book*. New York: Crown, 1976.

Crosby, R. M., with Liston, Robert A. *The Waysiders: Reading & the Dyslexic Child*. New York: John Day, 1976.

Davis, Albert J., and Schubert, Robert P. *Alternative Natural Energy Sources*. New York: D. Van Nostrand Co., 1974.

Dichter, Ernest. *Motivating Human Behavior*. New York: McGraw-Hill, 1971.

Diffrient, Niels, Tilley, Alvin R., and Bardagjy. *Humanscale 1/2/3*. Cambridge, Mass.: M.I.T. Press, 1974.

Eden, John. *The Eye Book*. New York: Penguin Books, 1978.

Egan, M. David. *Concepts in Architectural Acoustics*. New York: McGraw-Hill, 1972.

Ellsworth, Ralph E. *Planning the College and University Library Building*. Boulder, Colo.: Pruett Press, 1968.

Faulkner, Waldron. *Architecture and Color*. New York: Wiley-Interscience, 1972.

Fisher, David Hackett. *Growing Old in America*. New York: Oxford University Press, 1977.

Fitch, James Marston. *American Building*. New York: Schocken Books, 1975.

Friedman, Arnold, and Farrell, Philip F., Jr. *Common Sense Design*. New York: Scribner's, 1976.

Gatz, Konrad, ed. *Modern Architectural Detailing*. Vol. 3. New York: D. Van Nostrand Co., 1967.

Goldberg, Robert L. *A Systems Approach to Library Program Development*. Metuchen, N.J.: Scarecrow Press, 1976.

Hall, Edward T. *The Hidden Dimension*. Garden City, N.Y.: Anchor Books, 1969.

Hamilton, Beth A., and Ernst, William B., Jr., eds. *Multitype Library Cooperation*. New York: R. R. Bowker, 1977.

Harkness, Sarah P., and Groom, James N. *Building without Barriers for the Disabled*. New York: Watson-Guptill, 1976.

Harmon, M. H. *Psycho-Decorating*. New York: Wyden Books, 1977.

Heismath, Clovis. *Behavioral Architecture*. New York: McGraw-Hill, 1977.

Hennig, Margaret, and Jardin, Anne. *The Managerial Woman*. Garden City, N.Y.: Anchor Press, 1977.

Hicks, Warren B., and Tillin, Alma M. *Developing Multi-Media Libraries*. New York: R. R. Bowker, 1970.

————. *Managing Multimedia Libraries*. New York: R. R. Bowker, 1977.

Holland, Winford E., Szilagyi, Andrew D., and Oliver, Christie. "Employee Behavior Affected by Changes in Social Density." *Contract* 20 (1978): 64–67.

Illuminating Engineering Society. *Recommended Practice of Library Lighting*. New York: Journal of the Engineering Society, 1974.

Johnson, Sidney M., and Kavanagh, Thomas C. *The Design of Foundations for Buildings*. New York: McGraw-Hill, 1968.

Kuller, Rikard, ed. *Architectural Psychology*. Stroudsburg, Pa.: Dowden, Hutchinson & Ross, 1973.

Kuppers, Harald. *Color*. New York: D. Van Nostrand Co., 1973.

Lang, Jon, et al., eds. *Designing for Human Behavior*. Stroudsburg, Pa.: Dowden, Hutchinson & Ross, 1974.

Langer, Susanne K. *Problems of Art*. New York: Scribner's, 1957.

Leinwand, Gerald, ed. *Growing Old*. New York: Pocket Books, 1975.

McGuiness, William J., and Stein, Benjamin. *Mechanical and Electrical Equipment for Buildings*. New York: John Wiley, 1971.

Marx, Ellen. *The Contrast of Colors*. New York: D. Van Nostrand Co., 1973.

Mehrabian, Albert. *Public Place and Private Spaces*. New York: Basic Books, 1976.

Metcalf, Keyes D. *Planning Academic and Research Library Buildings*. New York: McGraw-Hill, 1965.

Michelson, William, ed. *Behavioral Research Methods in Environmental Design*. Stroudsburg, Pa.: Dowden, Hutchinson & Ross, 1975.

Modley, Rudolf. *Handbook of Pictorial Symbols*. New York: Dover Publications, 1976.

Morrisey, George L. *Management by Objective and Results*. Reading, Mass.: Addison-Wesley, 1970.

Mount, Ellis, ed. *Planning the Special Library*. New York: Special Libraries Assn., 1972.

Muther, Richard. *Systematic Layout Planning*, 2nd ed. Boston: CBI Publishing Co., 1973.

Muther, Richard, and Wheeler, John D. *Simplified Systematic Layout Planning*. Kansas City, Mo.: Management and Industrial Research Publications, 1977.

National Paint and Coatings Association. *The Household Paint Selector*. New York: Barnes & Noble, 1975.

Newman, Oscar. *Defensible Space*. New York: Macmillan, 1973.

Nuckolls, James. *Interior Lighting for Environmental Designers*. New York: John Wiley, 1976.

Nyren, Karl, ed. *LJ Special Report #1: Library Space Planning*. New York: R. R. Bowker, 1976.

Palmer, Alvin E. *Planning the Office Landscape*. New York: McGraw-Hill, 1977.

Poole, Frazer G., and Trezza, Alphonse F., eds. *The Procurement of Library Furnishings*. Chicago: American Library Assn., 1969.

Propst, Robert. *The Office—A Facility Based on Change*. Elmhurst, Ill.: The Business Press, 1968.

Propst, Robert, and Wodka, Michael. *The Action Office Acoustic Handbook*. Ann Arbor, Mich.: Herman Miller Research Corp., 1975.

Rasmussen, Steen Eiler. *Experiencing Architecture*. Cambridge, Mass.: the M.I.T. Press, 1962.

Reader's Digest Association. *Reader's Digest Complete Do-it-Yourself Manual*. Pleasantville, N.Y.: Reader's Digest Assn., 1973.

Ruesch, Jurgen, and Kees, Weldon. *Nonverbal Communication*. Berkeley: University of California Press, 1972.

Samuels, Mike, and Samuels, Nancy. *Seeing with the Mind's Eye.* New York: Random House, 1975.

Sargent, Walter. *The Enjoyment and Use of Color.* New York: Dover Publications, 1964.

Scott, Ian, ed. *The Luscher Color Test.* Translated by Ian Smith. New York: Pocket Books, 1971

Sharry, John A., ed. *Life Safety Code Handbook.* Boston: National Fire Protection Assn., 1979.

Shoshkes, Lila. *Contract Carpeting.* New York: Whitney Library of Design, 1974.

———. *Space Planning.* New York: Architectural Record Books, 1976.

Sommer, Robert. *Personal Space: The Behavioral Basis of Design.* Englewood Cliffs, N.J.: Prentice-Hall, 1969.

———. *Tight Spaces.* Englewood Cliffs, N.J.: Prentice-Hall, 1974.

Stein, Richard G., and Stein, Carol. *Low Energy Utilization School.* Phase I: Interim Report. Washington, D.C.: U.S. Government Printing Office (#2800-00194).

Thompson, Godfrey. *Planning and Design of Library Buildings.* New York: D. Van Nostrand Co., 1974.

Whitaker, Ben, and Browne, Kenneth. *Parks for People.* New York: Schocken Books, 1971.

Wiegel, Robert L., ed. *Earthquake Engineering.* Englewood Cliffs, N.J.: Prentice-Hall, 1970.

Wittkower, Rudolf. *Architectural Principles in the Age of Humanism.* London: Alec Tiranti, 1971.

Wright, Frank Lloyd. *The Future of Architecture.* New York: The New American Library, 1963.

INDEX